>> 中国

U0500365

# 我国应急物流体系建设研究

任丽丽　张娜 ◎ 著

RESEARCH ON THE CONSTRUCTION OF
CHINA'S EMERGENCY LOGISTICS SYSTEM

(中英文)

知识产权出版社
全国百佳图书出版单位
—北 京—

**图书在版编目（CIP）数据**

我国应急物流体系建设研究：汉、英/任丽丽，张娜著. —北京：知识产权出版社，2024.4

ISBN 978 - 7 - 5130 - 9044 - 5

Ⅰ.①我… Ⅱ.①任… ②张… Ⅲ.①突发事件—物流管理—研究—中国—汉、英 Ⅳ.①F259.221

中国国家版本馆 CIP 数据核字（2023）第 226960 号

责任编辑：国晓健　　　　　　　　责任校对：潘凤越

封面设计：臧　磊　　　　　　　　责任印制：孙婷婷

**我国应急物流体系建设研究（中英文）**

Research on the Construction of China's Emergency Logistics System

任丽丽　张　娜　著

| | | | |
|---|---|---|---|
| 出版发行：知识产权出版社 有限责任公司 | 网　　址：http：//www.ipph.cn |
| 社　　址：北京市海淀区气象路 50 号院 | 邮　　编：100081 |
| 责编电话：010 - 82000860 转 8385 | 责编邮箱：anxuchuban@126.com |
| 发行电话：010 - 82000860 转 8101/8102 | 发行传真：010 - 82000893/82005070/82000270 |
| 印　　刷：北京中献拓方科技发展有限公司 | 经　　销：新华书店、各大网上书店及相关专业书店 |
| 开　　本：787mm×1092mm　1/16 | 印　　张：16.75 |
| 版　　次：2024 年 4 月第 1 版 | 印　　次：2024 年 4 月第 1 次印刷 |
| 字　　数：322 千字 | 定　　价：88.00 元 |
| ISBN 978 - 7 - 5130 - 9044 - 5 | |

# 前　言

我国到 2035 年的总体目标之一是实现经济实力、科技实力和综合国力大幅跃升，而要增强经济实力，就要从各个方面发展经济。现代物流作为我国经济发展的一项重要产业，一头连着生产者，另一头连着消费者，因而国家高度重视物流产业发展对国民经济发展的重要性。应急物流作为现代物流的一个重要组成部分，是为应对各种自然灾害、事故灾难、公共卫生事件和社会安全事件等突发危机时的专门用途物流，已成为物流学科研究的一项重要内容。我国第一个物流行业的"十四五"发展规划中强调，物流产业的发展方向之一即提升现代物流的安全应急能力，现代物流可挖掘的潜力之一即提升应急物流发展水平。

我国近些年来遭受了多次自然灾害，如 1998 年的特大洪水灾害、2008 年的汶川大地震等，又多次受到公共卫生事件的威胁，如 2003 年的非典疫情和 2019 年的新型冠状病毒感染疫情（以下简称新冠疫情）。尤其是新冠疫情，持续时间长，影响范围广，使应急物流的运作经受了巨大的挑战。要提高物流运作的效率，最大限度减少自然灾害、公共卫生事件等突发事件对人们的生命和财产造成的损失，建设完善的应急物流体系尤为重要。因此，本书从应急物流体系建设的角度出发，研究了应急物流的定义、属性和应急物流体系的构成，从理论上探讨了应急物流的指挥系统、信息系统、管理系统和保障系统这些子系统的建设原则、组成部分、工作机制等内容，最后从实践角度出发，探讨了自然灾害条件下和突发公共卫生事件时应急物流体系的建设问题。

本书的创新点在于对应急物流体系建设的各个方面进行了系统的探

讨,为应急物流体系建设提供了理论依据和实践经验。另一个创新点在于本书融入了应急物流领域的最新研究成果、政策文件、实践案例等,为本领域的研究提供了前瞻性的参考。

# Preface

One of the overall goal of China by 2035 is to significantly increase its economic strength, scientific and technological strength and comprehensive national strength. To increase economic strength, we must develop the economy from all aspects. As an important sector in China's economic development, modern logistics "connects production at one end and consumers at the other", so the country attaches great importance to contribution that the development of logistics industry makes to the development of national economy. Emergency logistics, as an important part of modern logistics, is a special-purpose logistics for dealing with various natural disasters, accident disasters, public health events, social security events and other emergencies, and has become an important part of logistics research. The *Fourteenth Five-Year Plan* of China's first logistics industry emphasizes that one of the development directions of the logistics industry is to improve the safety and emergency capability, and one of the potentials that modern logistics can tap is to improve the development of emergency logistics.

In recent years, China has suffered from many natural disasters, such as the catastrophic flood in 1998, the Wenchuan earthquake in 2008, and many public health events, such as the SARS pandemic in 2003 and the COVID-19 pandemic in 2019. In particular, the COVID-19 pandemic, which lasts for a long time and has a wide range of impacts, poses a huge challenge to the operation of emergency logistics. To improve the efficiency of logistics operation and minimize the loss of people's lives and property caused by emergencies such as natural disasters and public health events, a sound emergency logistics system is particularly important. Therefore, from the perspective of the construction of the emergency logistics system, this book studies the definition, attributes and composition of the emergency logistics system, theoretically discusses the construction principles, components and working mechanisms of the command system, information system, management system and security system of the emergency logistics, and finally from the practical perspective, discusses the construction of emergency logistics system under natural disasters and public health emergencies.

The originality of this book lies in the systematic discussion of all aspects of the construction of emergency logistics system, which provides theoretical basis and practical experience for researchers in the construction of emergency logistics system from both theoretical and practical perspectives. Another novel idea is that this book integrates the latest research results, policy documents, practice cases, etc. in the field of emergency logistics, thus providing a forward-looking reference for researchers in this field.

# 目　录

## 理论篇

# 实践篇

# Theory

## Practice

理论篇

# 第1章　应急物流概述

应急物流是一种特殊的物流活动，与常规物流相对。"物流"一词来自军事活动，最初是为了满足军队后勤保障的需要。随着社会经济的发展，商品的流通日益增多，物流逐渐用来指代人类社会中物品的流通，其目的是满足人类的经济需求。在面临天灾人祸时，人们除自救、邻里互助或依赖当地政府的管理和决策外，"一方有难、八方支援"更是体现了社会经济发展、文明进步和人道主义意识的增强。不管是自救还是外部救援，不可避免地会涉及人员和物资的召集、流动、管理和维护等，这种面临公共紧急事件时对物流的管理日益得到重视。近些年来，应急物流从萌芽到逐渐发展，在我国经历了从无到有、从点到面再到迫切需要系统化的过程。

在应急物流这一概念提出之前，国内外学者已经对与这一概念相关的军事物流、企业物流、人道主义物流、灾害物流等进行了研究，为应急物流这一概念的提出提供了研究思路和土壤。随着各国对自然灾害、事故灾难等应急事件的重视，各国相继成立了应急管理机构，这促进了紧急事件下对物流活动的筹划与管理。最早成立应急管理机构的国家是美国，早在20世纪70年代成立了联邦应急管理署（Federal Emergency Management Agency，FEMA）。随后，加拿大、俄罗斯、日本等国也陆续建立了本国的应急管理模式（邹逸江，2008）。各国政府应急管理或相关组织机构的相继成立，有力地推动了突发性事件下物流理论与实践的开展，也为应急物流这一概念的最终提出提供了理论支持与政策依据。我国的应急管理机构则成立较晚，中华人民共和国应急管理部于2018年3月根据国务院机构改革方案设立。

但是，"应急物流"这一明确表述却最早出现在中国。2003 年的非典疫情给中国乃至东南亚甚至全球的经济都造成了严重损失。人们深刻认识到，面对突发紧急事件，物资保障的好坏会影响到对抗突发事件的成败，不规范、不完善的物流活动也会直接造成经济损失。仅在中国，非典疫情期间物流活动所造成的成本损失至少达到 30 亿美元（何明珂，2003）。鉴于非典疫情对整个社会包括物流行业的强烈冲击，2003 年 10 月 17 日由中国物流学会召开的第二届"中国物流"学术年会设计了一个"应急物流"的研究专题，与会专家学者的 10 篇研究成果发表在 2003 年 12 月《中国物流与采购》杂志特别策划的"应急物流专题系列报道"中，这也是"应急物流"这一概念的最早表述。2004 年 3 月，欧忠文等人发表了《应急物流》一文，其摘要中提到"在国内外首次提出了'应急物流'概念"，这一说法尚且存疑，但"Emergency Logistics"这一英文表达的确应是首次出现。相比之下，根据在中国知网的查询情况，国外研究虽然早在 20 世纪七八十年代就有人道主义物流（humanitarian logistics）或灾难物流（logistics of a disaster）等相似概念的表达，90 年代末甚至出现了"logistics of emergency departments"（应急部门物流）和"emergency medical logistics"（应急医药物流）这样的表述，但明确出现"emergency logistics"（应急物流）这一表达却是在 2004 年 7 月，稍晚于中国学者的研究成果。由此可以断定，无论中文还是英文，"应急物流"这一概念的确源自中国学者的研究成果，并由此成为一个专业术语。

## 1.1　应急物流的定义

在 2003 年最先发表的应急物流研究专题报道中，中国学者虽谈及了对"应急物流"这一概念的理解，但仅限于对这一概念的解释，并未形成一个明确的定义。何明珂（2003）指出，"在本文中，应急物流指由于突发性因素导致的物流活动，包括由突发性因素产生的应急物流需求和满足这些物流需求而进行的应急物流供给活动"。徐东提到，"顾名思义，应急物流主要是为了应对重大疫情、严重自然灾害、军事冲突等突发事件而实施的物流活动"。高丽英（2003）开篇提及，"应急物流从字面上可以理解为应对突发事件（包括战争、灾情、疫情）所采取的一系列紧急物流保障措施"。高东椰、刘新华（2003）认为，"应急物流是指各类突发事件中对物资、人员、资金的需求进行紧急保障的一种特殊物流活动"。赵新光等人（2003）认为，"应急物流是指危机发生时对物资、人员、资金等需求进行紧急保障的一种特殊物流活动"。这些对"应急物流"这一术语的解释虽然较为简单，但均强调了"突发而紧急""物流保障"这些核心要素。更难得的是，这一术语从创设之初就有学者认识到，应急物流不仅包括对物资需求的保障，还包括对人员和资金需求的保障。

欧忠文等人（2004）挖掘了应急物流的内涵，即"应急物流是指以提供突发性自然灾害、突发性公共卫生事件等突发性事件所需应急物资为目的，以追求时间效益最大化和灾害损失最小化为目标的特种物流活动"。这一定义虽局限于物资保障，却另有所长，指出了应急物流与其他物流相区别的"损失最小化"这一目标。

随着应急物流的概念被广泛接受，这一术语也得到了政府机构的认可。2006 年，中国国家标准化管理委员会出版的《物流术语》（GB/T 18354—2006）纳入了"应急物流"一词，将其定义为"针对可能出现的突发事件已做好预案，并在事件发生时能够迅速付诸实施的物流活动"。这一定义强调了应对突发事件要做好预案，虽对于有些突发事件预案难以做到足够有效且准确，但也将人们对应急物流的认识进行了拓展，应急物流不只是在突发事件后被动地应对，而且是可以主动地提前进行部署准备。2021 年版的《物流术语》（GB/T 18354—2021）则将应急物流定义修订为"为应对突发事件提供应急生产物资、生活物资供应保障的物流活动"。与之前相比，新版定义明确了应急物流活动供应的物资既包括生产物资，还包括生活物资。此定义发布正当新型冠状病毒感染疫情肆虐之时，面临生产企业随时可能发生的停工停产，这一新版定义的提出充分考虑到了重大公共事件长期影响下生活物资的应急生产和持续稳定供应。

孟参、王长琼（2006）仿照现代物流的定义，在借鉴前人研究基础上尽可能规范地给出了如下定义，"应急物流是指以提供自然灾害、公共卫生事件、重大事故等突发性事件所需应急物资为目的、以追求时间效益最大化和灾害损失最小化为目标，借助现代信息技术，整合应急物资的运输、包装、装卸、搬运、仓储、流通加工、配送及相关信息处理等各种功能而形成的特殊的物流活动"。这一定义表面上看虽较为规范全面，却较为机械地套用了现代物流中物资流通的各个环节，单方面强化了物资流通的全过程，却忽略了对人员和资金的筹措与管理。

王丰等（2007）在《应急物流》这一专著中将应急物流定义为"为应对严重自然灾害、突发性公共卫生事件、公共安全事件及军事冲突等突发公共事件而对物资、人员、资金等的需求进行紧急保障的一种特殊物流活动"。这个定义第一次较为全面地总结了突发公共事件的种类，而且借鉴了前人对于"物资、人员、资金等"需求方面的较为全面的描述。

各研究者对应急物流的定义或有相似，或各有侧重，可谓众说纷纭，但由于应急物流发展的历史还很短，理论研究仍须继续深入，至今尚没有形成统一规范的定义。基于已有的研究与实践，博采众长，并对疏漏之处进行补充完善，本书试将应急物流定义如下：

应急物流是指面对造成或可能造成严重危害的自然灾害、事故灾难、公共卫生事件和社会安全事件等突发危机，运用现代信息技术，由政府、军队、专业社团组织、企业、民众等一方或多方参与，参照相应或相似预案对人员、资金、物资等需求进行紧急保障，以最大化减少人员伤亡、财产损失、生态环境破坏的一种专门用途物流。

在这一定义中，"自然灾害、事故灾难、公共卫生事件和社会安全事件等突发事件"是应急物流的激发要素，这一表述参照了 2007 年 11 月 1 日施行的《中华人民共和国突发事件应对法》中第三条对突发事件类型的描述。"政府、军队、专业社团组织、企业、民众"是参与的主体对象，根据实践经验总结得出。"参照相应或相似预案"既考虑到了突发事件的必然性，因而一定要有预案，又考虑到了突发事件有些可预测有些不可预测的特点，所以那些不可预测的紧急事件可参照相似预案。"对人员、资金、物资等需求进行紧急保障"借鉴了前人的研究成果，也符合现实中紧急事件突发时的紧急需求。"最大化减少人员伤亡、财产损失、生态环境破坏"是目标，这不仅体现了对生命安全和财产的重视，还创新性地融入了生态保护的思想，对比 2019 年澳大利亚森林火灾和 2022 年重庆森林火灾的应对方式和结果，就会意识到应急物流对生态环境的重要性。"专门用途物流"用来取代很多学者定义的"特殊物流活动"，首先是因为应急物流属于物流的一个分支，应该纳入常态管理，它的特殊就在于它的特殊用途。正如语言学中有英语和作为分支的物流英语、科技英语等专门用途英语一样，故而采用"专门用途"这一表达。其次，应急物流不应只是涉及运输、包装、装卸、搬运、仓储、流通加工、配送及相关信息处理等各种功能的物流活动，它的范畴远远大于常规物流，而是集组织、管理、信息、物流等不同领域于一体，因此，不能简单地将应急物流仅仅定义为一种物流活动。

## 1.2  应急物流的属性

基于对应急物流这一术语的界定，有必要进一步挖掘应急物流的属性，以便对应急物流这一概念有更深入的理解和认识。前面已经提到，不能简单地将应急物流仅仅理解为一种物流活动。相比常规物流，应急物流虽然同样涉及物品从供应地到接收地的实体流动过程，但其应对突发事件的本质使其有着不同于普通物流的属性。

首先，应急物流具有社会性的本质属性。根据物流的不同目的，军事物流是为满足军队常规的后勤保障或紧急行军的物资保障，本质上是一种军事活动；商业物流的目的是实现商品的经济价值，即便也会出现应急供货或产品召回等紧急物流活动，但其本质上仍是一种经济活动；与前两者不同，应急物流的目的是减少人员伤亡、财产损失和生态环境破坏，它是通过紧急应对突发事件实现社会稳定、体现社会人文精神的价值体现，其本质上是一种社会活动。

其次，应急物流具有多元性。虽然应急物流属于物流的一个分支，但其并不只局限于物流这一个领域。从促发因素来看，军事物流的促发因素是行军、打仗等军事活动，由军事指挥中心对接；商业物流的促发因素是经济活动，由工厂、企业、消费者等商业链参与者对接；应急物流的促发因素却是多元的，仅暴雨、台风、蝗灾、森林大火、地震等自然灾害就可能需要与气象部门、农林部门、地震局等不同部门对接，更不用说事故灾难、公共卫生事件和社会安全事件，这些更是需要与各行各业的相关部门对接。从参与主体来看，军事物流的参与主体是军队后勤部门，商业物流的参与主体是物流公司或物流部门，应急物流的参与者并不只是单一部门，而是涉及政府、军队、专业社团组织、企业、民众等多种机构或团体的集体参与和相互配合。从需求保障来看，军事物流和商业物流主要是对物资的需求保障，军事领域和商业领域对人员和资金的需求保障则分别属于人事部门和金融部门的职责范围，只有应急物流的需求既有对物资的需求，又有对人员和资金的需求，仅靠物流部门无法解决所有需求，只有多部门进行联动才能实现多方面的需求保障。总之，应急物流的启动对接部门多元，参与主体多元，需求多元，保障部门多元，应急物流的多元性也就成了区别于其他物流的一个属性。

最后，应急物流具有即时公益性。商业物流以经济效益原则和成本分析原则为其核心考虑要素，相比之下，以人民群众生命、财产及生态环境安全为目标的应急物流不再把经济效益作为第一选择，而是秉承"人民至上、生命至上"的理念，在突发事件后为了确保生命安全甚至会不计成本进行救援。与军事物流的经济成本由政府专项拨款不同，应急物流的经济成本虽离不开政府的专项救助资金，却经常有企业、各种机构和民众的慷慨救助，或捐款或捐物或出力当志愿者，与政府、部队官兵一起给予受灾遇险人员人力、物力和财力的需求保障。因而，在突发事件发生后进行救援的一定时间内，应急物流具有即时的公益性。

# 1.3　我国应急物流体系建设的指导思想

当今社会不可避免地会发生造成严重危害的自然灾害、事故灾难、公共卫生和社会安全事件等突发危机，应对这些危机是任何国家和地区都可能面对的强有力的挑战之一。近些年来，随着我国经济发展、科技创新、交通物流业得到长足进步，国力逐步增强，应对突发紧急事件的应急处理能力也不断得到提高，但同时也暴露出不少问题。在应急物流方面，以 2008 年汶川大地震为例，虽然地震发生后，各种救援物资与设备从全国甚至世界各地源源不断涌向灾区，但由于道路等基础设施损毁严重，交通通信中断，为抗震救灾带来很大困难，物资设备无法及时运往灾区。不同渠道、不同类型的物流缺乏统一的调度指挥，存在杂乱无序的现象。各个震区收容点的需求也不尽相同，信息纷繁复杂难以统计，很难做到供需的匹配。因此，有必要建成一套指挥有力、信息畅通、管理到位、配送及时、保障完善的应急物流体系，这既是应对突发事件时确保人民生命和财产安全的迫切需要，也是我国经济建设和社会稳定发展的现实需求，同时符合国家的重要发展战略，具有十分重要的现实意义。然而，应急物流体系是一个庞大复杂的系统，涉及诸多领域、诸多层面、诸多要素，为了确保实现完善建设的目的，就必须要遵循科学的指导思想。

## 1.3.1　以人为本的指导思想

以人为本，是科学发展观的核心思想。在建立健全我国应急物流体系的过程中，要遵守以人为本的科学指导思想，就是要以最大化保障人民群众的生命和财产安全为主要目标，把人民群众的利益作为一切工作的出发点和落脚点，维护人民群众的尊严，保障人民群众的生命和财产安全，在人民群众处于危难时刻施行紧急的人道主义救援。

首先，要以人为本救助人。应急物流体系应急人民所急，想人民所想，快速向灾民提供急需的食物、水、衣服、被褥、帐篷、药品等基本生活物资，确保灾民的生命安全和健康需求。同时也要考虑到特殊群体的差异化物资需求，如婴儿奶粉、纸尿裤、妇用卫生巾等，真正做到保障人的正常生活需求。

其次，要以人为本调动人。应急物流体系应本着以人为本的思想，将政府、军队、社团组织、企业、民众等众多参与者有效调动起来，充分发挥各自优势，激发人的积极性、主动性、创造性来开展应急物流活动，实现多元主体协同。

最后，要以人为本培养人。应急物流体系应加强培养应急物流各环节的专业人员，有意识地对他们进行系统的理论培养和应急物流活动工作规范和工作能力的培养，提高专业人员的业务素质和工作能力，增强他们的大局意识、责任意识和奉献意识。

## 1.3.2 可持续发展的指导思想

在建立健全我国应急物流体系的过程中，要坚持可持续发展的指导思想，就是要建立应急物流长效机制，实现可持续发展的应急物流能力建设。可持续发展的应急物流体系至少应该包含以下几个方面的内容：

首先，可持续发展的应急物流决策和管理体系。提高应急物流决策与管理能力是可持续发展能力建设的重要内容。要培养高素质的应急物流决策人员与管理人员，就要综合运用规划、法制、行政、教育等手段，建立和完善可持续发展的组织结构，形成应急物流综合决策与协调管理的机制。

其次，可持续发展的应急物流科技系统。只有将高水平的科学技术应用到应急物流体系中，才能实现可持续发展的目标。科技可以有效地为可持续发展的应急物流决策提供依据与手段，促进可持续发展应急物流管理水平的提高，提升应急物流供应链的效率，为应急物流保障系统提供动力和助力。

再次，可持续发展的应急物流供应链系统。要将绿色环保理念贯穿应急物流供应链的各个环节，提升应急物流可持续发展能力。如采用绿色可循环包装材料，减少过度包装和二次包装，加快标准化应急物流周转箱的推广应用等。

最后，可持续发展的多元主体参与。多元主体参与是实现应急物流可持续发展的必要保证，因为可持续发展的目标和行动，仅仅依靠政府和军队的政军力量是远远不够的，还需要企业、社团组织、民众的广泛参与。企业、社团组织和民众的参与方式和参与程度，将决定应急物流可持续发展目标实现的进程。

### 1.3.3 协同发展的指导思想

协同发展论目前已被许多国家和地区确定为实现社会可持续发展的基础。协同发展不仅是应急物流体系的发展手段，也是应急物流体系的发展目标。应急物流体系是一个复杂的系统工程，其运转既依赖政府、军队、社团组织、企业、民众等多元主体的协同配合，又依赖应急物流体系各子系统间的协调运作。遵循协调发展的指导思想，可以确保应急物流体系中的各个要素充分发挥职能优势，通过相互协调、相互支撑，促进应急物流体系实现系统性、整体性和协同性发展。

## 1.4 我国应急物流体系建设的主要内容

应急物流体系作为突发紧急事件下应急管理体系的一个子系统，在整个应急管理体系中起到后勤保障的作用。应急物流体系的建设已得到国家的充分重视，如在 2020 年 3 月 6 日国务院联防联控机制举行的新闻发布会上，国家发展改革委副秘书长高杲提到正抓紧研究制定加强我国应急物流体系建设的政策。他特别强调，针对自然灾害、重大突发公共卫生事件、重大安全事故等紧急情况，要建立应急物流的分级响应和保障体系，统筹利用国家储备资源和网络，发挥好行业协会、骨干企业的组织协调能力和专业化优势，提高包括快速运转、冷链物流在内的应急物流快速响应和保障能力。

《中华人民共和国国民经济和社会发展第十四个五年规划和 2035 年远景目标纲要》（以下简称《"十四五"纲要》）指出，应急物流体系是指突发事件条件下保障应急物资供应、生产生活运转的物流体系。"十四五"时期，将加快建立储备充足、反应迅速、抗冲击能力强的应急物流体系，充分利用现有各类物流资源，以健全机制为主、硬件建设为辅，坚持政府统筹、企业运营、平战一体、全社会共同参与，建立以企业为主体的应急物流队伍，增强物流设施应急保障能力，提高应急物流技术装备水平，健全应急物流运转保障机制，强化应急物流政策保障措施。

应急物流体系建设的意义十分重大，关系到国计民生，关系到国家与社会的稳定和谐和国防安全的巩固，关系到人民的幸福安康，关系到民众日常生活的保障与生命财产安全。为了有效应对突发事件，避免为社会稳定和人民生命财产安全带来重大的破坏和负面影响，毋庸置疑，应急物流体系的建设极其重要，亟须形成一个科学规范、系统全面、专业智能、协调保障的建设体系。

对于应急物流体系建设的内容，不同的专家学者有不同的角度和观点。王旭坪、傅克俊、胡祥培（2005）认为，应急物流系统包括控制层、决策层、数据层和环境层 4 个层次。李睿、佘廉（2007）对枢纽城市紧急事态下的应急物流系统进行研究，将应急物流系统设计为组织指挥系统、资源保障系统、交通保障系统和信息共享系统。陈方建（2008 年）认为，一个有效完备的应急物流体系必须由应急物流保障系统、应急物流指挥系统、应急物流信息系统、应急物流配送系统组成。余朵苟、何世伟（2008）指出应从指挥决策、运作框架、保障机制等 3 个层面构建应急物流体系。李艳琴、张立毅、郭纯生（2010）认为，应急物流体系的建立健全，包括基础设施的建设与完善、应急物资的筹措与采购模式的研究、应急物资的储备与调度方式的探讨、政策法规的制定实施、专业技术人才的培养等诸多方面。高晓英（2011）认为，有效的应急物流系统应当包括应急物流指挥系统、应急物流信息系统、应急物流保障系统、应急物流配送系统这 4 个子系统。刘同娟、马相国（2013）认为，应急物流体系建设至少应包括五个方面：应急物资供应体系、应急物流运作体系、应急物流组织体系、应急物流基础性支撑体系、应急物流法律法规和政策体系。陈慧（2014）则认为，应急物流一般由组织系统、指挥决策系统、物资储备系统、物流配送系统、信息管理系统、专业人员系统、理论系统、政策法规系统等相关要素构成。以上各种观点都有其可取之处，或精简或细致，有的仅集中在物资物流层面，有的则将范围延伸到指挥决策、信息管理和政策法规保障领域。

本书在借鉴各位学者观点的基础上，延续本书中对应急物流的定义所涵盖的内容，将应急物流体系建设的内容分为以下 4 个子系统：应急物流指挥系统、应急物流信息系统、应急物流管理系统、应急物流保障系统。应急物流体系是一个复杂庞大的系统，涉及政府、军队、专业社团组织、企业、民众等不同机构或个人，涉及信息的收集、整理、共享、运用，涉及人、财、物的分配、调度、管理以及法律法规等保障。每个不同部分的要素都来自不同的子系统，同时各个子系统又相辅相成，有机融合，共同组成紧急事件下从应急启动到实现救助保障目的的整套应急物流体系。

（1）应急物流指挥系统。负责根据紧急事态的严重程度启动相应级别的应急物流行动，进行快速决策和指令的布置、下达及指导工作，使整个物流体系高效有序地运行。

（2）应急物流信息系统。该平台可运用计算机和网络构建一个专门的应急物流信息平台，为全过程的信息传达、收集、整理、共享提供技术支持。通过信息系统，可为指挥系统提供信息的上传下达，为管理系统提供对人员、资金和物资的统一调度，为保障系统提供信息的收集和共享。

（3）应急物流管理系统。对应急物流相关的人员、资金和物资进行统一管理。负责对应急物流人员的招募与动员、培养与培训、委派与调用、考核与评估，对应急物流资金的筹集、使用与监管，对应急物资的规划、采购与生产、储备、调度与征用、运输与配送、回收与处理等进行全方位的管理。

（4）应急物流保障系统。既为整个应急物流活动提供法律法规政策的保障，还为参与应急物流任务的人员提供后勤保障，以及道路交通设施等保障协调服务。

# 第2章　我国应急物流指挥系统的建设

当突发事件发生时，短时间内需要大量应急物资和大量应急人员，如何协调相关部门提供救灾专用设备、通信设备、医疗设备、生活用品等供应，如何对各类各级别管理人员、救援人员和后勤保障人员进行调配，这需要一个自上而下、各有分工、相互协作的指挥系统。比如，当应对重大地震灾害时，震区需要交通、通信、电力部门对遭到地震破坏的基础设施进行紧急修复，需要抢险救援的工程设备及食品、药品、帐篷、棉衣等物资供应，这需要地震局、政府、军队、交通、通信、电力、医疗、企业等不同机构部门进行紧密协作，如果这些单位相互间没有一个成熟的协调机制，就容易造成责任不明确、多头指挥、各自为战，不利于及时有效地发挥应急物流的作用。

应急物流的社会属性也必然需要整个社会的参与，包括政府、军队、专业社团组织、企业、民众等。不同级别、不同领域的人员要做到合理分工、发挥专长、有效配合，也离不开一个统一的指挥系统进行统筹部署和任务策划。在对各种信息进行整合、筛选的基础上，统一的指挥系统可以统揽全局，有效地对各种资源进行协调和分配。

应急物流指挥系统是国家或地区在应对自然灾害、事故灾难、公共卫生和社会安全事件等突发公共危机中，按照相应预案对应急物流级别、联络机构、应急物流过程等进行指挥决策、联络协调和监督评估，以确保应急物流的快速反应和顺利运作的指挥系统。

应急物流指挥系统的主要任务是：对可预测的紧急突发事件制定相应的应急预案，并将预案按照分类，如自然灾害、事故灾难、公共卫生事件和社会安全事件等，制定针对性的措施和方案；及时启动应对紧急突发事件的应急物流行动，结合实际情况根据相应预案做好行动部署；对应急物流行动的过程进行整体的监控、协调和评估，及时进行必要的指导和行动计划的适当调整。

# 2.1 我国应急物流指挥系统的建设原则

应急物流的指挥系统是应急物流行动的发起者，也是应急物流体系的指导中枢，它对整个应急物流体系的高效有序运行起到了至关重要的作用。建立有效的应急物流指挥系统，需要遵循以下几个原则。

## 2.1.1 统一指挥、科学决策

应急物流是应对重大公共危机的生命线，也是非常时期保障民生的动脉管，是维持国民经济健康运转的基本能力，它的重要性决定了它必须由政府统一指挥。政府对应急物流进行统一指挥，可以充分发挥政府的职能优势，将党、政、军、企、民有效地组织起来，形成合力，将专业力量和社会力量结合起来，形成高效应急反应机制。同时，在党和政府的领导下，充分发挥专家库的智囊团作用，根据专家的专业意见形成科学决策，保证应急决策的科学性。

## 2.1.2 灵活应对、快速决断

在应对突发事件的过程中，由于突发事件可能不断升级或变化，对物资的需求种类、数量也会发生相应变化。指挥人员需要根据形势变化灵活应对并快速做出决断，确保在救援的黄金时间内起到应急物流的保障作用。

### 2.1.3　统筹规划、协调运作

在政府统一领导下，根据灾害易发的类型做好应急物流的预警和统筹规划，既要做好充分的物资储备，又要避免重复建设和过度浪费。当灾害来临时，及时对应急物资进行补充和调拨，广泛调动政府、军队、企业和社会的各种资源，发挥各方力量的优势，形成整体效能和合力，实现物流、信息流、资金流的有效运转。

## 2.2　我国应急物流指挥系统的组织构建

应急物流指挥系统是应急物流体系的"大脑"，是紧急事件发生时应急物流行动的领导机构。在应急物流的实施过程中，经常需要好几个部门进行统一行动，而这些部门相互间并没有形成一个成熟的协调机制，沟通渠道不畅、责任不明、多级指挥，导致应急物流不能发挥其快捷和高效的特性和作用，往往造成严重后果。在我国目前的应急管理体制中，国家应急管理部设有救灾和物资保障司，其主要职责为：承担灾情核查、损失评估、救灾捐赠等灾害救助工作，拟订应急物资储备规划和需求计划，组织建立应急物资共用共享和协调机制，组织协调重要应急物资的储备、调拨和紧急配送，承担中央救灾款物的管理、分配和监督使用工作，会同有关方面组织协调紧急转移安置受灾群众、因灾毁损房屋恢复重建补助和受灾群众生活救助。虽然该司承担了国家应急物流指挥机构的核心功能和任务，但同时也兼有救灾的部分职能，在应急物流方面侧重于制订计划和协调物资和款物，尚未对整个应急物流体系起到应有的监督和指导作用。另外，全国范围内尚未形成一个明确的从上而下的指挥体系。这样的体系既能在组织机构上实现从上而下的指导和监督，还能根据公共危机事件的等级调度相应级别的指挥机构来进行更有针对性的领导和指挥。

## 2.2.1 纵向构建

应急物流指挥系统的建设要重视自上而下的应急物流指挥中心的分级组成，形成上下组织机制畅通的应急物流指挥系统。在以政府为主导的应急管理体制中，明确设立应急物流管理部门，以更有效地实现政府应对紧急公共事件的需求保障。与我国的行政区域体制相对应，应急物流管理部门可按照中央、省、市、区（县）四个级别设置。这个体系机动灵活，可以根据灾害的危害程度实现分级指挥。当灾害波及的范围较小时，可以由灾区所属地的应急物流指挥中心制定方案指挥救灾。当出现全国性的公共危害时，全国性的指挥中心把各级指挥部门统一到全国的指挥系统中，形成全国的快速响应网络。在应对新冠疫情的全国性公共卫生事件中，我国已经形成了从中央到各省市、从各省市到区县、从各区县到乡镇或街道的遍布全国每个角落的疫情防控网络，在严格防控下有效遏制了从原始毒株到阿尔法（Alpha）、贝塔（Beta）、伽马（Gamma）、德尔塔（Delta）、奥密克戎（Omicron）等变异株数轮的攻击，最大限度地延缓遏制了病毒给人民生命安全造成的严重危害，同时也为全国大面积公共危机下应急物流体系的建设积累了宝贵的经验。

在国家层面上，依托国家应急管理部，成立专门的国家应急物流部，负责在全国范围内或跨省级区域特别重大公共安全事件中对应急物流行动进行统一领导、统一指挥和特别重大紧急决策，必要时可根据危害类型和影响程度临时组成专项应急物流国家指挥工作组。

在省级层面上，在国家应急物流指挥部门指导下，依托省级应急管理部门成立省级应急物流指挥中心，负责在全省范围内或本省跨市级区域重大公共安全事件中对应急物流行动进行统一领导、统一指挥和重大紧急决策，必要时可根据危害类型和影响程度临时组成专项应急物流省级指挥工作组。

在市级层面上，在省级应急物流指挥中心指导下，依托市级应急管理部门成立市级应急物流指挥中心，负责在全市范围内或本市跨区（县）级区域较重大公共安全事件中对应急物流行动进行统一领导、统一指挥和较重大紧急决策，必要时可根据危害类型和影响程度临时组成专项应急物流市级指挥工作组。

在区（县）级层面上，在市级应急物流指挥中心指导下，依托区（县）级应急管理部门成立区（县）级应急物流指挥中心，负责在全区（县）范围内或本区（县）所属村镇或街道一般公共安全事件中对应急物流行动进行统一领导、统一指挥和紧急决策，必要时可根据危害类型和影响程度临时组成专项应急物流区（县）级指挥工作组。

当下一级政府的应急物流能力和资源不足时，可以提请上一级政府物流指挥中心提供支持，上一级物流指挥中心应视情况给予必要的援助。

## 2.2.2  横向构建

应急物流指挥部门是应急管理系统中承担应急物流服务的核心机构。根据我国国情，充分发挥制度优势，在各级政府统一领导下成立的各级应急物流指挥部门内部，可根据所属行政区域内可能发生的公共安全事故的种类和特点，设置应急物流指挥部、应急物流办公室、应急物流专家咨询委员会、应急物流监督反馈处四个组成部分。

### 2.2.2.1  应急物流指挥部

中央和地方各级应急物流指挥部门应设立应急物流指挥部，在紧急公共事件发生后，要在充分收集信息的基础上，对于紧急应对内容进行火速商讨，随即迅速、切实地采取相应措施并且将相关行动具体化。以四川省为例，四川省是地震灾害频发的省份，省级应急物流指挥中心设立的应急物流指挥部则可由政府应急物流管理部门、交通运输部门、军队后勤部门、地震局等机构派出专人组成，也可根据突发公共灾害类型由其他的相关机构参与应急物流指挥部的工作，必要时可派指挥人员进驻灾区现场亲临指挥决策。多部门联手形成联防联控指挥中心，可以形成统一指挥意见，负责预案制定、灾难紧急响应等决策，从而避免多头指挥、指挥混乱、信息沟通不畅等带来的各种问题。

### 2.2.2.2 应急物流办公室

各级应急物流办公室负责及时整理灾区的需求信息，在应急物流指挥部授意下紧急协调与灾情相关的各个部门，做好多部门多主体的应急物流信息沟通和工作协调，保障指令和决策的紧急发布以及各种信息的上传和下达。

### 2.2.2.3 应急物流专家咨询委员会

根据本行政区域内应急物流工作需要，聘请有关专家、学者组成应急物流专家组，为应急物流领导组提供决策咨询和行动建议，必要时参与现场应急物流处置工作。

### 2.2.2.4 应急物流监督反馈处

对应急物流行动的全过程进行监督和评估，将新形势新变化及时汇报给领导组，以便对指挥决策进行灵活调整，实现动态的应急物流监督评估反馈机制。

## 2.3 我国应急物流指挥系统的工作机制

基于应急物流指挥系统的工作任务及其建设的基本原则，我国应急物流指挥系统要形成以下工作机制，以实现指挥科学、响应快速、协同高效的指挥功能。

### 2.3.1 应急物流监测预警与预案演练机制

监测与预警是预防一切公共突发事件造成严重后果的前提。应急物流体系要注意监测一切公共安全事件突发的可能性，随时做好启动应急物流行动的准备，甚至在灾害救援行动尚未开始之前就提前启动应急物流行动，这也就是古语所称的"兵马未动，粮草先行"。各级政府应急物流办公室应通过有效的信息共享平台，随时关注地质、气象、消防、卫生、防疫等部门上传共享的灾害预警信息，及时汇报应急物流指挥部，指挥部会同专家咨询委员会的相关专家进行风险预测评估，提供预警意见，及早采取应对措施。应急物流的监测预警机制将应急物流行动提前预测、提前规划，可以极大提高应急物流指挥工作的效率和反应速度，做到"有备无患，有患即战"，形成应急物流指挥系统的柔性和韧性。

监测预警机制可以确保应急物流行动的及时性，完善的应急物流预案与演练机制则是实现应急物流指挥任务有效性的前提和关键。作为应急物流行动的根本依据，应急物流预案的应用性和可操作性很强，能在紧急公共事件发生时迅速有效地提供行动纲领。自 2006 年国务院发布《国家突发公共事件总体应急预案》以来，各级人民政府，相关部门，重点企事业单位、学校、医院、人员密集场所等都各自制定了较为完善的应急预案，但应急物流的预案还未得到充分重视，未形成较为完善的预案体系。为了尽快改变这种局面，区（县）级及以上各级应急物流部门应根据本地区发生大规模公共安全事件的特点和规律，会同有关部门制定本行政区内的应急物流预案。在预案制定之后，还要定期组织相关机构和人员进行应急物流预案演练，促进各部门、各主体、各子系统间的协作和磨合，根据暴露出来的问题及时进行改进调整和丰富完善。由于应急事件的不可预测性及影响的不可预知性，各级应急物流指挥机构还应具有灵活应对的意识和指挥经验，不可机械地完全套用预案，而应根据突发公共事件的类型特点、发生地环境、影响范围等情况，采用动态调整的应变策略。

## 2.3.2　应急物流分级响应与联络机制

反应是否迅速、响应是否及时是应急物流成败的关键之一，也是应急物流体系建设的一项基本要求。这首先离不开一个反应迅速、响应及时的应急物流指挥系统。上下纵向分级的应急物流指挥系统既可满足事发当地应急物流快速启动的紧急需求，同时也可根据紧急公共事件的危害程度和范围，及时申请上级请求相邻地域的支援和协助。对于小范围区域的突发公共事件，一般由当地政府领导应急物流指挥部门进行及时响应，同时报请上一级政府紧密关注事态发展，必要时给予协调和援助。对于跨省或全国范围内突发公共事件，则直接由国家应急物流管理局启动应急物流的指挥任务。上下分级的响应机制，责权明确、分工科学，体现了应急物流指挥系统分级响应的速度和效率。除了组织机制的上下分级响应，应急物流指挥机构还应根据突发公共事件的规模和态势明确响应的级别。根据国务院颁布的《国家突发公共事件总体应急预案》，按照可能造成的危害程度、紧急程度和发展势态，可以将突发公共事件划分为四个级别：Ⅰ级（特别重大）、Ⅱ级（重大）、Ⅲ级（较大）和Ⅳ级（一般）。各级政府在制定相应的应急物流预案时，应根据突发公共事件的四个级别的特点，制定相应的应急物流的四个级别，明确每个级别的应急物流实施标准。当突发公共事件时，应急物流指挥机构首先要确定该次危机级别，综合各方信息做出及时响应，启动相应级别的应急物流行动。当然，根据事态的发展和物资的紧缺程度，可以适时调整应急物流行动的级别，以更科学地指挥应急物流行动。

分级响应机制可以提高应急物流指挥系统的速度和效率，联络机制则是提高整个应急物流体系运转的速度和效率的关键。应急物流的参与主体广泛，包括政府、军队、企业、社团组织、民众，甚至还包括他国政府、海外组织和机构。应急物流的各个环节还很复杂，既包括应急物流人员的召集、培训、调拨，也包括应急物流资金的筹集、使用、监管，还包括应急物资的规划、采购、储备、调拨、运输等，甚至包括法律法规、基础设施、交通设施等保障，这几乎涉及社会的各行各业和方方面面。只有一个政府领导下的强有力的应急物流指挥系统，才能做到联络社会各界力量，协调社会各方资源，为应急物流的顺利实施铺平道路。为了有效地发挥指挥系统的联络机制，可在各级应急物流办公室设置专人专岗，加强与其他部门的联络与信息共享，如应急管理部门、军队、民政部门、交通部门、消防局、防汛抗旱部门、地震局、市场监督管理局等。

### 2.3.3　应急物流监督评估机制

应急物流指挥系统需要具备把控物流全局的能力，其中既包括宏观层面的全局把控，也包括微观层面的全局把控。这需要应急物流指挥部门在应急物流行动中起到评估和监督的作用。宏观把控指的是，应急物流指挥系统应具备对重特大突发事件的发生、发展和结束的总体物流情况进行全局评估的能力，及时对应急物流行动进行调整，并有效协调和调整供应，以免出现供需不一致、大量应急物资闲置或浪费的情况发生。微观层面的全局把控指的是，应急物流指挥系统能够有效监督每个子系统中各要素的职能发挥，如应急物流专业人才的数量和培养质量是否能够满足日常需求，应急物资的结构和种类是否能够满足灾区人民的需求等。根据评估的结果和监督过程中发现的问题，应急物流指挥部可以及时调整决策和方案。

然而，目前情况下，我国的应急物流体系缺乏动态的监督评估机制。除政府和军队有计划地应急物流行为外，企业、社会团体和个人的捐款捐物和人力物力的支援未能及时纳入有效的管理体系，导致管理混乱、物资大量浪费。指挥部门不了解现场志愿者的规模、能力和企业实际捐助的应急物资状况，也就无从做到有效指挥、统筹协调。要实现应急物流指挥系统的监督评估机制，就要借助现代信息技术，将各方庞杂的信息进行智能化技术处理，及时纳入决策支持信息网络。如，针对某种应急物资的需求，指挥部门应根据受灾人员数量和救灾预计持续时间等要素，制订指导性的供应计划。同时对比当地的政府应急储备情况，及时向社会发布说明，以便更好地管理和引导来自社会的捐助。

# 第3章　我国应急物流信息系统的建设

应急物流信息系统的目标，是运用现代信息技术，更加及时准确地传递应急物流所需的各种信息，以配合应急物流行动的全过程。作为我国应急物流体系的一个子系统，应急物流信息系统承担着为整个体系提供信息收集与发布、分析与处理、沟通与协调、共享与反馈等服务的重要任务。

## 3.1　我国应急物流信息系统的建设原则

应急物流信息系统是我国应急物流体系的"神经网络"，为整个系统提供各种必要的数据信息。建设有效的应急物流信息系统，就要遵循以下几个原则。

### 3.1.1　集成化原则

应急物流体系各个子系统的顺利运行都离不开信息的有效传递。每个子系统所需的信息不尽相同，却又相互支撑，构成一个纷繁复杂的信息海洋。功能单一的信息系统无法满足系统内部及系统间的信息支撑，因而需要对信息系统进行整体设计，进行集成化建设，将支撑不同系统的各种有效信息综合在一起，消除信息传递壁垒，实现整个应急物流体系信息渠道的畅通。

### 3.1.2　标准化原则

标准化既指信息系统的搭建要遵循科学、规范的标准，又指信息采集与处理的标准化。应急物流体系中既有很多原始信息，又有很多加工信息，要实现信息的多部门多领域共享，就必须制定统一的标准和格式，以确保信息流在应急物流体系中的畅通无阻。

### 3.1.3　动态化原则

在应急物流行动中，信息的作用至关重要，它是指挥、管理、运输、配送等各个环节的基础。信息是否准确可靠，甚至可以影响整个应急物流行动的成败。应急物流中的不可预测性使某些需求随时发生变化，要确保信息的准确性，就需要对各种信息及时更新和调整。因而，采用动态化的建设原则是确保应急物流信息系统可靠性的有力保障。

### 3.1.4　可视化原则

为了满足对公共突发事件的服务保障，应急物流既需要社会各界的广泛参与，又需要媒体和公众的普遍关注。以可视化的原则建设应急物流信息系统，实现应急物流信息的公开、透明，既有利于实现系统内及系统间信息的有效共享，提升应急物流体系运行的整体效率，又有利于实现公众对政府应急处置工作的监督，提升各级政府应对突发事件的能力和政府公信力。

### 3.1.5　智能化原则

应急物流信息系统不仅需要采集原始数据，还需要采用多种技术手段对原始数据进行智能加工，为应急物流的各个环节有针对性地提供信息支持，以提高整个应急物流体系的工作效率。例如，在应急物资分配中采用优化方法及仿真技术，减少人工处理信息的不足，实现信息对指挥系统决策的支持。

## 3.2　我国应急物流信息系统的层级构建

应急物流信息系统是我国应急物流体系中不可缺少的神经网络，不仅要自成体系，还要延伸到各个子系统，为应急物流的各环节提供信息保障。我国应急物流信息系统可以采用层级的构建方法，以完善的通信基础设施为基础，打造汇集各方信息于一体的智能化应急物流信息平台，进而实现信息在应急物流各专业领域中的应用。沿着这个思路，我国应急物流信息系统可以按照基础层、平台层和应用层进行三级构建。

### 3.2.1　基础层

基础层是指支持应急物流信息传播的基础设施、设备及其系统。在基础层上，完善的应急物流信息系统既包括硬件也包括软件。硬件既指信号塔、线路等大型基础设施，又指系统的硬件资源和物理设备，如计算机、服务器、通信设备等。硬件是构建信息系统的基础，构成了信息系统运行的硬件平台。软件指的是维持信息系统运行的各种功能的模块所组成的系统。软件既有为整个系统所共享的数据和程序，又有为支持某一系统功能的专用数据和程序。软件主要包括系统软件和应用软件两大类。其中，系统软件主要用于系统的管理、维护、控制及程序的装入和编译等工作。应用软件则是指挥计算机进行信息处理的程序或文件，包括功能完备的数据库系统，实时信息收集和处理系统，实时信息检索系统，计划规划、资源调配、实时监控、情况预测等系统（袁渊、杨西龙，2009）。

完善的信息系统基础层是信息流动的载体，对信息的有效传递起着决定性作用。良好的信息系统可以及时传达预警信号和救灾物流信息，大幅度提高救灾的快速反应能力，缩短救灾时间，提高救灾效率。政府可以考虑建立灾害情况下进行信息传递的特殊通道，拥有独立于商用和公众通信网络的应急通信网络，保证在民用通信网络瘫痪时能够启动特殊通道指挥救灾及应急物流活动。鉴于信息系统在应急物流过程中发挥的作用不可或缺，作为搭载应急物流信息系统的基础层，其作用尤其应该得到加强。因而，"通信网络运营商要加大资金投入，加紧建设通信网络基础设施，优化和加强网络信号，扩大信号的覆盖区域范围，增强网络数据传递承载能力，特别是在灾害发生后出现通信盲点时，要第一时间抢修设施设备，尽快消除盲点，确保通信畅通"（韦琦，2010）。

### 3.2.2　平台层

平台层是指应急物流各环节所需各种信息的综合汇集平台。虽然我国把突发事件分为自然灾害、事故灾难、公共卫生事件和社会安全事件四个类型，但每一类下面都涵盖数种不同的突发事件，每一种与突发事件相关的应急物流活动所需的信息则更是纷繁复杂，但又不可缺乏，任何渠道的信息对应急物流行动的开展都具有一定的价值和作用。遗憾的是，由于我国还没有建立统一的应急物流信息平台，所以导致各种信息来源较为分散。应急物流指挥者和管理者有时苦于缺乏关键信息，有时又面对大量信息高度重合，不得不投入很多时间精力进行信息的收集和筛选，严重影响工作效率。因此，建立统一的应急物流信息平台，将各种信息资源集中在一起，方便各环节各领域随时调取查找，才能使信息资源在应急物流活动中发挥出最大作用。

平台层的主要任务是对突发事件的各种信息进行采集，包括危害类型、发生地点、伤亡情况、受灾程度、气候条件、交通设施损毁情况、物资需求情况等。在尽可能不对原始信息进行处理的前提下，要按照统一规范的数据采集格式进行原始信息的采集和录入，储存在应急物流信息平台中。对于信息平台的信息，要求相关部门随时上传并更新，以确保信息及时、可靠、迅速，便于相关应急物流人员根据信息的动态变化调整工作部署。在对原始信息进行收集的过程中，目前我国应急物流资金投入不足、专业化人才短缺，缺乏将信息进行二次利用的意识，因而信息利用率较低，处理成本较高。因此，在应急物流信息系统的建设中，还要注意将平台层的信息以原始数据的形式进行保存，这样便于进行二次分析和处理，提高数据利用效率，提高信息资源的可视化管理。

按照突发事件的类型，应急物流信息系统可以建设不同灾难类型的应急物流信息平台，如自然灾害应急物流信息平台、事故灾难应急物流信息平台、公共卫生事件应急物流信息平台和社会安全事件应急物流信息平台。每类信息平台还可以进行细分，如自然灾害应急物流信息平台可以细分为地震灾害应急物流信息平台、雪灾应急物流信息平台、台风应急物流信息平台、洪水应急物流信息平台等。信息平台的设置越有针对性，信息的收集和汇总就越精准化，越能有效地实现信息服务的智能化和集成化。以应急物资的统计为例，如果按照自然灾害、事故灾难、公共卫生事件和社会安全事件这些灾难类型汇集不同来源的应急物资的数据，打破多层级、多部门之间物资资源共享壁垒，将原有各自分散的、不同格式的、不同类别的应急物资资源数据统一接入应急物流信息平台，加强各类物资资源数据通用性整合，就可以实现应急物资从筹集到使用的全过程跟踪管理，确保国家应急物资资源得到有效利用。

### 3.2.3 应用层

应用层是指在平台层加工处理的信息在应急物流行动中各个领域的应用。当前，我国应急物流信息化程度普遍较低，这极大地制约了应急物流各环节的效率。为提升应急物流信息化水平，就要加强信息技术在应急物流体系中的应用。《"十四五"纲要》也强调指出，"加快构建数字技术辅助政府决策机制，提高基于高频大数据精准动态监测预测预警水平"。只有将信息平台提供的信息在专业领域进行深度融合，利用系统集成手段对应急物流体系中各环节信息进行整合，及时实现应急物流信息的智能化运用，才可以为应急物流指挥、管理、协调等具体工作提供有力的信息支持。

应用层的主要任务是在各种灾难应急物流信息平台的基础上，根据应急物流体系中不同环节的信息需求，构建统一高效、上下贯通、左右衔接的应急物流信息应用中心。按照应急物流体系各环节的信息需求，应急物流信息系统可以建成为应急物流各子系统服务的信息系统，如应急物流指挥信息系统、应急物流管理信息系统、应急物流保障信息系统，以及保障系统间信息互通的应急物流综合信息系统。例如，在对应急物资进行运输和配送环节的管理中，应急物流信息平台可以通过整合全球定位系统（GPS）、全球移动通信系统（GSM）、地理信息系统（GIS）等现代信息技术，对应急物资运输车辆进行全天候、高精度、大规模、大范围地实时动态定位，提高车辆的运行效率和行进安全，有效提高应急物资的运输能力。

## 3.3　我国应急物流信息系统的功能构建

作为应急物流体系的神经中枢，信息系统的信息网遍布各个子系统，因而需要建构多重功能，以便为应急物流各系统各环节提供信息保障。从应急物流行动的启动，到应急物流指挥决策，再到应急物资管理部门的沟通协调以及应急物流保障系统的运行，应急物流体系各个环节的高效可靠运转都离不开信息系统的支撑。按照信息系统在应急物流体系中的功能和作用，我国应急物流信息系统可以分为应急物流指挥信息系统、应急物流管理信息系统、应急物流保障信息系统和应急物流综合信息系统。

### 3.3.1　应急物流指挥信息系统

应急物流指挥信息系统是信息技术在应急物流指挥工作中的应用系

统。虽然我国在部分行业和领域的信息化程度和规模已经比较成熟，但与许多发达国家相比，在应急物流方面的信息化程度还很低。在应急物流指挥决策方面，不仅面临着信息传递不及时、准确度不高、数据分析能力有限等问题，还缺乏统一的指挥信息共享平台。在紧急情况下，即便有了各种信息的及时采集，但缺乏完善的、行之有效的应急物流信息平台支撑，海量的信息资源也无法有效利用，第一手的信息也难以转化成决策依据。建立应急物流指挥信息平台，采用先进的技术手段处理各种数据和信息，实现信息的集成化、智能化处理，可以极大地提升应急物流指挥工作的效率。例如，在事故灾难发生后，可以通过遥感技术、数据库和网络通信等技术的应用，准确定位受灾区域，快速获取受灾信息，以便根据有关信息快速进行应急物流的决策，为应急物流指挥工作提供信息化保障。

按照应急物流指挥机构中央、省、市和区（县）四个级别的纵向构成，有必要构建四级指挥信息共享制度。在紧急突发事件爆发后，灾区所属区域应急物流指挥机构迅速根据灾区需求启动应急物流程序，同时上报上级应急物流指挥机构，借助信息系统的信息支持形成决策。在必要的情况下，可以申请上级应急物流指挥机构进行指导，或申请其他临近区域应急物流指挥中心的支援和配合。在这个过程中，各个相关部门需要及时交换信息，借助必要的设备和软件进行视频、微信或电话等有效沟通。同时，应急物流指挥信息系统还要遵循一定的信息共享标准，基于网络信息技术提高信息共享能力。

### 3.3.2 应急物流管理信息系统

应急物流管理信息系统是信息技术在应急物流管理工作中的应用系统。应急物流管理不只是狭义的对物资流通的管理，而是涉及对应急物流人员、资金、物资的全方位综合管理。离开信息化技术手段的支持，如此庞杂的管理系统势必会陷入管理混乱、条目不清、难以协调的境地。虽然应急物流体系将人、财、物纳入统一管理，但管理对象间的巨大差异使得管理内容和手段大不相同。《"十四五"国家应急体系规划》指出，"建设绿色节能型高密度数据中心，推进应急管理云计算平台建设，完善多数据中心统一调度和重要业务应急保障功能"。只有通过运用"大数据""云计算"等现代信息技术对各管理对象进行数据分析，才能有效地掌握各方信息，对人、财、物多项内容进行统一规划、调度、分配等管理，实现应急物流行动对人员、资金和物资的保障需求。

应急物流管理信息系统可以分为应急物流人员管理信息系统、应急物流资金管理信息系统和应急物流物资管理信息系统三个部分。应急物流人员管理信息系统将对应急物流人员的管理信息统一汇聚在一起，包括应急物流人员的招募与动员、培养与培训、委派与调用、考核与评估等。通过打破体制和制度壁垒，将政府、军队、企业、社会团体、民众等诸多应急物流专业人员和志愿者纳入应急物流人员管理信息网，实现应急物流人员信息共享，既方便对应急物流人员的统一指挥和调度，又可以为应急物流从业者提供一个开放、公平、便捷的信息使用环境。应急物流资金管理信息系统将政府应急物流专项资金、企业赞助资金、社会团体和个人的捐款纳入统一的管理信息系统，接受政府和公众的信息监督和共享，更有利于实现应急物流资金使用的透明度，实现资金使用效率最大化。应急物流物资管理信息系统更是将应急物资的一切相关信息综合在一起，包含应急物资的规划、采购与生产、储备、调度与征用、运输与配送、发放与回收等。通过建立信息共享标准规范，实现应急物资准备阶段的科学化、应急物资运输配送阶段的可视化，以及应急物资回收处理阶段的绿色环保化。

### 3.3.3　应急物流保障信息系统

应急物流保障信息系统是信息技术在应急物流保障工作中的应用系统。应急物流既需要应急物流相关的法律法规和规章制度等政策文件的保障，又需要"交通运输基础设施、通信基础设施、物资储备基础设施、物流信息网络基础设施等"（汪莹、樊九林，2022）基础设施的保障。当然，应急物流还离不开社会其他方方面面的保障。建立统一的应急物流保障信息系统，可以利用保障信息系统的公开共享功能，有效避免保障需求的片面化和重复化，为应急物流系统的顺利运转充分做好各方面的准备。

从法律法规等政策制度的保障方面来说，将与应急物流相关的国家和各地方的政策法规、预案等各种相关文件统一纳入保障信息系统，既方便应急物流相关人员进行工作参考，还有利于各级、各地应急物流相关机构相互学习和借鉴，完善相应的法律法规和各种预案等政策文件。

从基础设施的保障方面来说，将交通运输、通信、物资储备、物流信息网络等基础设施纳入保障信息系统，可以为应急物流活动的开展构建良好的物理环境基础。通过信息系统的资源共享和信息传递功能，既有助于应急物流相关基础设施的日常维护和完善，又能在危害发生、基础设施受损时及时反馈相关信息，确保灾后基础设施的及时修复和重建。

### 3.3.4　应急物流综合信息系统

应急物流综合信息系统是为整个应急物流活动提供信息保障的应用系统，是要综合解决从受灾信息各个渠道的信息收集，到应急物流活动各环节的信息协调和沟通，再到应急物流活动结束后的评估和反馈信息，这一贯穿始终的信息传递问题。应急物流综合信息系统既要有支撑信息系统自身运转的功能，又要有维护信息子系统间沟通协作的功能，还应成为各防灾相关机构进行信息交换和沟通的场所。

首先，应急物流综合信息系统要有支撑信息系统自身运转的功能。作为一个信息类的应用系统，应急物流综合信息系统需要具备数据的收集、整理、存储、加工、统计、检索等功能。这就需要融合各种先进的信息技术，以维持信息系统的正常运行。

其次，应急物流综合信息系统要有维护信息子系统间沟通协作的功能。《"十四五"国家应急体系规划》指明，"系统推进'智慧应急'建设，建立符合大数据发展规律的应急数据治理体系，完善监督管理、监测预警、指挥救援、灾情管理、统计分析、信息发布、灾后评估和社会动员等功能"。应急物流信息系统正是涵盖了这诸多功能的应急数据治理系统，但这些功能并非各自独立，而是相辅相成，需要一个专门的应急物流综合信息系统进行子系统间的沟通和协作，形成应急物流体系各子系统间的"神经网络节点"，构建信息纵横畅通的应急物流信息系统。

最后，应急物流综合信息系统还要具备为各防灾相关机构提供信息交换和沟通的功能。按照日本的建设经验，日本政府建设的"防灾相互通信网，可以在现场让警察署、海上保安厅、国土交通厅、消防厅等各防灾相关机构彼此交换各种现场救灾信息，以更有效、更有针对性地进行灾害的救援和指挥"（左小德，2011）。为了加强我国防灾相关机构的信息交流和协作，应急物流综合信息系统可以将各个防灾相关机构连接在一起，共建"防灾相互通信网"，为各防灾机构打造信息沟通和共享的平台，从而为应急物流指挥和决策部门的信息来源搭建崭新的平台。

# 第4章　我国应急物流管理系统的建设

作为应急物流体系的一个子系统，应急物流管理系统主要涉及与应急物流相关的人、财、物三个方面的管理，核心目的是更好地满足应急物流行动对人员、资金和物资的需求。将所有与物流相关的需求统一纳入应急物流管理系统下，有利于集中规划、统筹管理、灵活匹配和及时补给。

## 4.1　我国应急物流管理系统的建设原则

我国应急物流管理系统从应急物流的角度出发，结合各要素的特点，遵循管理学的科学管理方法，将应急物流行动中的人、财、物纳入统一管理。为了对多方面要素实施科学有效的管理，就要遵循以下建设原则。

### 4.1.1　统一领导，分级负责

不管是中央还是地方，要将应急物流保障人员以及资金、物资的管理纳入党和政府的统一领导下，才能充分发挥集中规划和统筹管理的优势，避免多方管理带来的混乱和沟通不畅。具体的管理可由各级政府分别进行，以利于上下联动。

### 4.1.2　依法规范，加强管理

要依法规范应急物流中人、财、物的管理，在符合国家法律、法规和规章的前提下确保人力、财力、物力的供给稳定可靠，能够充分满足各级各类公共安全事件的紧急物资保障，从而为实施有效的管理打下坚实的基础。

### 4.1.3　节省资源，专常兼备

对应急物流的保障人员、资金与物资的管理要做到专常兼备，就要充分考虑到平时和"急"时两种状态下的管理特点。既要居安思危，做好应急条件下的管理，还要优化日常管理，在平时的管理中不浪费人财物资源。

### 4.1.4　依靠科技，清晰透明

应急物流管理系统中对人、财、物的管理是多层次、多方面、多渠道的动态管理，不依靠科技的力量，就无法实现管理的科学和高效。只有借助科学的管理方法和强大的技术支撑，才能使人、财、物各阶段的管理信息和状态清晰显现出来，才能使复杂的管理系统变得清晰透明。

### 4.1.5　快速反应，协调应对

为了及时满足应急物流对人、财、物的需求，就需要快速反应，及时地将这些资源进行部署分配。由于公共突发事件的不可预测性，不可避免地会涉及将资源进行区域内、区域间甚至上下级间借调和调拨的情况。快速协调应对是实现应急物流对人、财、物的需求保障的重要一环。

## 4.2 我国应急物流的人员管理

应急物流人员是维护应急物流体系各个子系统和应急物流活动各个环节顺利运转的人力保障。应急物流人员泛指一切为应急物流行动付出努力的人员，包括应急物流指挥决策人员、应急物流信息技术人员、应急物流管理人员、应急物流运输配送人员和应急物流保障人员等。从人员自身归属及提供应急物流服务的性质来说，有属于政府和军队的公共服务人员、属于市场的商务服务人员、属于社会团体的慈善服务人员，以及民众自发的志愿服务人员。对于应急物流人员的管理，要充分发挥不同人员的特点，将不同功能不同服务性质的应急物流人员纳入统一的管理系统中，形成优势互补、协同服务的应急物流人员管理机制。在应急物流体系中，对应急物流人员的管理主要包括应急物流人员的招募与动员、培养与培训、委派与调用、考核与评估。

### 4.2.1 应急物流人员的招募与动员

我国公共安全事件在特定区域内应急物流行动的次数可谓屈指可数，因而作为"未雨绸缪"的服务保障队伍，应急物流可以保持一定数量的常设人员，在有应急行动时也要招募一定数量的应急人员临时加入。应急物流人员的来源广泛，构成复杂，不仅包括专业性强的技术人员，也包括一些基层劳动人员、社会志愿者等，这就需要一个统一的应急物流人员管理系统，对多主体、多来源的应急物流人员进行招募和动员。

本着节省资源、专常兼备的原则，政府可以建立"应急物流人力资源库"，将各种突发公共安全事件下应急物流所涉及各领域的专业人才和志愿者纳入"应急物流人力资源库"进行统一管理。资源库人员是可供随时任命或调遣的机动人员，经个人及所在单位同意纳入应急物流管理体系，建立应急物流人员个人档案。各地可根据地域内可能发生的公共安全事件类型，按照统一领导、分级负责的原则，由各地政府负责进行自属地应急物流人员的招募和动员工作。除维持日常必需的岗位需要专职人员外，其他非日常岗位则可根据具体灾情在人员预备库中选任。资源库人员日常服务于所在的工作单位和岗位，在紧急物流行动需要的时候听从政府紧急调遣，积极完成所分配的任务。

另外，在面临重大公共安全事件时，还需要调动全民积极性，动员民众广泛参与，以完成应急物流的保障任务。在我国新冠疫情期间，不乏民众自发加入应急物流行动，甚至自发组织开展紧急物资互助和自救的事例，这都极大地提高了应急物流的效率。

## 4.2.2　应急物流人员的培养与培训

虽然大多数应急物流人员是来自各领域的专业力量，能够胜任所分派的应急物流工作，但是基于应急物流的专业性及行动的特殊性和紧急性，仍需要重视对应急物流人员的培养和培训，以便更好地发挥不同人员的优势和特点，更好地开展应急物流行动。

首先，加强高校应急物流专业及相关课程体系的建设。随着我国对应急物流的日益重视，已经有个别高校开设了应急物流的相关课程，以满足社会对应急物流专业人才的需求，如物流学院开设应急物流课程，应急管理学院开设应急物流与供应链管理课程等。但是，应急物流体系是一个庞大的系统，它的运行涉及各行各业与应急物流的交叉应用，目前对应急物流人才的培养只局限于个别学校个别相关课程的点状开设，缺乏全面性、综合性、系统性的专业培养，这无疑会极大地制约对应急物流专业人才的有力补充。从根本上有效培养应急物流专业人才，就要从高等教育入手，加快应急物流专业和相关课程体系的建设，全方位培养应急物流专业人才。

其次，建立应急物流人员的常态培训制度。由于目前我国尚未构建统一的应急物流人员管理系统，因而对现有应急物流人员的管理缺乏针对性的培训制度。实现有效的应急物流人员管理，就要根据预案对不同环节的应急物流人员进行分类管理，定期进行应急物流行动的专业技能和流程培训，甚至进行应急物流行动的预习演练，以更好地促进应急物流体系的正常运转。如，"根据应急物流岗位能力需求，重点培养统筹能力强、管理素质高、专业技能全的指挥管理人才；重点锻炼快速分仓布局、港口装卸搬运、集装包装作业、大货司机等一线关键岗位人才；重点扶持精研保障预案、演练指导、辅助决策的专家型人才"（黄剑炜、贺电、杨朝江，2021）。同时，建立应急物流人员培养培训信息数据库，对应急物流人员的培养和培训进行数字化管理，形成动态的应急物流人员培养培训机制。

### 4.2.3　应急物流人员的委派与调用

应急物流人员既有专编的常备应急管理人员，又有应急物流预备库人员、科研工作人员、专业技术人员、军地一体化物流人员、企业应急物流人员和社会志愿者等。针对每次的紧急公共安全事件，都需要紧急委派和调用各种应急物流人员组成应急物流队伍，统筹规划人员分配，根据个人专长进行委派和调用。

首先，要做到知人善用。应急物流人力资源库人员个人档案及其培训培养记录要公开透明。各地需要结合各地易发公共安全事件的性质，熟练掌握人力资源库人员的专长和特点，以便紧急集结应急物流队伍，进行任务委派，紧急响应应急物流行动。

其次，要完善征调制度。除了常规的专职应急物流人员，大多数的应急物流人员都日常服务于原工作岗位。因而在紧急事件发生后，要根据征调制度进行临时的调动，以快速满足应急物流的人员需求。另外，应急物流行动经常面临跨地区的支援，因而除了区域内征调，还要完善跨区域征调制度，依法办事，规范应急物流行动。

最后，要建立用人薪资补偿机制。对于紧急征调的应急物流人员，要根据当地薪资水平制定用人薪资补偿措施。对紧急加入应急物流行动的人员给予合理的薪资补助和津贴，保障应急物流人员的正当权益，提高应急物流人员的工作积极性。

### 4.2.4　应急物流人员的考核与评估

对应急物流人员加强管理，还要建立考评机制，对应急物流人员进行考核和评估，以保障从事应急物流人员的素质、能力及工作态度和热情。

首先，对报名应急物流人力资源库的人员进行资质考核，合格人员发放应急物流人员资质证明，纳入应急物流人力资源库。

其次，各地可根据实际情况自行制定政策，对参与应急物流行动的人员进行过程考核与评估。在考核中，既可针对具体地应急物流行动对应急物流行动参与者进行考评，也可结合相关培训等情况进行年度考评。考核既要鼓励先进，又要查找问题，并及时进行反思整改，在确保应急物流人员业务素质和工作能力的同时，增强他们的大局意识、责任意识和奉献意识。

## 4.3　我国应急物流的资金管理

应急物流资金是支撑应急物流体系各个子系统顺利运行、应急物流活动各个环节顺利运转的财力保障。我国对应急物流资金的管理主要包括应急物流资金的筹集、应急物流资金的使用以及应急物流资金的监管与评估三个方面。

### 4.3.1　应急物流资金的筹集

与应急物流行动一样，应急物流资金的筹集需要各方的共同参与和努力。但是，由于应急管理部门的性质和作用，除以个人身份进行捐款外，部门并不具备整体筹集资金的能力。因而，对于应急物流资金的筹集来说，应以政府专项拨款和社会公益捐款相结合的方式进行，建立多元化的资金投入机制。

首先，完善应急物流资金储备制度。加强制度建设，建立健全应急物流资金储备及管理条例，将应急物流资金的筹集纳入法治体系进行规范和保障。

其次，加强政府专项拨款。充分发挥政府职能，将应急物流资金纳入政府专项拨款范畴，努力消除地区和城乡差异，建立应急物流资金池，加强应急物流资金的储备。

最后，引导多元化资金投入。发挥政策导向作用，鼓励自然人、法人或者其他组织（包括国际组织）按照《中华人民共和国公益事业捐赠法》等有关法律、法规的规定进行捐赠和援助，引导企业、社团、个人等多元化的资金投入。

## 4.3.2  应急物流资金的使用

作为专项资金，应急物流资金的使用必须与应急物流行动密切相关。应急物流资金的流向可以覆盖应急物流行动之前、之中、之后的全过程。在应急物流资金的使用中，要整合优化各种资源，形成政策合力。

首先，应急物流行动前准备资金的使用。为了做好应急物流的准备，需要人力、财力和物力的投入，而人力和物力都离不开财力的保障。从应急物流的演练费用、应急物流人员的培训、应急物流设施设备的完善，再到应急物资的采购与储存，各个环节均需要资金的支持才能顺利完成。

其次，应急物流行动中资金的使用。应急物流行动启动后，需要大量专业人员的临时调用和专家委员会的咨询服务，需要运输车辆到应急物资储存库和储存基地进行装运和运输，有时还需要临时采购紧缺物资，这些都需要资金的支撑，来满足购买应急物流服务的费用。

最后，应急物流行动结束后资金的使用。即便应急物流行动结束，灾区得到了充足的物资保障，仍需要资金投入来进行收尾工作。例如，对部分应急物资进行回收处置，对紧急征用物资进行事后补偿，对于各种相关设施设备进行维修、维护和保养，等等。

### 4.3.3 应急物流资金的监管和评估

《国家突发公共事件总体应急预案》指出，"要对突发公共事件财政应急保障资金的使用和效果进行监管和评估"。有了应急物流资金专项储备金制度，就要对资金的筹集和使用进行有效的监管和评估，以规范资金运作，提高资金使用效率。

首先，完善应急物流资金管理法律法规。在遵循应急物流资金管理法律法规的基础上，建立应急物流资金使用责任制，严肃查处应急物流资金管理制度的违规行为。加强应急物流资金专款专用，杜绝挪用占用。

其次，健全监督机制，实现应急物流资金动态化监督。设立专门的监督部门，加强应急物流资金全过程的动态监管，切实发挥各级应急物流管理机构的作用，提高应急物流资金监督的权威性。

最后，健全应急物流资金评估机制，开展应急物流资金常态化审查评估。按照职责分工，组织上级领导部门对年度应急物流资金实施审查评估，提交审查评估报告，将审查评估结果作为改进应急物流资金管理的重要依据。

## 4.4 我国应急物流的物资管理

应急物资是指在紧急公共安全事件即将发生前用于控制事故发生，或事故发生后用于疏散、抢救、抢险等应急救援的工具、物品、设备、器材、装备等一切相关物资。应急物资是实现应急物流服务的重要内容，也是应对紧急公共突发事件中物资保障的核心目的所在。对于不同种类的紧急公共突发事件，应急物资的目录不同，用途也不一。应急物资种类繁多，由于我国尚未形成统一的分类标准，这也造成了物资管理的难度。根据《国家突发公共事件总体应急预案》，要确保应急所需物资和生活用品的及时供应，做好受灾群众的基本生活保障工作和医疗卫生保障。做好

"基本生活保障"，就是要确保灾区群众有饭吃、有水喝、有衣穿、有住处、有病能得到及时医治。而做好医疗卫生保障，就离不开及时为受灾地区提供药品、器械等卫生和医疗设备。根据灾区群众的总体需求，应急物资基本可分为生命救助类物资、生活类物资和灾后重建物资（孟祥娟、许耀坤，2016）。对于应急物资的管理，则要考虑到各类应急物资的性质和特点，既要准备充足，又要节省资源，实现应急物资的科学有效管理。当突发事件发生后，应当立即启动应急物流行动，由指挥机构根据突发事件的类型、影响范围、灾区气候情况等因素，结合应急物流指挥信息系统中的数据，初步判断应急物资的需求情况，做出应急物流决策。应急物流管理机构根据管理信息系统中存储的信息，查询应急物资的准备情况，包括物资的分布、品种、储备等，根据查询到的信息紧急筹措和采购应急物资，必要时进行应急物资的调度和征用，组织应急物资绿色通道的运输与配送，及时将应急物资送到灾区。根据救灾进展情况和应急物资使用情况，还要对应急物资进行必要的回收与处理。总之，对应急物资的管理至少应当包括应急物资的规划、采购与生产、储备、调度与征用、运输与配送、发放与回收这些环节。

### 4.4.1 应急物资的规划

应急物资的规划指的是应急物资种类、数量、来源、存储地点等方面的规划。各级应急物流指挥机构要按照应急物流预案做好应急物资的规划，根据所属地的地域特点和可预计危害类型做好应急物资目录，明确所属地应急物资的种类、数量、来源及存储地点等信息。

首先，对应急物资的种类要进行科学规划。根据所属地易发生公共安全事件的类型和特点制定应急物资目录，除普遍需要的食品、饮用水等生活必备物资外，各地区要有针对性地丰富特定的应急物资种类，如，地震多发区的帐篷、宿营车、移动房屋、棉衣、棉被等生活物资，海难多发区的救生衣、救生艇（筏）、救生缆索等水上救助物资，雪灾多发区的棉衣、融雪剂、防滑料等防寒救助物资。

其次，对应急物资的数量要进行科学规划。根据区域内突发公共安全事件发生的性质和频率，以及各物资储备中心的服务范围，进行适当数量的储备，以确保在事件发生后能满足需求，同时严格控制数量过多导致损耗或变质。对易于存放且保质期较长的物资，如帐篷、棉衣、棉被等，要有数量充足的储备。对于保质期短不易存放的物资，如食品、药品等，则可采用定期定额补给的方式，保持物资的循环补充和更新，避免造成大规模的损耗和浪费。

再次，对应急物资的来源要进行科学规划。要以储备为主，辅以及时采购、调拨以及社会的爱心捐赠。各地的应急物流管理部门要根据当地预案，对符合属地特点的常规应急物资进行一定规模的储备，确保基本满足中等程度的突发公共安全事件。当发生重大突发公共安全事件时，如果储备不足以满足需求，则可通过向合作供应商进行紧急采购、邻区调拨的方式及时进行物资补充。同时，企业、社团和民众的爱心捐赠也是应急物资的重要来源之一，为抗灾救灾发挥着不容忽视的作用。但是社会捐赠物资品类复杂、规格不等、质量良莠不齐，这不仅会增加应急物流的额外负担，还会造成物资供需失调。因此，政府应该根据突发事件的性质、级别及物资需求等反馈信息，向公众传达应急物资捐赠的侧重点。

最后，对应急物资的存储地点要科学规划。应急物资存储地点的设置，要最大程度地接近事故多发地，同时考虑交通便利性。这样既可以降低应急物流活动成本，发挥更大的物流效应，还便于紧急运输，及时将应急物资运往灾区，为保障受灾人民的生命财产安全节省宝贵时间。

## 4.4.2　应急物资的采购与生产

应急物资的采购既包括应急物资储备性的常规采购，也包括公共安全事件突发时紧缺物资补给性的紧急采购。应急物资的常规采购可以根据预案，按照应急物资规划的种类和数量进行，做到品种适宜、质量可靠、数量充足、常备不懈，确保应急物资之需。而应急物资的紧急采购则需要根据突发事件的性质和危害、灾后救援的具体需求、物资储备情况等因素有针对性地进行。由于我国尚未建立完善的应急物资存储体系，再加上突发事件的不可预测性，不可避免地会造成某些应急物资的短缺，况且许多基本生活物资和医疗卫生物资并不适宜大量储备，因而常规采购通常无法完全满足救灾的需求。尤其是在经济较为落后的地区，存在应急物资储备点少、分布不均衡、硬件设施不完善、存储物资种类单一、数量不足等各种问题（陈慧，2016），物资需求更是难以保障。社会捐赠的应急物资不仅响应速度慢，种类还容易过度集中，这导致受灾初期部分种类物资缺乏而后期又超常饱和，造成严重浪费，而有些紧缺的应急物资却得不到有效补充。因此，除了应急物资的常规采购，还需要应急物资的紧急采购，这也是紧缺应急物资紧急补给的重要方式。

应急物资的采购要在政府的统一领导下，由各地应急物流管理中心负责，建立应急物资采购预案和应急物资采购体系。不管是常规采购还是紧急采购，应急物资的采购都属于政府行为，因而要依据政府采购法进行。应急物流的常规采购方式以公开招标为主，但也允许采用其他采购方式，如邀请招标采购、竞争性谈判采购、单一来源采购、询价采购等其他采购方式，实现应急物资的实物储备。对于应急物资的紧急采购方式，则可以采用较为灵活的采购方式，除单一来源采购、询价采购外，还可以在完善应急物资采购法规的前提下，实现政府与市场合作，建立合同储备制度。合同储备制度是指由应急物流管理中心事先与生产应急物资的企业签订预购合同，一旦突发事件发生则立即启动预购合同，签约企业以合同价位迅速提供质量可靠的物资。这样既可减少实物储备所消耗的费用，又能及时满足应急物资的需求，也可避免紧缺物资坐地起价，降低应急资金的效益。

应急物资的采购行为能否顺利完成，与应急物资的生产能力密切相关。在我国新冠疫情的三年中，不少民众都经历过医用口罩、酒精、药品等防护用品的短缺，这都与生产企业的生产能力密不可分。因此，政府在完善应急物资采购法的同时，还要加强应急物资生产法等配套法规的建立和健全，规范应急物资的生产行为，保障应急物资的优先生产。同时，"实施应急产品生产能力储备工程，建设区域性应急物资生产保障基地"

（《"十四五"纲要》），引导企业加大应急物资生产能力建设投入，支持应急物资领域有实力的企业做强做优，培育一批在国际、国内市场具有较强竞争力的应急物资大型企业集团，鼓励特色明显、创新能力强的中小微应急物资企业利用现有资金渠道加速发展。另外，采用推荐目录、鼓励清单等形式，引导社会资源投向先进、适用、可靠的应急物资生产和服务。

### 4.4.3　应急物资的储备

应急物资的储备对应急物流行动的顺利运行至关重要。我国目前的应急物资储备面临着物资储备主体结构不合理、储备库布局不科学、储备物资种类数量不灵活、物资储备管理不清晰、物资储备技术不先进等问题。《"十四五"国家应急体系规划》中强调，"建立中央和地方、政府和社会、实物和产能相结合的应急物资储备模式"。建立科学合理的应急物资储备模式，就要着重加强对物资储备主体、物资储备库分布、物资储备种类和储量、物资储备管理、物资储备技术等方面的完善和优化。

从应急物资储备主体结构来看，要建立"五级五位一体化"的应急物资储备体系。我国目前虽然形成了一定的应急物资储备网络，从中央到地方、从政府到民间都有一定的应急物资储备，但不同行政级别、不同主体的储备意识并不统一，尤其是部分地区和民众的储备意识不足。要完善应急物资储备的主体结构，就要健全中央—省—市—县—乡五级纵向以及政府—应急部门—企业—社团—民众五位横向的应急物资储备体系，实现中央和地方结合、政企社民合作的"五级五位一体化"应急物资综合储备网络。

从应急物资储备库分布来看，要建设辐射全国的应急物资储备库新布局。首先，完善中央级应急物资储备库布局。2003 年我国已经建立 10 个中央级应急物资储备库以及 31 个省级储备库，但是中央级储备库大都分布在中东部，西部地区仅在西安设置，布局存在很大不合理性。要扩大应急物资储备库的西部辐射范围，可以在西南地区新增昆明、重庆和拉萨三个应急物资储备库，西北地区新增兰州和乌鲁木齐两个应急物资储备库，以覆盖整个西部地区。同时，还要完善其他区域的储备库布局。华北地区新增石家庄，和天津一起负责山西、北京、内蒙古大部的地区。在保有合肥储备中心地位的同时，在华东地区新设福州应急物资储备库。在华南地区新增广州，广州储备库不但可以保障两广地区应急物资需要，同时，对香港和澳门也具有较强的服务作用，并且可以更好地接收国际支援物资（孙永春，2013）。其次，充分发挥政军企的专业储备力量，加强各地应急物资储备基地建设。在政府方面，依托现有中央和地方物资储备库，在交通枢纽城市、人口密集区域、易发生重特大自然灾害区域建设一批综合性应急物资储备基地；在军队方面，建设完善军队救援队伍应急物资储备库及战勤保障站；在企业方面，依托大型快递物流企业建设一批应急物资调运平台和区域配送中心。

从应急物资储备种类和储量来看，建立实物和产能结合的应急物资储备体系。除优化应急物资储备库布局，做好实物的应急物资储备外，还要"实施应急产品生产能力储备工程，建设区域性应急物资生产保障基地"（《"十四五"国家应急体系规划》），将季节性强、保质期短、周转周期短的物资生产纳入产能储备，动态调整实物和产能储备的种类和数量。首先，完善鼓励、引导重点应急物资产能储备企业扩能政策，持续完善应急物资产业链。其次，将符合条件的企业纳入产能储备企业范围，制定应急物资产能储备目录清单，加强应急物资生产能力动态监控。最后，还要加强对重大灾害事故物资需求的预判研判，完善应急物资储备和集中生产调度机制。

从应急物资储备的管理来看，要建立制度化的管理理念和科学的管理模式。由于"我国尚未建立明确的应急物资储备机制及管理办法，应急物资储备多由当地政府结合地区实际情况开展"（陈慧，2014）。在缺乏规范的制度指导的前提下，我国的应急物资储备管理就无法做到规范合理，带有较大的主观性和随意性。另外，有些地区应急物资的储备种类不合理、数量不够用、存储环境差、仓储作业机械化较低。要加强应急物资储备的管理，首先，要建立严格的应急物资储备制度。只有在相关法律、法规和应急预案的指导下，才能做好物资储备工作。各地应急物资机构应通过明确应急物资储备的基本原则，建立应急物资储备目录，健全使用情况报告制度等措施，科学调整应急物资储备品类、规模和结构，规范对应急物资储备的管理。其次，采用对应急物资存储进行分类管理的方法。在对应急物资储备进行管理的过程中，可以借鉴企业物流管理中对库存进行管理的ABC 分类法，科学确定应急物资的储备规模，实现应急物资的库存控制。在分类时要注意不同突发事件对应急物资的不同需求，如地震多发区大量储备救灾帐篷、医疗器械等物资，矿难易发区重点储备救生器材、消防设备等。按照不同的类别对应急物资进行分类管理，可以采取不同的库存策略来降低成本，提高利用率和综合效益。

从应急物资储备的技术层面来看，要加强应急物资储备库的科技含金量。首先，从硬件上配置专业化的仓储设备。我国目前应急物流储存库的机械化程度较低，不少储备中心的作业还是靠人工，叉车等专业化的仓储工具使用较少，因而无法在短时间内完成作业，导致应急物流行动的延误。其次，从软件上采用先进的分拣技术，进行集装化储存管理。采用分拣组套技术对应急物资进行管理，形成综合性单元模块，便于精准调拨、快速配送。

### 4.4.4　应急物资的调度与征用

应急物资的调度与征用是对应急物资进行统筹管理的具体体现，有利于提升应急物资的使用率和最大效益。当公共安全事件突发时，如果地方某一级或来自政府、公共应急部门物资的供应不能满足需求时，可以充分利用"五级五位一体化"的应急物资储存网络对应急物资进行紧急调度或征用，以期在最短时间内实现应急物资的保障。首先，推进中央、省、市、县、乡五级应急物资指挥调度平台的建设，实现各级政府应急物资调度的互联互通。其次，建立政军企社民五体应急物资的协调联动。

除了政府和应急管理部门的公共物资，将企业、社会团体、民众多方的社会应急物资进行统筹管理，按照相关政策进行调度或征用，这也正是对"一方有难、八方支援"精神最好的阐释。当然，还要建立社会物资征用的补偿机制。除捐助性质的社会物资外，政府还要按照相关政策对统一调度或征用的社会应急物资进行适度的补偿，以实现"五级五位一体化"应急物资储备系统的可持续发展。

### 4.4.5　应急物资的运输与配送

应急物资的运输是指运用各种运输方式将应急物资从各级应急物资储备库、应急生产企业、社会团体甚至民众手中运送到灾区的过程。这是应急物流得以真正实现的重要环节。长期以来，我国应急物资运输的主要方式为铁路和公路，这对道路设施、交通条件等因素依赖性很高。当发生地震、泥石流等自然灾害导致道路损毁时，应急物资的运输很可能因为道路不通被迫中断，而等待道路修复或找到替代运输方式则使应急物流的时间效益大打折扣，造成灾害损失的扩大。另外，由于应急物流的公益性质，我国目前主要依靠军队作为应急物资运输的主体，这显然难以将不同来源的应急物资及时运送到灾区，实现应急物资的统筹利用。要改善目前应急物资的运输现状，首先要深化应急交通联动机制，落实铁路、公路、航空应急交通保障措施。深化应急交通联动机制，就是要充分发挥不同运输方式在规模、速度、覆盖范围上的优势，构建快速通达、衔接有力、功能适配、安全可靠的综合交通应急运输网络。其次，依托大型骨干物流企业，统筹建立涵盖铁路、公路、水运、民航等各种运输方式的紧急运输储备力量，发挥高铁优势构建力量快速输送系统，保障重特大灾害事故应急资源快速高效投送。依托大型骨干物流企业，就是要充分发挥物流企业的专业优势，推动建立以企业为主体的应急物流运输队伍。最后，还要加强紧急运输绿色通道建设，完善应急物资及人员运输车辆优先通行机制。加强紧急运输绿色通道建设，可以按照"优先计划、优先安排、优先运输、优先入关、优先停靠、优先放行、优先装卸"（陈慧，2014）的原则为应急物流提供"绿色通道"，保障应急物流交通运输线路全时段免费畅通。

应急物资的配送是指对大型车辆集中运送到灾区的大批量应急物资进行分装、分拣和分配，按照具体需求送到各个灾民聚集地的过程。应急物资的配送是应急物流活动的最后一个关键环节，也是我国目前由于效率较为低下造成物流损失较大的一个环节。据统计，"在突发性自然灾害造成的巨大人员伤亡和财产损失中，由于低效的应急物流配送造成的损失约占总损失的 15% ~ 20%"（冯海江、张卫刚、彭春露，2010）。要提高应急物资的配送效率，降低配送过程中造成的物流损失，就要在应急物资的管理中注意以下几个很重要的细节问题。首先，应急物资的包装、分类、标记等管理细节要严谨、科学、规范。考虑到应急物资可能面临的特殊环境，有可能在道路中断时采用直升机、无人机运送等配送方式，因而既要注重包装的密封性和抗撞击性，以减少应急物资被迫空投时被损毁的程度，还要提前做好分类、标记等细节工作，便于灾民快速识别和查找急需物资。其次，应急物资的配送规格要"小型化和便携化"（李艳琴、张立毅、郭纯生，2010）。在应急物资大批量大包装到达灾区等待配送时，为了方便各种小型运输工具甚至人工紧急搬运，要将大包装拆分成小型化、便携化的小规格包装，这样既便于根据实际需求灵活拆分进行配送，又便于配送人员以及志愿者徒手搬运，以确保应急物资配送的"最后一公里"尽快完成。

### 4.4.6　应急物资的发放与回收

应急物资的发放指的是将紧急配送到灾民聚集地的应急物资向灾民进行发放的过程。这是应急物流活动的终级目标，也是实现应急物流物资保障的最后一步。通常情况下，应急物资发放点设在灾民聚集地或救助点附近，或者是学校、体育场、广场这样的公共场所。应急物资发放点要与灾民居住活动场所有适当距离的间隔，以便规划出应急物资发放时的进出通道，避免物资发放过程中引起管理混乱，造成人身安全事故或物资财产的损失。另外，应急物资的发放要统筹规划，按照"先急后缓，突出重点"的原则进行发放。例如，对于需求迫切的紧急类物资如食品、饮用水、药品等优先发放，对于需求迫切性较低的消耗类物资稍晚发放，对于补充类非关键物资则最后发放。在救灾初期，应急物资的发放应以政府为主，确保应急物资及时到达灾民手中。如果物资发放持续时间过长，则可以按照相关法规制度，委托社会专业团体或物流企业开展。这样，既可以及时满足灾民需求，提高应急物资的发放效率，又可以有效避免应急物资发放过程中的腐败或人为不公现象。此外，还可以减轻政府负担，充分发挥社会和企业的专业优势，调动广大社会公众的监督力量。

应急物资的回收指的是将供给过剩或救灾结束后可重复利用的应急物资进行回收，以备二次利用的过程。虽然应急物资按实际需求进行了前期规划，但是灾情发展的不可预测性以及应急物资来源的多渠道性仍会造成某些应急物资过多运往灾区，如果不及时进行回收将会造成物资的极大浪费。总结经验教训之下，首先应当制定相关的规章制度，当应急物资到达灾区后，如果一些保质期短的应急物资因为某些因素导致无法顺利发放，可以按照规定进行灵活处理，如由相关企业接收处理或捐给慈善机构等。对于帐篷、照明灯这些可重复利用的应急物资，则要完善逆向应急物流，在救灾结束后交由相关企业或社会机构进行必要的清洁、维修和回收，既避免对环境产生污染或造成物资浪费，又能进一步完善应急物资的管理，提高应急物资的回收率和修复率。

# 第5章 我国应急物流保障系统的建设

　　我国在应对自然灾害和突发公共卫生事件方面积累了很多经验，尤其是应急物流体系在不断完善、优化，也不难看到我国的综合应急物流体系存在诸多问题。对于自然灾害多发的中国来说，建立应对气候变化和突发公共事件的综合应急物流体系至关重要。建设综合应急物流体系，不但需要各个相关主管部门通力合作，建立一定的协调机制，还需要完善与应急物流相关的法律法规，为体系的建设提供法律保障。该体系还应该能将全社会力量动员起来，使全民参与到社会重大公共事件的应急工作中，并且能够支撑应急物流的信息化设备、交通运输设施的建设等。本章梳理了美国、日本在应急物流保障方面的先进经验，重点研究了我国与应急物流相关的应急管理机制，法律、法规、政策保障机制，应急物流的动员机制，以及物流基础设施建设的保障。

## 5.1　美国的应急物流保障系统建设

　　美国作为发达国家之一，对于突发性灾害事件的应对机制也相对完善，本节简要介绍其应急管理机构的设置、应急管理体系、应急物流的法律法规保障。

## 5.1.1 美国的应急物流管理体系

美国联邦以及州政府层面所有应急事务由联邦应急管理局（Federal Emergency Management Agency，FEMA）实行统一应对和处置。美国联邦应急管理局成立于1979年4月，该机构的主要职责是在联邦政府层面做好全面的防灾、减灾、备灾、救灾工作，同时也要负责灾后的重建工作；其工作的主要目标是将突发性灾害事件的破坏程度降到最低，将公民的生命和财产损失降到最小。在2001年"9·11"事件之后，该机构与其他22个机构一起并入国土安全部，成为国土安全部的一个重要独立机构。该机构可以直接向总统报告事务，专门负责重大灾害应急事务，其主要的应急响应措施之一即是向灾民提供住宿、衣物和食物，保障灾民的生活物资供应。

美国的应急管理体系包括联邦、州政府、地方政府（市政府）三个层次的管理与响应机构，其特点是：统一管理、属地为主、分级响应、标准运行。联邦政府的职责是从全国层面组织协调抗灾救灾等工作。由于美国属于联邦制国家，各州政府的具体做法不尽相同，但大致的应急管理方式都是由州一级政府成立的应急服务办公室，市政府负责管理和协调辖区内的应急响应和灾害恢复活动。有突发性紧急事件发生时，应急行动指挥权属于当地政府，尤其是跨区域的应急事件发生时，当地政府向上一级政府提出求助，上级政府才调用资源进行救助。但上级政府并不能完全接替地方政府的应急事务处置权，而是根据实际情况帮助当地政府协调应急资源，支持地方政府进行灾后救援活动。上级政府可以在灾后对地方政府的救灾物资及资金使用情况进行审计和监督。

应急救援的核心力量是消防、警察和医疗部门，参与救援的主要部门有联邦应急管理局、红十字会、交通、通信、农业、国防等部门。

应急物流管理体系也是遵循应急管理的组织原则。联邦应急管理局设有专门的物流管理单位进行救灾物资的管理和储备，对救灾物资的需求进行监测和预测。在国家突发公共事件时，联邦应急管理局的专门物流管理单位会迅速做出响应，保障救灾物资的筹备和运输。美国法律规定，应急救灾处置权属于当地政府，当地政府救灾能力和资源不足时向州政府提出支援请求，但州政府并不能完全接替当地政府的应急物资等各项资源的处置权；州政府救灾能力和资源不足时可向联邦政府提出支援请求。

### 5.1.2　美国应急物流的法律法规保障

美国早在 1988 年就通过了《斯塔福德灾难与紧急援助法》（*Robert T. Stafford Disaster Relief and Emergency Assistance Act*），简称《斯塔福德法案》，该法规定了自然灾害发生时的救助原则，并规定了联邦政府和州政府、地方政府的协调机制。该法律还明确规定了防灾、减灾和援助的程序，重大灾难与紧急援助机构的设立，重大灾难的援助计划，紧急状态的援助计划和应急预案的制定。该法第 307 条明确规定联邦政府的救援资金应该首先保证受灾地区的物资供应、重建以及其他的救援行动；第 309 条明确规定，在征得允许的情况下，总统可以要求美国红十字会等一系列救援机构来进行应急物资、食物、药品的发放。这些条文的规定，都保障了国家有重大危害事件发生时应急物资的运输和发放畅通。美国还先后于 1977 年颁布了《国家地震灾害减轻法》（*National Earthquake Hazards Reduction Program*），1994 年制定了《美国联邦政府应急反应计划》（*Federal Response Plan*），这几项法规都对应急物流、应急物资的发放进行了描述，保障了应急物流的运作畅通。

## 5.2　日本的应急物流保障系统建设

日本属于太平洋上的岛国，由于其特殊的地理位置和条件，全国处于地震多发带，地震、台风等自然灾害发生频繁。因此，日本在应对自然灾害方面的经验非常丰富，其应急保障机制建立较早，发展也比较完善。

### 5.2.1　日本的应急物流管理体系

日本的应急物流管理体系经历了初步建立、基本建立和基本完善的三个阶段（姜旭，2021）。目前，日本的应急管理体系比较完善，日本设立了中央防灾委员会，应急管理机制为中央政府、都、道、府、县地方政府和市、町、村的三级应急机制，实行"政府为主，政企协同为辅"的应急物流管理体系。政府起到总指挥的作用，同时注重调动各大物流企业及各种协会，包括日本的卡车协会、国际航空联合会、通运联盟、航空货物运输协会，在自然灾害等应急事件发生时，政府协同这些企业和协会进行物资的调拨。应急物资调拨的顺序是"受灾地外—受灾地一级区域物流中心—受灾地二级市物流中心—避难所"（姜旭等，2021），中央政府与相关的物流企业和协会共同协作，保证在最短时间内将应急物资配送到位。

### 5.2.2　日本的应急物流法律法规保障

鉴于日本特殊的地理因素，日本的应急物流体系相关的法律也比较完善，涉及应急物流的主要相关法律按其性质可以分为一般性立法和专门性立法；按其内容可以分为基本法、灾害预防法、灾害应急法和灾后重建与恢复法。一般性立法中，主要法律有 1947 年颁布的《灾害救助法》和 1961 年颁布的《灾害对策基本法》。

《灾害救助法》关于应急物流管理的规定中，专门有对灾害救援的食物、饮用水和医疗物资的紧急调拨的规定条款，还有对地方行政官员合理调拨紧急物资和对地方民用资源的临时征用问题的规定。

《灾害对策基本法》规定了在突发性灾害事件的预防和应急处置中，国家的职责，都、道、府、县的职责和市、町、村的职责，以及各级公共机关和公民的职责。其中，第四章的灾害预防规定必须将防灾物资的储备计划列入灾害预防计划中，规定了防灾和应急物资的储备、调拨和运输等相关事宜；第五章灾害应急对策中也规定了要确保紧急运输的相关事项。

除了对灾害预防和应急措施的规定，日本对灾后重建和补偿机制也有相对完善的法律。《灾害对策基本法》的第六章专门对灾后重建进行了详细的规定，包括灾后重建的实施主体、重建费用的使用以及财政金融的措施。该法的第 82 条和第 84 条分别对从事应急救灾主体的补偿以及对曾经从事应急救灾的人员因救灾受伤、致残或死亡的补偿进行了规定。

# 5.3　我国应急物流保障体系的建设原则

应急物流是为应对各种突发的公共事件而对人力、财力、物力进行流通的一种活动。为提高应急物流运作的效率，降低突发公共事件对人民生命和财产造成的损失，必须要建立一套完善的应急物流保障体系，包括应急物流管理体系、应急物流法律法规保障体系、应急物流的社会动员机制和应急物流基础设施建设的保障体系。而保障体系的建设必须遵循以下四个原则。

## 5.3.1　政府主导，企业参与

我国的各项应急法律法规中都规定，在国家突发重大公共事件时，应急指挥应由中央统一领导、组织；地方发生重大公共事件时，由各级地方政府组织实施应急处置措施。在各级政府的主导下，各大物流企业参与应急物流的运作，发挥企业在物流运作实战方面的优势，将物流行业的专业知识应用到应急物流运作中，提高应急物流的效率。

## 5.3.2　健全法规，完善政策

为保障应急物流的运作畅通，必须健全应急物流相关的各种法律法规及政策，为应急物流的运作提供法律保障。从最初的在《国家突发公共事件总体应急预案》《突发事件应急预案管理办法》等文件中只能找到关于应急物流的只言片语，到后来的《物流业发展中长期规划（2014—2020年)》《国家突发事件应急体系建设"十三五"规划》《"十四五"现代物流发展规划》等文件，将应急物流规划作为一项重要的国家发展规划任务。可以看出，应急物流体系的建设正是由于有了法律法规和国家政策的保障，才得以逐渐完善。

### 5.3.3　政府动员，全民参与

在重大公共事件发生时，除了政府的统一领导、协调组织，联合物流企业完成应急物流的运作，政府还有一项重要的工作即进行社会动员，动员广大人民群众参与到应急物流的运作实践中。具体包括防灾阶段的全民危机意识培养、应急物流人才的培养；抗灾减灾阶段广泛动员社会各界力量，全民参与抗灾救灾工作；灾后重建阶段动员社会各方力量参与到灾后重建中，使灾区尽快恢复经济活力。

### 5.3.4　规范设施建设，提高利用效率

应急物流基础设施的建设包括交通运输通道、物流园区、仓储设备、搬运设备、物流信息技术等的建设。在交通运输通道合理布局的前提下，应急物流要利用好公路、铁路、航空运输等主要运输通道，常态下作为普通物流的交通运输通道在紧急突发事件发生时应迅速转化为应急运输通道，提高基础设施的利用率，避免资源浪费。物流设备和物流信息技术的建设，要依靠高新科技手段，将普通物流设备和信息技术应用到应急物流运作中。同时要注重应急物流专门设施的建设，如停机坪、紧急避难场所等的建设。

# 5.4　我国应急物流的管理体系建设

本书对应急物流管理体系的定义，借鉴姜旭等（2021）的定义：能正确评估、有效预测预警和高效保障事故灾害、自然灾害、社会安全事件和公共卫生事件发生过程中物资、信息流通的系统。我国应急物流起步较晚，应急物流管理体系的发展可以分为两个阶段。1949—2003 年为突发公共事件分类管理阶段，我国当时没有应急管理的概念，当自然灾害等紧急事件发生时，由水利、地震等相关部门负责自然灾害的应对；2003 年非典疫情结束后，我国开始建设应急物流管理体系，正逐步形成了以"应急预案，应急管理体制、机制、法制"的"一案三制"为核心的应急物流管理体系（姜旭等，2021）。目前，应急物流管理体系处在一个探索和逐渐完善的过程中。

我国在重大紧急公共事件突发时，应急物流管理遵循党中央、国务院统一领导，各级地方政府分级负责的组织方式。目前，我国实行中央、省、市、县（区）的四级联动机制（杨山峰，2020），成立各级应急物流组织管理机构。在常态下，由国务院应急管理办公室牵头，协调交通运输部、商务部等制定完善的应急物流预案。在突发重大紧急公共事件后，由国务院应急管理办公室统一协调交通运输部、公安部、商务部等各部门进行应急物流的运作。应急物流的运行在政府主导下，鼓励各个物流企业参与，将企业的行业知识、企业物流运作的经验应用到应急物流中，发挥企业和行业的优势，同时在必要时会动员军事力量的参与，借助军事运输力量、运输设施和运输通道，提高应急物流的效率，缩短应急物流的时间，最大限度降低受灾地区人民群众的生命和财产损失。

## 5.5 我国应急物流的法律法规和政策保障体系建设

应急物流的运作与实践要依靠完善的法律法规和政策的保障，使应急物流的运作能有法可依。我国应急物流相关法律法规的发展经历了很长的时间，也是一个逐步发展完善的过程。本节对我国重要的应急物流法律法规和政策等文件进行梳理，为本领域的研究者提供重要的参考。

我国于 2006 年 1 月 8 日发布并实施《国家突发公共事件总体应急预案》，将突发公共事件分为自然灾害、事故灾难、公共卫生事件，以及社会安全事件。预案强调各有关部门要按照职责分工和相关预案做好突发公共事件的应对工作，做好物资保障、人民的基本生活保障、医疗卫生保障、交通运输保障。

2006 年 6 月 15 日发布的《国务院关于全面加强应急管理工作的意见》（国发〔2006〕24 号）强调，要加强应对突发公共事件的能力建设，包括：推进国家应急平台体系建设，提高基层应急管理能力，加强应急救援队伍建设，加强各类应急资源的管理，全力做好应急处置和善后工作。

2007 年 8 月 30 日，第十届全国人民代表大会常务委员会第二十九次会议通过《中华人民共和国突发事件应对法》，第十七条规定，"国务院制定国家突发事件总体应急预案，组织制定国家突发事件专项应急预案；国务院有关部门根据各自的职责和国务院相关应急预案，制定国家突发事件部门应急预案"。第三十二条强调国家要"建立健全应急物资储备保障制度，完善重要应急物资的监管、生产、储备、调拨和紧急配送体系"。第四十五条第二款强调，"调集应急救援所需物资、设备、工具，准备应急设施和避难场所，并确保其处于良好状态、随时可以投入正常使用"；第四十九条第七款规定政府要"保障食品、饮用水、燃料等基本生活必需品的供应"。

2009 年国务院发布《物流业调整和振兴规划》，首次提出了"应急物流工程"，应急物流成为国家战略规划的一部分。

2009 年，《国务院研究发展中心调查研究报告》指出，要加快应急物流体系建设，增强应急物资保障能力。

2013 年，国务院办公厅印发《突发事件应急预案管理办法》（国办发〔2013〕101 号），该办法将应急预案制定的主体分为政府及其部门应急预案、单位和基层组织应急预案两类。该管理办法将政府及其部门应急预案分为国家层面专项和部门应急预案、省级专项和部门应急预案、市县级专项和部门应急预案、乡镇街道专项和部门应急预案的四个层面的应急预案，各个层面应急预案的侧重点各有不同。针对突发事件应对的专项和部门应急预案，分为对重要基础设施、生命线工程等重要目标物保护的专项和部门应急预案、针对重大活动保障制定的专项和部门应急预案、针对突发事件的应急预案，以及联合应急预案。其中，针对突发事件应对工作的应急预案中，提到应对突发事件时，要制定物资、装备、资金等资源保障的专项应急预案，要确保突发事件发生时资源的顺利调用。

2014 年国务院发布《物流业发展中长期规划（2014—2020 年）》（国发〔2014〕42 号），明确了"应急物流工程"的概念。在规划的 12 项重点工程中，其中一项即应急物流工程，规划要求"建立统一协调、反应迅捷、运行有序、高效可靠的应急物流体系，建设集满足多种应急需要为一体的物流中心，形成一批具有较强应急物流运作能力的骨干物流企业。加强应急仓储、中转、配送设施建设，提升应急物流设施设备的标准化和现代化水平，提高应急物流效率和应急保障能力。建立和完善应急物流信息系统，规范协调调度程序，优化信息流程、业务流程和管理流程，推进应急生产、流通、储备、运输环节的信息化建设和应急信息交换、数据共享"。

2014 年，国务院办公厅发布《关于加快应急产业发展的意见》（国办发〔2014〕63 号），将应急物流作为应急服务的重要内容。在该意见的第三条"重点服务"的第十项"应急服务"中强调要提高突发事件防范处置的社会化服务水平，在社会化救援方面，发展紧急医疗救援、交通救援、应急物流等应急服务。在第四条"主要任务"的第十五项中提到"健全应急产品实物储备、社会储备和生产能力储备管理制度，建设应急产品和生产能力储备综合信息平台，带动应急产品应用。加强应急仓储、中转、配送设施建设，提高应急产品物流效率"。该意见还将健全应急物资的储备、应急物资的中转，提高应急产品的物流效率等任务细化到具体的部门。

2015 年 8 月，国家发展改革委印发《关于加快实施现代物流重大工程的通知》，通知要求将"应急物流工程"作为主要任务之一，重点是建设应急仓储、中转、配送设施，提升应急物流设施设备的标准化和现代化水平。

2017 年，国务院办公厅发布《国家突发事件应急体系建设"十三五"规划》，规划提出了"十三五"的总体目标是："到 2020 年，建成与有效应对公共安全风险挑战相匹配、与全面建成小康社会要求相适应、覆盖应急管理全过程、全社会共同参与的突发事件应急体系……"在分类目标中，明确提出将快速提升应急物资综合保障能力作为一个主要目标，明确提出将完善应急物资保障体系、提高紧急运输保障能力作为规划的主要任务。

2021 年，我国颁布了《中华人民共和国国民经济和社会发展第十四个五年规划和 2035 年远景目标纲要》，在这样国家层面的重大规划中，将"实施应急产品生产能力储备工程，建设区域性应急物资生产保障基地"和"实施加快建立储备充足、反应迅速、抗冲击能力强的应急物流体系"作为两个重要的目标。

2022 年 5 月 17 日，我国物流领域的第一个五年规划《"十四五"现代物流发展规划》颁布，规划提出要提升现代物流安全应急能力，提升战略物资、应急物流等保障水平，充分发挥社会物流作用，推动建立以企业为主体的应急物流队伍。规划还强调要提升应急物流发展水平，完善应急物流设施布局，完善应急物流设施网络，统筹加强各类应急物资储备设施和应急物流设施在布局、功能、运行等方面相互匹配、有机衔接，提高紧急调运能力。

综上可以看出，我国最初制定的《国家突发公共事件总体应急预案》只提出了"做好物资保障、交通运输保障"的要求，并没有对应急物流做出具体规定或指导；《国务院关于全面加强应急管理工作的意见》也只强调了加强各类应急资源的管理。从 2009 年国务院发布的《物流业调整和振兴规划》中首次提出"应急物流工程"开始，各项关于物流业发展的法规、政策开始重视应急物流的发展，从《物流业发展中长期规划（2014—2020 年）》中明确了"应急物流工程"的概念，到将"应急物流工程"作为我国经济发展的主要任务之一，再到明确提出将完善应急物资保障体系、提高紧急运输保障能力作为《国家突发事件应急体系建设"十三五"规划》的主要任务，再到我国物流领域的第一个五年规划《"十四五"现代物流发展规划》颁布，强调要提升应急物流发展水平，完善应急物流设施布局，完善应急物流设施网络。我国应急物流体系的建设正是由于有了法律法规政策的保障，才得以逐渐完善。但与应急物流相关的法律法规政策都体现在应急事件或普通物流的法规、政策等文件中，我国并没有专门的应急物流法，在我国应急事件处理经验越来越丰富的今天，国家应出台专门的应急物流法律法规，对应急物流的组织，应急物资的储备、管理、运输、配送等环节，应急工作人员和社会参与人员的责任和权限加以明确，并提供法律保障。

完善应急物流法规的过程中，要健全应急物流补偿制度。我国关于突发事件应对的各项法律法规中，对于补偿机制并未进行系统、明确的规范，在《国家突发公共事件应急预案》中仅提到对于突发事件应急处理工作中受伤、死亡以及其他工作人员"按照规定给予抚恤、补助或补偿"；在《中华人民共和国突发事件应对法》中规定，各级政府"根据本地区遭受损失的情况，制定救助、补偿、抚慰、抚恤、安置等善后工作计划并组织实施"。其他的相关法律中也对补偿制度的问题提及很少。因此，我国在相关应急物流法规的完善过程中，要将补偿制度，包括补偿的标准、补偿范围和补偿形式等予以明确规定。在补偿制度完善的过程中，要充分调动社会和市场资源以弥补国家财政补偿能力的不足（刘晶芳，2014），建立政府补偿为主的多元化补偿机制（尚希桥，2017）。除政府的补偿以外，保险公司也要发挥其在突发事件后的补偿作用，履行其对个人及其他组织的意外险、财产险的理赔责任，保险公司还可以通过设置专门的灾害补偿部门和灾害准备金，缩短灾后补偿金到位的时间（徐慧敏，2014），来履行保险公司的社会责任。在政府补偿和保险公司赔偿之外，政府还可以发挥社会动员的功能，号召社会捐助，使用社会捐赠资金进行补偿。通过对与补偿相关的法律法规和制度的完善，使补偿制度有法可依，使参与救援的个人及单位的利益得以保障，对社会动员起到正面积极的影响作用。

## 5.6 我国应急物流的社会动员机制建设

在应对自然灾害、突发公共卫生事件或安全事件时，单靠政府的力量很难快速、准确地响应，因此，政府必须进行应急动员，充分调动各方面的力量，发挥各方力量的积极性，以此全面提升应对突发事件的能力和效果，而强有力的动员机制对应对各种突发事件起着至关重要的作用。我国2007年颁布的《中华人民共和国突发事件应对法》也规定了国家应建立有效的社会动员机制，增强全民的公共安全和防范风险的意识。

### 5.6.1 应急动员

"动员"一词曾经只作为军事术语，专门指战争动员。百度百科把"动员或战争动员"定义为：国家或政治集团的武装力量从平时状态转入战时状态，以及把所有的经济部门（工业、农业、运输业等）转入供应战争需要的工作，即统一调动人力、物力、财力为战争服务。广义上的动员是指在应对社会或国家的特定突发事件时，政府调动社会各方面的力量进行积极应对的过程，动员包括人力动员、技术动员、生产能力动员、物流动员等。

战争动员的三大任务是，动员各方力量进行武装作战、作战的同时维护社会生产和生活的稳定、最大限度减少战争灾害。广义上，应急动员的任务也可以分为三个方面，一是最大限度减少灾害对人们生命和财产的危害；二是要在抗击灾害的同时，维护社会生产和生活的稳定；三是最大限度减少次生灾害和衍生危机。

动员分为应急预警阶段的动员、应急准备阶段的动员、应急响应阶段的动员和灾害恢复阶段的动员（薛莹莹，2018）。在应急预警阶段，主要的任务是对于可避免的突发事件进行干预，防止其继续恶化，比如食品安全事件，在发现极个别问题时能迅速制止食品安全事件大规模发生。对于不可避免的事件，比如自然灾害、公共卫生事件等，预警阶段的动员则主要体现在政府对广大群众防灾、减灾知识的宣传教育方面，培养公众的危机意识，明确在危机发生时要积极主动配合政府的动员，发挥社会力量的抗灾减灾作用。应急准备阶段的任务主要是完善相关的应急法规、应急预案，完善应急预警系统，进行应急教育、培训，开展应急演练等，动员社会力量，明确应急响应时的任务。应急响应阶段的主要目的是抢救生命，减少人民群众的生命和财产损失，此阶段的主要任务是动员社会力量和社会资源参与到抗灾减灾的工作中。政府部门可通过媒体、网络等各种渠道及时向社会传达灾害信息，动员社会力量并指导社会力量的抗灾救灾行为，通过动员，有效发挥社会力量和社会资源的优势，也有利于加强全社会的团结。此阶段的另一个任务是动员部队的力量，在自然灾害发生时，各地方驻军、武警消防官兵等都是抗灾减灾的主要力量，在抗灾过程中，部队发挥其"召之即来，来之能战"的作用，对于社会和军队力量的动员能有效地发挥党、政、军、民齐心协力一致抗灾的作用。灾害恢复阶段的主要任务是灾后重建，此时广大社会力量是主要力量，政府应动员全社会力量参与灾后恢复，增强社会凝聚力。此阶段，政府还有一个重要的职责是协同相关组织，对受灾民众的心理恢复进行干预，帮助受灾群众尽快平稳度过心理危机。社会力量参与抗灾减灾工作也受到我国相关法律的保护，《中华人民共和国突发事件应对法》规定，公民在参加应急救援工作或在灾害期间参与维稳工作时，其工作单位的工资待遇等不变。

## 5.6.2　应急物流动员机制

应急物流动员是应急动员的一个方面，应急物流动员是指政府在应急物流过程中调动非政府资源来应对突发公共事件或紧急状态所需的物资、人员、资金的行为过程（王丰等，2007）。

重大自然灾害或公共卫生事件具有不可预见性，而通常突发事件发生时，短时期内需要大量的救灾物资，从基本生活保障用品到救灾专用物资和医疗物资，都需要在第一时间送达灾区，而此时灾区会有道路中断、通信设备破坏等情况发生，所以给应急物流运作带来更大的难度。物流动员在应急情况下，能把社会各方面的力量集中起来，并通过持续的物流动员，保障救灾和灾后重建过程中资源的持续供应。政府在动员全社会力量的过程中，凝聚了全国各方面的力量，提高了特殊时期的应急效率。

应急物流动员分为应急物流动员准备、应急物流实时动员和应急物流灾后动员三个方面（王丰等，2007）。

应急物流动员准备阶段的主要任务是开发和储备应急物流资源，在平时的物流潜力建设中实施应急物流动员准备，以便在突发事件发生时，更好、更快、更高效地利用物流资源。此阶段应是为自然灾害或公共卫生事件未发生时做好准备工作，应急物流动员准备包括应急物资的储备和应急物流的财政保障。因为应急事件的不可预测性，应急物流所需的物资也存在不可预测性，因此，应急物资的储备除了常规的抗灾减灾物资、生活物资、医疗物资的实物储备，更主要的是生产能力和生产技术的储备、与供应商的合同储备。物流动员准备将应急资源与常态下的物流系统建设相结合，在突发事件发生时，通过正常的社会动员程序，将常态的物流资源迅速转化为应急物流资源。政府也应从财政预算上支持应急物流资源的储备，加大对应急物流资源的投入，财政支持可以是实物的储备，也可以是生产能力、生产技术或合同储备。除了资源和资金的储备，政府还应培养应急物流管理方面的专业技术人才和高效的应急保障队伍。实施应急物流动员，需要具有专门应急物流知识的管理人才和能快速响应的应急保障队伍，因此，政府应注重应急物流人才的培养和具有应急物流知识的人才储备。同普通的应急动员一样，应急物流动员也需要在平时对公众进行危机意识的培训、应急处理能力提升的培训、应急演练等普及工作，提高公民的危机防范意识和危机应对能力。

应急物流动员准备还要包括应急物流预案的制定，根据《国家突发公共事件总体应急预案》制定合理、完善的应急物流预案，才能使应急物流资源和各方保障力量在紧急事件发生时高效、有序完成物流保障任务。各级地方政府和相关部门，应该根据所在地的实际情况和历史相关灾害情况，尤其是地震灾害频发地区、洪涝灾害易发地区等，政府在对可能发生的突发事件进行预测的前提下，制定相应的应急预案，必要时做到一种突发情况多种预案、多手准备。比如，应急物资储备的预案，不仅涉及实物储备，还要涉及合同储备供应商、技术研发单位、生产储备单位的应急预案。应急物资的运输预案也要考虑到自然灾害发生的各种突发情况，将道路中断、通信设施损坏等情况纳入应急物流预案中。

应急物流实时动员发生在突发事件发生后，政府部门对非政府资源的调配、动员。根据《中华人民共和国突发事件应对法》的规定，各级人民政府应立即调动各个有关部门，调动应急救援队伍和社会力量，组织公民参加应急救援工作，并有权要求有特定专业的人员参与应急救援工作。在突发事件发生后，各级政府应结合具体的应急救援任务，迅速组建高效的物流保障队伍，并根据灾害的性质，比如根据地震灾害、洪水灾害、冰雪灾害等不同灾害性质，制定合理的应急物流运作模式，将应急物资第一时间运送到受灾地。应急情况下，根据《民用运力国防动员条例》，政府可以采取临时交通管制，实施交通运输动员，对运输路线和运输工具进行统一管制，必要时可以征用社会力量的交通运输工具。

应急物流实时动员还包括宣传动员，对外可以开展外交宣传，将灾害的真实情况呈现给国际社会，既可以提示国际社会提前应对类似灾害，还可以争取广泛的国际认可和同情，争取国际支援；对内将真实的灾害信息公布给广大民众，尊重公民的知情权，同时开展全民动员，动员广大人民群众积极参与到应急物流保障工作中。

应急物流灾后动员是灾后修复和重建阶段的动员，受灾地区基本恢复到常态，应急处理保障队伍有序撤离，受灾地区开始对灾情、人员伤亡和财产损失进行评估，并对紧急征用的民用物资进行补偿，开始对受灾地区进行重建，使受灾地区恢复经济活力。此时政府需要动员广大人民群众参与到重建工作中，并对积极参与应急救援的单位和个体进行褒奖，通过奖励有功人员起到再次动员更多群众参与到灾后重建任务中的作用。

## 5.7 我国应急物流的基础设施、设备保障建设

法律法规、动员机制等是应急物流系统运行的机制保障，而基础设施的完善是应急物流系统高效运行的物质保障。

根据黎红、陈御钗（2021）的分类方法，物流基础设施包括物流园区、物流中心、公路、铁路、水路、航空等各类运输通道、运输枢纽、场站、仓储设施等；物流设备包括运输设备、仓储设备、装卸搬运设备、流通加工设备、物流信息技术设备等。

从本书研究的内容来看，主要涉及突发公共卫生事件和自然灾害事件下的应急物流，所以本节主要研究公路、铁路、航空的基础设施建设。根据国家统计局数据截至 2022 年，我国公路总里程达 535 万千米，形成了以高速公路为骨架、普通公路干线为脉络、农村公路为基础的公路网，其中高速公路里程位居世界第一。截至 2022 年，我国铁路营业里程达 15.5 万千米，其中包括高铁营业里程 4.2 万千米，高铁营业里程位居世界第一。截至 2022 年，我国共有定期航班航线 4670 条，航线的国内通航城市（或地区）249 个（不含香港、澳门和台湾地区）。从交通通道的全国布局来看，我国铁路形成了"五纵三横"的铁路网线，公路形成了"五纵七横"的国道主干线以及主线和联络线相连通的公路网线。我国的航空运输网络也已经形成了纵横交错比较完善的运输网络。2021 年民航总局制定的"十四五"发展规划中，明确表明要完善"国内航空运输网络、国际航空运输通道、航空枢纽功能 3 大体系"。我国的铁路枢纽主要有北京枢纽、天津枢纽、沈阳和哈尔滨枢纽、郑州枢纽、武汉枢纽、广州枢纽、兰州枢纽、重庆枢纽、昆明枢纽、贵阳枢纽等，公路运输枢纽主要分布在北京、天津、石家庄等 45 个大中型城市，所有的铁路、公路枢纽都分布在运网发

达、运量集中、经济较发达的大型城市或水路联运中心。我国公路、铁路、航路等运输通道基础设施的大力发展，为应急物资和应急人员的高效运输提供了强大的物质基础条件。这些交通运输通道，在常态下为普通物流提供便利，在紧急突发事件状态下，可迅速转化为应急运输通道。应急管理部门在制定各种突发事件的应急预案时，应规划好将交通运输通道迅速转化为应急运输通道的方案，提前规划好应急路线，提高应急运输的效率。

在现有的交通运输通道、交通运输枢纽建设的基础上，我国应急物流的运输通道建设要尝试建立基础设施战备储备机制（陈媛、李靖，2011），根据各地的地形特点和气候条件建设货运站、中转场站等基础设施，合理布局各个物流节点，合理利用现有的交通主干道和主网线，建立辅助公路与主干道的联系，使交通运输网络覆盖广泛，在紧急事件发生时，交通运输通道能实现快速转化为紧急救灾运输通道，使救灾物资及时到达灾区。

应急物流中心或物流园区的建设要着眼于为应急救援提供快捷便利的服务。中心或园区的选址应在自然灾害频发、易发区周边交通便利的地方，而且应急物流中心或园区的建设要有一定规模，要保证装卸应急物资有可操作空间，保证多辆运输车辆能够同时通行。应急物流中心和园区的建设规模还要参考周边城市的人口规模，人口数量决定了应急物资存储或运输的数量，城市经济发展程度也是应急物流园区建设应考虑的因素之一。

将现代化科技手段运用到应急物流设备和技术的建设中，能够进一步提高应急物流的效率，将突发事件损害降到最低。从物流设备发展的角度看，我国研发了大型自动化立体仓库，将电子计算机技术应用到巷道堆垛、自动化出入库输送、仓库管理等的作业中。2008 年 3 月，我国出台了《联运通用平托盘主要尺寸及公差》（GB/T 2934—2007）标准，规定了通用托盘的材质和尺寸大小，为应急物资的联合运输提供了便利。自动分拣系统的使用可以在货品入库时，根据货品上的标签进行品质、数量、货位以及货主信息的识别，并通过自动输送装置将货品送入系统设定的货位，甚至可以脱离主输送机进入集货区域通道。同时，货架、输送设备的更新换代，由电磁感应引导、激光引导或磁铁陀螺引导的自动搬运车的应用，以及电子标签、条码打印机、数据采集技术的应用，都大大提高了应急物资的储备管理、库存管理效率。从物流信息技术的发展看，条码技术和射频识别技术在现代物流系统中的广泛应用，不仅为普通物流，也为应急物流在运作时能快速识别物品、迅速响应分拣运输系统等提供便利。应急物流运作中，应全方位使用普通物流技术和设备发展的成果，既节约了专门开发应急物流技术和设备的资源，又提高了应急物流运作的效率。

物流运输通道、物流设备和物流技术的发展，为应急物流的高效运作提供了物质基础保障，除此之外，应急物流的专门设施、设备建设也必不可少。首先是区域应急救助点的建设，救助点规划建设时按紧急避难场所设计，在常态下可做其他用处，比如作为运动场、文化广场等，具体用途根据救助点所在地的实际需求来定，在紧急事件发生后，这些场所可紧急转化为应急救助点或避难场所用于存放应急物资，或用于发放应急物资的场所。其次，为建立立体化救援网络，一些自然灾害频发易发地区可以进行大型停机坪的建设，有需要的地区可以根据国家民航局的规定，建设消防救援设备、气象设备等设备完善的大型停机坪，以备在应急事件发生时，直升机可以安全起飞和降落，为应急救援赢得宝贵的时间。

综上所述，物流运输通道和大部分的物流设备和物流信息技术，都是依托于普通物流在运输通道、物流设施设备方面的建设和发展，但要在建设初期规划好的前提下，并在应急物流管理部门的协调下，能在紧急状态时迅速转化为应急物流的设施、设备，并配合应急物流的专门设施、设备，才能更好地发挥应急物流在应急救援中的作用。

实践篇

# 第6章 我国自然灾害应急物流体系

　　我国国土面积辽阔，地理环境复杂，属于自然灾害频发的国家，而且自然灾害种类繁多，灾害造成的损失在一定程度上制约了我国的社会经济发展，因此，我国在应对自然灾害方面也制定了许多相关的法律法规，让应对自然灾害的处置行为有法可依。同时为应对自然灾害，国家和各级地方政府也制定了许多自然灾害应急预案，其中包括对应急物资的储备、管理、运输等的预案。另外，高效的应急物资运输是抗灾减灾工作的一个重要组成部分，可以为抗灾减灾赢得宝贵时间，从而大大减少人员伤亡和财产损失。本章将从应急物资的分类、储备、管理、运输和配送等方面阐述自然灾害应急物流体系的建设。

## 6.1 自然灾害概述

　　葛全胜（2008）认为，凡是危及人类生命财产和生存条件的各类事件均可称为灾害。黄崇福（2009）将自然灾害定义为自然界中发生的，能造成生命伤亡与人类社会财产损失的事件。本书认为，只要是给人类的生命财产、自然环境带来损失的自然现象均可称为自然灾害。

　　我国2013年2月1日开始实施的《自然灾害分类与代码》（GBT 28921—2012）将自然灾害分为气象水文灾害、地质地震灾害、海洋灾害、生物灾害、生态环境灾害共五大类。气象水文灾害包括干旱灾害、洪涝灾害、台风灾害等 13 种自然灾害。地质地震灾害包括地震灾害、火山灾害等 9 种自然灾害。海洋灾害包括风暴潮灾害、海浪灾害、海冰灾害、海啸灾害、赤潮灾害等共 6 种自然灾害。生物灾害包括植物病虫害、鼠害等共 7 种自然灾害。生态环境灾害包括水土流失灾害、盐渍化灾害等共 5 种自然灾害。根据灾害的起因，郗蒙浩（2021）将自然灾害分为气象水文灾害、海洋灾害、地质灾害、地震灾害、生物灾害、土地退化灾害共 6 个大类。

对于自然灾害的定义，众多的学者、专家有不同的描述，但本质基本相同。对于自然灾害的分类虽然也不尽相同，但本质基本类似。本章所研究的内容为应对自然灾害的应急物流体系建设，由于篇幅限制，本章内容所涉及的自然灾害主要包括地震灾害和洪水灾害。地震灾害是指地震引起的强烈地面震动导致地面产生裂缝、变形，各类建筑物或设施设备倒塌或损坏，并由此引起火灾、爆炸、场地破坏等人类生命财产和牲畜伤亡的自然灾害。洪水灾害是指因为暴雨、冰山急骤融化等造成的水量超过江河、湖泊、水库、海洋等水域的承受能力，导致水量剧增或水位急涨而造成的自然灾害，通常会给人类的正常生产、生活，甚至人类的生命财产带来损失。

# 6.2　我国近几十年来重大地震灾害和洪水灾害概述

本节概述我国近几十年来影响范围大、灾害损失严重的几次特大自然灾害，并简单梳理在灾害应急过程中应急物流发挥的作用。

## 6.2.1　1998 年特大洪水

1998 年特大洪水是一场包括长江、嫩江、松花江等江河流域地区的大洪水，是一次全流域型的特大洪水，据统计，全国有江西、湖南、湖北、黑龙江等 29 个省（区、市）遭受了不同程度的洪涝灾害，直接经济损失达 1660 亿元。此次洪灾于 6 月 27 日在嫩江发生第一次洪峰，7 月 2 日，长江上游出现第一次洪峰，7 月 14 日，国家防总发出《关于进一步做好防汛工作的通知》，要求全面落实各项防汛措施，干部、劳力、物资都要全部到位。8 月，哈尔滨抗洪一线官兵出现防雨御寒衣物短缺、大庆出现救生器材短缺、内蒙古出现御寒衣物短缺等现象，时任总理朱镕基批示要求立即解决物资短缺问题，要求组织有计划的生产，要保证应急救灾物资的供应。9 月 25 日，长江中下游水位全线回落至警戒水位以下，至此全国人民抗灾救灾工作顺利结束。在此次特大洪涝灾害的救灾过程中，出现了短暂的物资短缺现象，暴露出救灾物资储备、运输方面的问题。当时我国还没有应急物流的概念，因此在自然灾害发生时，物资储备和运输都未能做到迅速响应。

## 6.2.2　2008 年汶川大地震

汶川大地震，又称 "5·12" 汶川地震，地震发生于四川省阿坝藏族自治州汶川县映秀镇，时间是 2008 年 5 月 12 日下午 2 点 28 分。中国地震局将汶川大地震的震级定位 8.0 级，地震波及了中国的大部分地区以及亚洲多个国家和地区。遭受此次地震破坏的地区面积达 50 万平方千米，因地震丧生的人员达 69000 多人，失踪人员 17000 人，受灾人口达 4625 万人之多。汶川大地震是新中国成立以来影响最大的一次地震，灾区的住房、校舍、交通、地貌、水利、少数民族文化均受到严重的破坏。

地震发生后，中共中央、国务院、国务院抗震救灾总指挥部以及四川省政府带领四川人民积极抗震救灾。在总指挥部的部署下，各有关部门紧急调配大量的救灾物资前往灾区，并拨付大量救灾资金，各方力量紧急救援四川灾区。四川省政府在地震发生后，迅速启动应急 I 级响应，省委、省政府立即成立抗震救灾指挥部，迅速、积极、有效、有序组织抗震救灾工作。四川省指挥部在震后实施有效的交通管制和交通保障，保障救灾物资和救灾人员的交通畅通，集中力量保障了 "生命线" 的畅通。四川省委、省政府积极组织协调各方力量做好物资筹集、管理，保障救灾通信畅通，做好交通保障，使各方救灾运力迅速到位，通过以上各种措施保障各方救援物资和救灾队伍顺利到位。

### 6.2.3  2020 年南方洪灾

2020 年中国南方洪涝灾害被应急管理部公布为 2020 年全国十大自然灾害之一。2020 年南方洪涝灾害指的是 2020 年入汛以来，中国南方地区发生多轮强降雨过程造成的多地发生的严重洪涝灾害。截至 2020 年 6 月，全国 16 个省区的河流均发生了超警戒水位，上海、重庆、四川、广西、贵州、浙江等省市分别启动了防汛应急响应，其中浙江省曾一度将防汛应急响应调至 I 级响应。面对洪涝灾害，应急管理部多次组织调度会议，对灾情和救灾工作进行研判，曾先后向贵州、广西、广东、四川、重庆等地调拨救灾帐篷、折叠床等中央救灾物资，支持地方开展抗洪救灾工作。截至 7 月 9 日，此次洪涝灾害共造成安徽、江西、湖南等省 3000 多万人受灾，60 多万人需要紧急生活救助，直接经济损失 600 多亿元。此次洪涝灾害直至 7 月底才得以缓解。此次救灾过程中，我国积累了较为丰富的应急物流经验，中央曾多次向灾区紧急调配应急物资，从中央到地方，上下团结一心，积极应对洪涝灾害并取得最终的胜利。

## 6.3  我国自然灾害应急物流保障机制

建设好应急物流系统各个子系统的保障机制，是应急物流成功运行的关键（余朵荷、何世伟，2008）。完善的自然灾害应急物流保障机制应该包括政府协调机制、灾害监测预警机制、应急预案机制、灾害信息发布机制、救灾应急物资储备机制、灾害应急社会动员机制和"绿色通道"机制。

遵循政府协调、企业参与、军民团结的组织机制。《中华人民共和国突发事件应对法》规定，在处置和救援过程中，由人民政府统一领导和组织处置突发事件。政府部门协调政府、军队、物流企业进行应急物资的保障。政府统一组织、调拨应急物资和资金，组织对社会进行动员，组织力量保障应急物资的顺利运输与发放。政府在紧急状态下，除了可以启用政府储备的应急物资和政府的运力，还可以调用军事力量、物流企业等其他社会力量的物资、设备、运力等。

重视监测与预警机制。监测机制是指对以往发生的突发事件的性质、规律、危害进行信息收集、核对，对可能发生的自然灾害等突发事件进行长期的监测、捕捉和预测，并及时将监测信息上报。预警机制是指根据科学的预测手段和技术，以及长期监测的数据，对可能发生的自然灾害发出警示，并上报相关部门，以便政府和民众及时采取正确的应对措施。在自然灾害事突发之初，市场的监测和预警信息部门，应该根据检测的数据以及灾害地的实际受灾人口数量，对应急物资的数量进行预测预警。比如，某些地震易发地区，地方政府应制定对本地区人口数量的监测和应急物资管理相结合的预警机制；地震灾害发生时，地方应急部门应根据受灾人口数量，迅速预测所需的救生类物资、生活保障类物资的数量，以最快速度提供应急保障物资。

根据实际情况，制定应急预案机制。对于某些自然灾害频发或易发地区，地方政府应当根据本地区的灾害特点制定相应的应急物流保障预案，包括如何对应急物资进行储备、管理、运输和发放，定期组织应对自然灾害的演练，加强对物流保障人员的培训，通过将减灾工作寓于平时的准备工作中，使各级政府在自然灾害发生时，能将应急预案迅速应用到实际的应急工作中，达到顺利、有效地应对自然灾害的目的。

制定长效的灾害信息发布机制。灾害信息发布包括对自然灾害灾情的信息发布，让全社会及时掌握灾情的信息、灾害程度和损失情况。同时也包括对救援物资的需求、使用、管理等信息的发布，让全社会及时掌握应急救灾物资的需求和使用情况，以利于政府筹集救灾物资，也方便社会捐助救灾物资。

实行多维的救灾应急物资储备机制。国家通过建立中央级的救灾物资储备中心和省级地方救灾物资储备中心，按各地自然灾害发生的可能性，对物资进行储备和管理。除实物储备外，政府还要跟企业签订合同储备，在灾害发生时，企业能迅速执行合同，进行救灾物资的生产。救灾应急物资储备还应包括资金储备，政府可以在每年的财政预算中预留出应对各种自然灾害的资金，尤其是一些自然灾害频发地区，这样才能在自然灾害发生时有效应对。

实施广泛的社会动员机制。自然灾害发生时，政府通过各种媒体和网络对灾情进行公布，并动员全社会参与抗灾救援工作，动员全社会筹集救灾物资，动员各物流企业参与救灾物资的运输与配送，团结全社会的力量进行抗灾救灾。除此之外，动员工作还包括对受灾地区人民群众的心理疏导，让受灾群众平稳度过焦虑紧张期，最大限度减少受灾群众发生创伤后应激障碍的可能性。

强化绿色通道机制。在自然灾害发生时，为保障救灾人员和物资顺利到达灾区，我国实行了"绿色通道机制"，为运送救灾人员和救灾物资的车辆提供快速通道，提高应急物流的效率。此时，航空、铁路、公路、水路等各交通部门有责任组织协调相关防疫部门、检查部门为保障车队或航班发放"绿色通行证"，减少检查手续、缩短检查时间以保障救灾人员和物资的运输畅通。

自然灾害发生时，有效的社会动员有助于高效的物流指挥，合理的资源调配，有效的资源流动，以及畅通的物流运作，为抢救生命、减少灾害损失和维护社会稳定起到了关键作用，而未来的社会动员要在灾害的动态变化中抓住中心和重点，将庞大的动员物资流和物资力量随主要任务方向的转变而进行有序的转变（张洪瑞、吴宏强，2009），动态变化的动员也是我国自然灾害应急动员的发展方向。

# 6.4　自然灾害应急物流信息系统的建设

应急物流信息系统是应急物流系统的一个子系统，自然灾害应急物流信息系统包括监测预警系统、信息共享平台和物流跟踪系统。通过建立完善的物流信息系统，可以高效发挥指挥系统的作用；通过信息系统的建设，各应急物流企业之间可以实现物流信息资源的实时共享，便于应急物资的调配和运输；通过信息系统的建设，公众也可以及时掌握应急物资的需求、使用情况，对应急物资的需求起到动员作用，也对应急物资的使用情况起到全社会监督的作用。应急物流信息系统的建设要遵循政府主导、企业参与的原则，在政府的组织协调下，各物流企业积极参与到自然灾害的救灾抗灾工作中。信息系统的建设要依靠现代化科学技术手段，更有利于精准抗灾救灾。

利用大数据的收集和分析处理功能，应急物流信息系统可实现信息的预警、监测功能。市场监测和预警对于有效应对自然灾害提供了强有力的数据支持，在自然灾害发生时，灾民对应急生活物资的需求量可以根据常态下灾害发生地的市场监测数据进行预估。常态下，政府部门应该协同生活保障用品市场监管部门，通过数据管理系统、市场实时监测和数据处理分析系统，对市民生活物资的需求量有所掌握。自然灾害发生时，政府可根据常态下掌握的市场数据进行救灾生活物资的供应。对于救灾抗灾的生命救援类物资的需求量，通常是在政府的指导下，结合受灾地的常住人口数量和实际受灾的灾民数量，确定生命救援类物资的数量。

利用信息共享平台，应急物流信息系统可实现物流信息的发布和共享功能。政府应建立各级政府部门间以及政府与企业之间的信息共享平台，通过核心数据的共享。纵向上，中央政府和地方政府之间，横向上，各级地方政府之间及政府和企业之间，通过信息共享平台，实时掌握受灾地区的救援物资需求和调配情况，通过掌握实时信息，优化救灾物资的调配。

自然灾害发生时，受灾地区可通过政府的官方平台公布救灾物资的需求量，向地方和中央政府请求支援。应急物流信息发布，除对应急物资的需求，还应包括对应急物资使用情况的信息公开，便于公众对救灾物资的使用情况和质量进行监督。

利用地理信息系统（GIS）、全球定位系统（GPS）等现代科技手段和现代通信技术，应急物流信息系统可实现救灾物资的物流跟踪功能。通过在救灾物资运输车辆上安装 GPS 和 GIS 相结合的复合导航系统，可为救灾物资运输车辆的路线规划提供技术和设备的支持。同时，目前已经在市场上非常普及的车载 GPS 安全监控系统或 GPS 终端定位系统，除可以规划线路以外，还可以实时定位车辆所在位置，便于救灾指挥中心了解救灾运输车辆和所运输物资的位置，以便对救灾工作进行进一步的部署。该系统还可以对车辆的行驶速度、驾车人员的驾驶情况进行跟踪监控，会对超速或驾驶员疲劳驾驶的情况发出报警，大大保障了应急物资运输车辆和驾驶人员的安全，也保障了应急物资的安全。当然除了 GIS、GPS 这样的定位技术，还可以利用现代化的语音、图像等通信技术手段，通过电话和视频通话等对物流车辆和人员进行直接的跟踪，及时、直接掌握物流运输车辆和人员情况。

## 6.5  自然灾害应急物资的储备

我国最早于 1998 年就颁布了关于中央级救灾物资储备的一些相关法规制度文件，对于国家级救灾物资储备进行了政策性的规范，包括救灾物资的种类、救灾物资储备点的建设等，后来又经过几次修订。截至 2023 年 7 月，我国应急管理部已在 31 个省（区、市）拥有 126 个中央级储备库。我国的救灾物资储备制度也在进一步完善。本节将从自然灾害的救灾物资种类、救灾储备中心的建立和救灾物资储备制度等方面进行详述。

### 6.5.1　应急物资的概念和分类

应急物资是指为应对突发公共事件，包括严重自然灾害、事故灾难、公共卫生事件和社会安全事件等全过程中所必需的物资保障。从广义上概括，凡是在突发公共事件应对过程中所用的物资都可以称为应急物资，包括灾前的防灾防备物资，突发事件发生时的救灾救援物资，以及灾后重建过程中用到的物资。狭义上来讲，应急物资是指在救灾救援过程中所需的物资。

对应急物资的分类，可以从几个角度出发。按突发公共事件性质不同，应急物资可以分为自然灾害类应急物资、事故灾难类应急物资、公共卫生事件应急物资、社会突发安全事件应急物资。按突发事件的严重程度，可以将应急物资分为一般级应急物资、严重级应急物资和紧急级应急物资（王丰等，2007）。一般级应急物资指用于救灾难度低、物资需求量相对较小的物资，该类物资有利于减轻突发事件的损失，如环保处理、工程设备类物资。严重级应急物资是指对减轻突发事件带来的损失或对缩小事件范围、应对救援工作能够发挥非常重要作用且非常必要的物资，如防护类物资。紧急级应急物资指对应急救援工作的开展、挽救突发事件受害者的生命财产损失、稳定局势起关键性作用，必须且极其重要的物资，如生命救助、生命支持、临时食宿类物资。

国家发展改革委编制的《应急保障重点物资分类目录（2015 年）》（发改办运行［2015］825 号）将应急保障物资按物资用途分为 13 类：防护用品、生命救助、生命支持、救援运载、临时食宿、污染清理、动力燃料、工程设备、器材工具、照明设备、通信广播、交通运输和工程材料，这 13 类产品名录共涵盖了 250 种物资。

本章只涉及抗震救灾类物资和防汛救灾类物资。抗震救灾物资可以分为救生类物资和生活类物资，比如探生仪器、破拆工具、小型起重设备、防寒毯、棉衣被、单帐篷、棉帐篷、睡袋、救生食物等。防汛救灾类物资有救生舟、救生艇、救生圈、救生衣、燃料燃具、防寒毯、棉衣被、单帐篷、棉帐篷、睡袋、救生食物等。综上可见，无论是防震还是防汛，都需要同时进行生命救助类的物资和生活类物资的物资储备。

不同的自然灾害所需的应急物资不同，为应对不同种类的突发自然灾害，对应急物资进行分类，可以有效地管理应急物资库存、高效运输和调配不同类型的物资，也有利于末端的物资配送。

## 6.5.2　我国救灾物资储备中心的建立

为应对重大自然灾害，我国于 1998 年颁布了《民政部、财政部关于建立中央级救灾物资储备制度的通知》，后又经过几次修订，制定了目前适用的《中央应急抢险救灾物资储备管理暂行办法》（国粮应急规〔2023〕24 号），对中央救灾物资的储备购置、储备保管、物资调用等进行了规定，并明确各省根据中央发文制定适合省内情况的救灾物资管理办法。

在 1998 年印发的《民政部、财政部关于建立中央级救灾物资储备制度的通知》中，将中央级救灾物资的品种暂定为单帐篷和棉帐篷，并在全国设立了 8 个代储点。各代储点的储备物资如表 1 所示：

**表 1　我国 8 个中央级救灾物资储备代储点（1998 年）**

| 地区 | 城市 | 救灾物资 |
| --- | --- | --- |
| 东北区 | 沈阳 | 棉帐篷、单帐篷 |
| 华北区 | 天津 | 棉帐篷、单帐篷 |
| 华中区 | 郑州 | 单帐篷 |
| 华中区 | 武汉 | 单帐篷 |
| 华中区 | 长沙 | 单帐篷 |
| 华南区 | 广州 | 单帐篷 |
| 西南区 | 成都 | 单帐篷 |
| 西北区 | 西安 | 棉帐篷、单帐篷 |

根据民政部等九部门联合印发的《关于加强自然灾害救助物资储备体系建设的指导意见》，截至 2015 年，民政部在北京、天津、沈阳、哈尔滨、合肥、福州、郑州、武汉、长沙、南宁、重庆、成都、昆明、拉萨、渭南、兰州、格尔木、乌鲁木齐、喀什等地设立 19 个中央救灾物资储备

库，在储备布局上，满足了"自然灾害发生 12 小时之内，受灾群众基本生活得到初步救助"的基本要求。截至 2023 年 7 月，根据国务院新闻办公室发布的新闻，我国在 31 个省市建立了 126 个中央级救灾物资储备库。

除了中央级的救灾物资储备库，我国在 31 个省、自治区、直辖市和新疆建设兵团也建立了省级、市级救灾物资储备仓库。比如云南省建立了云南省救灾物资储备中心，2010 年 5 月 11 日正式开始投入使用，中心建有 5 个大型仓库，5 个仓库同时储满救灾物资时，可以满足 70 万灾民的基本生活需求，同时，该中心建有一个 4800 平方米的停机坪，可以同时供两架大型直升机停靠。

无论从经济效益还是社会效益出发，建立健全的救灾储备中心，都可以迅速响应灾情，为挽救人民的生命和财产损失赢得宝贵的时间和资源。而我国建立的中央级救灾储备中心，大都集中在东部和南部，这样的布局对于西北部这样应急力量薄弱的省份应对突发自然灾害非常不利，本书建议应该增加新的救灾物资储备中心以加强西部地区如甘肃、西藏、青海、新疆等省或自治区的应急救灾能力。同时，除了中央级救灾物资储备中心，也要增加省级以下政府的应急储备仓库数量，形成完善的应急物流基础设施布局网络（王敏晰，2009）。

## 6.5.3　我国救灾物资的储备管理和储备形式

救灾物资的储备管理非常关键，除了救灾物资储备中心的地理布局，储备中心仓库内的物资存放布局、物资存放种类和储备量、对应急物资的日常维护和有效管理都是救灾物资的储备管理非常关键的内容。

应急物资的储备管理方式，完全可以借鉴企业物流管理中的库存控制管理方法，科学定制储备规模。对应急物资进行科学地分类管理存放，可以借鉴企业物流管理中物资分类的 ABC 分类方法对物资进行管理（孟参、王长琼，2006）。在储备管理时，可以将库存物品按应急物资的种类或针对某种自然灾害的种类以及占用资金的多少分为特别重要的库存（A 类）、一般重要的库存（B 类）和不重要的库存（C 类）三个级别，根据重要性等级分别进行管理与控制，这样可以有效压缩应急物资库存总量，释放一定的占压资金，使应急物资库存管理更加高效。

从救灾物资储备形式看，除了实物的储备，各省地方政府还可以通过建立救灾物资厂家名录、与生产厂家签订救灾物资紧急采购协议的方式进行合同储备，在自然灾害发生时，合同厂家可立刻根据灾害情况，投入救灾物资的生产。

## 6.6 自然灾害应急物资的运输

在地震或洪水灾害发生时，明确合理的物资运输规划是保证应急物资运输畅通的前提。应急物资运输的规划原则即优先保障救灾救援人员迅速到位、防灾救灾物资迅速到位；需要紧急疏散和撤离群众时，要保障疏散和撤离的交通工具的调配顺畅和交通道路畅通。应急物资运输的规划包括交通运输通道的规划、运输方式和运输路线的规划、运输力量的规划等。

自然灾害应急物资运输体系的建设可分为常态化建设和灾害发生时的救灾物资运输体系建设。在常态下，建立完善的交通运输通道，同时，在保障常态运输通道功能的前提下，完善其在应急状态下迅速转化为应急交通运输通道的能力。没有完善而有效的运输通道，就无法满足应急物流较强的时效性要求（陈慧，2014），所以在交通运输通道建设之初，就要设计其转化为应急通道的功能。交通运输通道的规划，可借助对历史自然灾害的大数据分析，预测运输路线，在发生自然灾害可能性较大的区域规划出多条应急运输通道，避免单线通道受阻，影响应急物流的运输。此外，还有各种港口、车站、仓库、集散地，都要完善其常态的交通枢纽功能和应急物流交通枢纽的功能。在交通运输通道和交通枢纽的建设之外，还要建设如停机坪等非常规备用通道，以满足应急物流的需求，保障道路中断的情况下应急物资能通过空运及时到达（陈慧，2014）。

合理的应急物资运输方式和运输路线可以大大提高救灾救援物资的运

输效率。救灾物资运输的方式可以是公路、铁路、航空、水运等多种运输方式，而物资运输方式和路线的规划应当以最短时间将救灾物资送达为根本目的，此时就体现出应急物流与普通物流的区别，在应急物流运输时可不考虑运输成本，只以提高效率为目的。当地震或洪水灾害发生时，运输方式和运输路线可根据实际的路况进行规划，如从全国其他地方运往灾区外围的物资，因道路、航线、水路畅通，可遵循日常的运输方式和路线；而从灾区外围向灾区中心运输物资时，往往会出现因洪水或地震灾害导致道路中断甚至通信中断的情况，这时就要根据道路情况重新规划运输方式和路线。如道路完全中断，车辆运输无法实现的时候，航空运输就是首选的运输方式，必要时还可以采用直升机、无人机等运输方式。为提高救灾运输的效率，尽量采用直达运输的方式，在条件不允许的情况下，可以采取多种方式联合的运输方式。

对运输力量进行合理安排。自然灾害发生时，一切运输力量的安排都要以保障救灾救援物资的顺利安全到达为主要原则，在政府主导下，可以动用水、陆、空各方的运力，此时也可以改变一些常规运输的运力安排，常规的航线、班列、长途汽车的运力都可以暂时征用为救灾所用，或暂停某些非紧急的常规运输，为救灾物资运输提供便利。运输部门也可以对救灾物资的运输实行特事特办、急事急办、简化手续等方式确保救灾物资运输安全、高效运送（王丰等，2007）。在民用运力不足的情况下，还可以由政府协调，动用军事运输装备和军事运输路线及相关设施来完成应急物资的运输。

2008 年汶川大地震发生后的第三天，交通运输部就发出紧急通知，要求各省交通主管部门全力配合做好汶川地震救灾物资和救灾人员的运输保障工作。当时的航空、铁路、公路各级交通运输部门紧急调用了飞机、机车、车辆，并加强铁路、公路的联合运输，实施空中和地面相结合的运输方式，全国各地的救援物资通过铁路运输、航空运输、空中投送的方式进入灾区。在灾区，由于公路的损坏，有些救灾物资是通过公路摩托化的方式运进灾区。救灾官兵也乘坐飞机日夜兼程赶往灾区，在飞机运输到达受灾地区外围后，改用车辆、步行等多种手段进入灾区中心。通过对各种运输方式综合运用和合理安排，大大降低了地震灾害带来的生命和财产损失。

2023 年 2 月 6 日，土耳其和叙利亚各发生一次 7.8 级大地震，截至 2 月 10 日，我国救援队共 288 人乘飞机前往土耳其救援。中国的救援物资先后于 2 月 8 日、2 月 12 日经空运到达土耳其。2 月 8 日随救灾人员到达的物资以食品和保暖用品为主，总重达 20 吨；2 月 12 日，50 多吨的救灾物资通过空运到达土耳其，物资以当地急缺的救灾帐篷为主。此次救援人员、救灾物资的迅速到位体现了我国的中华传统美德和国际人道主义精神，也反映了我国应急物流高效运作的能力。

应急物资运输还可以发挥物流企业的专业优势，采纳行业专家的专业技术，提高应急物流运输的效率。自然灾害发生时，虽然是政府主导，政府组织协调各方力量进行救灾抗灾，但政府部门可以动员、联合物流企业，采纳行业内专家的建议，让企业和行业内的专家参与应急物资运输方案的制定，参与救灾物资的运输，发挥物流企业的专业优势，提高应急物流运输的效率。

借助大数据、信息网络等现代化科学技术手段，打造智慧应急物流，提高应急物流效率。应急物流的运输，还可以采用 5G 等现代通信技术、现代网络技术、GPS /GIS 定位技术、数据库系统等各种高科技手段，实现对运输车队的车辆实时监控和调度，对应急物资的数量、种类、方位进行定位和远程管理，实现应急物流的智慧化，提高应急物流的运输效率。

以"七优先一免费"为原则，为应急物流提供"绿色通道"，为应急运输发放"绿色通行证"。"七优先"是指为保障应急物流交通运输线路的全时畅通，优先计划、优先安排、优先运输、优先入关、优先停靠、优先放行、优先装卸的原则。"一免费"是指对应急物资运输实行免费通行的原则（陈慧，2014）。在自然灾害发生时，政府部门应协同相关各部门，为应急运输提供专用通道，应急运输车辆等持"绿色通行证"在通过海关、检查站、跨省关卡等地点时，要简化检查程序、缩短检查时间，让其快速通过。政府主导，严厉打击私设关卡、私设收费站等的地方保护主义行为，确保专用通道的畅通，保障应急物资的运输。

# 6.7 自然灾害应急物资的配送与发放

救灾物资的配送、发放，一方面是将生活物资保障品投放市场，满足灾区人民生活物资的供应；另一方面是指将免费的救灾物资发放到灾民手中。

对于生活物资保障用品的市场投放，政府可通过市场监测和预警，掌握市场需求，将人民群众最需要的物资投放到市场。在配送方面，政府可协调经验丰富的物流企业临时完成物资配送任务，或是在常态时与物流企业签订配送协议，一旦有紧急事件发生，企业可迅速承担起应急物资的配送任务。这些企业往往都有丰富的配送经验，有固定的运力，有成熟的供应链网络等，可以在短时期内高效完成此类物品的市场投放。

免费救灾物资的发放原则是"先急后缓，突出重点"，物资的发放要统筹安排、合理使用（王敏晰，2009）。我国民政部于1991年颁布的《关于救灾物资接收、分发、使用、管理的规定》中，规定粮食、食品、蔬菜、生活用品类一定要发放给缺少此类物品的灾民，饮料、营养品等只发放给老年人、儿童或病人；对于药品和医疗器械一定交由灾区的医疗单位统一管理；对于建材类物资优先用于敬老院、福利院等机构的房屋修缮，其次才是无房的灾民；交通工具、通信工具等必须由民政部门统一分配使用，不得发放到个人。该规定的内容完全体现了"先急后缓，突出重点"的原则。该规定虽已被《民政部关于废止部分民政规章及规范性文件的通知》（2000年）所取代，但"先急后缓，突出重点"的原则一直适用于各类紧急救灾的工作中。

对于发放到个人的免费物资，以往的做法都是由政府工作人员和救灾部队直接发给群众，但实际发生灾害时，这种做法效率不高。本书建议可以实行层层发放的办法，比如由市级政府发放到县级，县级发放到村镇级政府，再由各个村政府按照一定的规则将全村再划分为单元，各单元指定负责人来发放免费物资，这样便于初级单位统计灾民数量，并按数量发放物资，避免造成物资浪费。

对于免费物资发放的地点，通常应设置在体育场、学校、村镇广场等开阔区域，并规划好领取路线，入口和出口应当采取两条线路，避免受灾群众在领取物资时造成拥挤踩踏事件。

# 第 7 章　我国突发性公共卫生事件应急物流体系

近二十多年来，我国先后受到非典疫情、新冠疫情等突发性重大公共卫生事件的影响，突发性公共卫生事件通常具有不可预测性，而且往往会对人民的生命、社会的稳定造成非常严重的危害，因此，我国早在 2006 年就制定了《国家突发公共卫生事件应急预案》，原卫生部也要求各级地方政府根据各地的实际情况制定当地的公共卫生事件应急预案，快速、积极响应突发事件。在应对突发重大公共卫生事件时，医疗资源和医务人员的高效率调配可以为应急处置赢得宝贵的时间。本章从应对突发公共卫生事件的应急物流体系建设的角度出发，探讨了突发公共卫生事件下我国应急物流的管理组织方式，应急医药物资的储备，医务人员的运输，医疗物资的运输、配送和发放。然后介绍了我国南方某市在新冠疫情防控期间的生活物资保供措施，为全国其他城市的生活物资保供提供了宝贵的经验。突发公共卫生事件时的应急物流信息系统的建设与自然灾害发生的应急物流信息系统建设类似，本章不再赘述。

## 7.1　突发公共卫生事件的定义、分类和特点

王丰等（2007）将突发公共卫生事件定义为已经发生或者可能发生的、对公众健康造成或者可能造成重大损失的传染病疫情，不明原因的群

体性传染病，还有重大的食物中毒事件和职业中毒，以及其他危害公共健康的突发公共事件。周宣开（2006）将突发性公共卫生事件定义为突然发生，造成或者可能造成社会公众健康严重损害的重大传染疫情、群体性原因不明疾病、重大食物和职业中毒以及严重影响公众健康的事件。

突发性公共卫生事件的分类，根据事件的成因和性质可分为：①重大传染病疫情；②群体性不明原因疾病；③重大食物中毒和职业中毒；④新发传染性疾病；⑤群体性预防接种反应和群体性药物反应；⑥重大环境污染事故，核事故和放射事故，生物、化学、核辐射恐怖事件，自然灾害导致的人员伤亡和疾病流行，以及其他影响公众健康的事件。

突发公共卫生事件的特点：①突发公共卫生事件通常具有不可预测性，某些事件可能在没有任何征兆的情况下突发；②起因复杂。突发公共卫生事件可能由自然灾害引起，也可能是交通事故、环境污染等，有时候也可能是由动物传播引起的；③传播速度快。某一种突发传染性疾病，由于现代社会的人口流动性大，可能会在短时期内迅速传播；④种类繁多。突发性公共卫生事件可以是突发性传染病，重大的中毒事件，或食品安全事件，或药品安全事件，或重大环境污染造成的卫生安全事件，可能会涉及社会的各个领域；⑤对社会危害严重。一旦发生公共卫生安全事件，就很有可能造成重症或死亡案例，而且波及范围大，可能造成群体性重症或死亡，也因此会引发社会不稳定事件。

# 7.2 我国应对重大突发公共卫生
# 事件时的应急物流措施概述

2003 年"非典"疫情期间，我国政府也曾采取多项措施保障物流运输的畅通。如，2003 年 5 月 6 日，公安部出台"五不准"：不准以防治"非典"为由阻断公路交通；不准在公路的省界交界处实行交通管制；不准在道路上设置路障，阻拦车辆正常通行；不准劝返正常行驶的车辆；不准因卫生检疫造成严重交通堵塞。该政策的实施为确保非典时期应急物资运输畅通起到了关键作用。应急物资运输在抗击非典疫情工作中也发挥了很大的作用，比如：2003年5月6日，国务院统一调拨抗击非典型肺炎物资援助香港，调拨物资为8万多件的防护服，物资重量超过14.5万吨，此次物资运输统一空运，飞机从浙江杭州起飞到达深圳，从黄岗口岸运抵香港，无论是空运还是航运，都一路畅通，高效的物资运输为我国香港地区的抗疫工作做出了很大的贡献。

新冠疫情期间，我国多省也出台了各项政策，保障应急物资的生产供应和运输。新冠疫情暴发早期正是我国农历新年，许多防疫物资生产企业的员工放弃与家人团聚，加班加点生产医用口罩和防护服等，保障了防疫物资的供应。有些省市出台各项政策保证应急物资运输的畅通，运输物资主要包括三大类：重要农产品、重要生活保障品、重要的防疫和医药物资。多个省级政府责令交通委和公安局联合印发"通行证"，为对应急物资车辆提供快速检查、绿色通行的政策，有些省市还向全社会公布了物资保障电话，市民可以通过电话了解物资保供情况。从中央到各地方政府都出台了多项政策从各个方面优先保证应急物资的运输。

# 7.3 我国突发公共卫生事件的应急管理组织方式

根据《国家突发公共事件总体应急预案》和《国家突发公共卫生事件应急预案》，全国突发重大卫生事件时的应急管理组织方式是在国务院的统一领导下，由国家卫生健康委（原卫生部）负责组织、协调、管理、应对全国的突发公共卫生事件。国家卫健委的重要职责中就包括制定并组织落实疾病预防控制规划、国家免疫规划以及严重危害人民健康公共卫生问题的干预措施，制定检疫传染病和监测传染病目录；负责卫生应急工作，组织指导突发公共卫生事件的预防控制和各类突发公共事件的医疗卫生救援。当全国突发特大公共卫生事件时，国家卫健委负责疾病的防控、诊断和治疗。在必要的情况下，国务院成立全国突发公共卫生事件应急指挥部。

各级地方突发公共事件时，发生地政府统一领导各级政府的卫生行政部门、卫生防疫机构，负责组织、协调、应对本行政区内的突发公共卫生事件。在必要的情况下，成立省级或市级等地方突发公共卫生事件应急指挥部。

全国和各级地方突发公共卫生事件指挥部负责突发事件的统一指挥和领导，做出处理突发事件的重大决策。

医疗应急司（原卫生应急办公室）、各级地方政府卫生部门负责突发公共卫生事件的预防、监测、预警等的管理工作。常态下，国家卫健委和各级地方政府可以成立突发公共卫生事件专家咨询委员会，对应对和预防公共卫生事件提出决策和咨询。在突发公共卫生事件发生时，应急指挥部可成立专家组，对突发公共卫生事件提供决策咨询和行动建议，配合各级政府进行突发公共卫生事件的应急处理工作。

在突发公共卫生事件时，除卫健委的疫情防控措施，国家和地方还要在防控公共卫生事件的前提下保障应急物资包括生活物资和医药物资的供应和运输畅通，此时，就需要全国各地多部门联合作业。国务院下属的商务部、发展和改革委员会、交通运输部、应急管理部等需要协调组织应急物资供应和运输的各个部门，以达到特殊时期物流的高效性，将突发公共卫生事件的损失降到最小。

# 7.4 突发公共卫生事件应急物资的储备

应急物资是指为应对突发公共事件，包括严重自然灾害、事故灾难、公共卫生事件和社会安全事件等全过程中所必需的物资保障。应急物资的概念和分类已在本书第6章进行详述，此处不再赘述。

突发公共卫生事件涉及的应急物资种类繁多，本章着重介绍医药物资的储备、运输和配送以及医护人员的运送问题。不同的突发性公共卫生事件所需的应急医药物资不同，为应对不同种类的突发公共卫生事件，对应急医药物资进行分类管理和储备，可以有效地管理应急医药物资库存、高效运输和调配。

### 7.4.1　我国突发公共卫生事件的医药物资储备制度

本节所研究的应急物资的储备主要涉及医药用品和生活保障物资的储备问题。加强医药储备的管理，不仅可以确保常态下公众用药的充足，而且可以积极应对突发公共卫生事件，对于维护社会稳定有非常重要的作用。比如，2022 年 12 月，随着我国新冠疫情防控政策的改变，全国出现大面积感染新型冠状病毒的患者，但多数都属于轻症或无症状感染者，可以居家治疗后自愈。12 月初，因为有居民大量囤积相关药物，导致各大药店退热类药品、清热解毒类药品和抗病毒药品大范围脱销，引起一部分民众的恐慌，但随着制药厂紧急制药和国家储备药的发放，脱销现象很快消失，退热药、清热解毒等药品的销售恢复正常，由此可见药品储备的重要性。

我国《国家医药储备管理办法（2021 年修订）》规定，我国医药储备包括政府储备和企业储备。政府医药储备分为中央和地方（省、自治区、直辖市）两级医药储备，要建立能应对各类突发公共事件和市场有效供应的保障体系。企业储备是根据医药产品生产经营状况建立的企业库存。政府医药储备管理由工业和信息化部会同国家发展改革委、财政部、国家卫生健康委、国家药监局共同管理工作。突发公共卫生事件时，原则上有地方医药储备负责本地的医药产品供应保障，地方医药储备不足时可向中央医药储备请求支援，中央医药储备有权、有偿调用其他地方医药储备。

### 7.4.2　我国突发公共卫生事件的医药储备形式

突发公共卫生事件，无论是重大传染性疾病、群体性原因不明疾病、重大食物和职业中毒、群体性预防接种反应和群体性药物反应，或是重大环境污染事故，核事故和放射事故，生物、化学、核辐射恐怖事件，自然灾害导致的人员伤亡和疾病流行，最首要的任务都是要及时救治受害群众的生命、及时防止卫生事件的蔓延、尽快缩小事件的影响范围。因此，医药储备的种类可以分为：进行流行病学的检验、检测、调查的药品和设备；对传染病患者的隔离、防护用品；对于已感染病人的救治、处置所需的药品、诊断试剂和器械等（王丰等，2007）。

根据我国《国家医药储备管理办法（2021年修订）》规定，政府储备医药产品的形式为实物储备、生产能力储备、技术储备相结合的形式，储备任务由符合条件的医药企业或卫生事业单位承担。除此之外，还要有一定的信息储备和资金储备。

对于部分可预测的医药用品需求实行实物储备。实物储备是指全部以实物的形式，将医药用品按要求储备在各个医药企业的仓库中，当突发事件发生时，企业按相关约定，在第一时间向有关部门或灾区提供医药用品。实物储备形式的优点是便于调用，当突发事件发生时，可以立即投入使用。但其弊端也显而易见：一方面，某些不常用的药品可能因为过期导致浪费，或有些药品作为储备药被贮存起来，造成不能在市场上有效流通；另一方面，药品的储存条件严格，库存管理成本较高。因此，在实物储备之外，还要有其他各种形式的储备方式作为补充。

以生产能力储备补充实物储备的不足。生产能力储备是指常态需求不确定的情况下，对于专门应对重大灾情、疫情的特殊医药产品，通过保证其生产线、生产技术和供应链的稳定来保障此类特殊医药用品的生产能力，在必要时能按照灾情或疫情的需要组织生产和应急供应的一种储备形式。生产能力储备对药品生产企业的生产能力、生产设备都有一定的要求，企业需在保证常态生产能力之余，可以承担公共卫生事件突发时的应急药品生产。

政府与研发机构合作，共同实施技术储备。技术储备是指对于一些无常态需求的潜在疫情用药，政府通过支持建设其研发平台，开发并储备此类药品的生产技术和研发技术，在必要时，该技术可迅速转化为疫情需要的医药产品的一种储备形式。技术储备适用于当突发公共卫生事件，某地区因为药品供应不足时，生产企业可以迅速将生产技术转化为生产力，生产某些特殊药品。技术储备的优点在于不会造成实物浪费或生产线闲置的浪费现象，但其弊端在于，生产技术可能因为疫情等事态的发展而出现技术落后的现象，造成技术浪费，同时也浪费了技术研发时投入的人力、物力和财力。

利用大数据、互联网技术等手段建立信息储备形式。信息储备是建立医药储备管理信息系统，收集并掌握全国医药企业的结构布局、产能产量、库存规模等信息，实现信息资源共享，为应对突发事件提供用药保障（袁韩时弼等，2018）。信息储备的优势在于可以加强各级政府部门之间、药企之间、政府与企业之间的信息沟通，便于政府掌握全国的相关医药用品信息，有助于在突发公共卫生事件时迅速掌握药品的库存情况，并立即调用。其弊端在于需要专人进行信息统计，并实时更新信息，如果信息更新不及时，滞后的信息会给应对突发事件带来不便，甚至误导应对策略的制定。

政府预留应急医药用品的资金，作为医药物资储备的最后一道保障。资金储备是指政府在做年度预算时，将用于购买应对突发公共卫生事件的药品的资金预留出来，资金储备适用于当实物储备、生产能力储备、技术储备都无法满足当前突发公共卫生事件所需的药品时，政府可启动资金购买或生产所需药品。其最大弊端在于，如果没有实物储备、技术储备或生产能力储备，资金储备再多也无法购买到应对突发事件所需的药品。

以上各种形式的医药物资储备，各有其优势或弊端，在突发公共卫生事件时，可能会同时启动多种形式的医药物资储备，最大限度地发挥各种储备形式的优势，为应对突发公共卫生事件提供充足的医药物资。

### 7.4.3　完善我国应对突发公共卫生事件的医药储备机制的建议

首先，在储备管理和保障机制方面，强调多部门合作的协作机制，由国家卫生健康委员会主责，科学技术部、国家发展改革委、商务部、国家市场监督管理总局、国家医保局等各部门要实施联动机制，在实物储备、技术储备方面共同合作。国家卫生健康委根据公共卫生应急等方面的需求，提出中央医药储备名录；工业和信息化部等对地方医药储备的政策和储备品类、规模等进行指导，地方与中央互补，形成全国集中统一的医药储备体系。

其次，在实物储备方面，中央和地方协同，科学动态地调整药品储备目录，运用国际通用的新兴技术探查方法，结合疾病风险预测模型、专家评估、国内外情报信息以及当前相应的突发公共卫生应急能力（赵锐等，2020）制定合适的药品储备目录。在实物储备管理方面，可以根据风险类型进行管理，如突发流感、禽流感、非典型性肺炎、新型冠状病毒感染等重大流行疾病时的药物储备，或突发食物中毒事件、突发职业中毒事件，突发群体性预防接种反应事件时的药物储备，根据风险类型的不同制定不同的药物储备名录，将各种不同的药物和器材实物储备在相关医药事业单位，在突发公共卫生事件时，根据储备名录迅速调用这些药品和器械，无须等待购买。但实物储备最大的问题是储存和库存管理的成本较高，还可能因为药品未使用即过期造成浪费。

最后，在技术储备方面，医药用品的技术储备可以有效解决药品过期浪费的问题，政府可以与科研机构、医药生产企业等签订合同，将应对突发公共卫生事件的医药用品提前研发，进行技术储备。因此，政府可以从政策、资金上，鼓励和支持科研机构和医药企业进行应对突发公共卫生事件的药品的研发和生产。除了科研机构和医药企业，政府还可以鼓励有研发基础的高校进行生命安全和生物安全的医药研发（赵锐等，2020）。

## 7.5 突发公共卫生事件应急物资的供应和运输

公共卫生事件发生时，应急物流运输通常多涉及药品、医药器械、防护用品以及参与救援的医务人员的运输。

为保障突发公共卫生事件后的应急物资供应，在常态下，要充分利用信息技术手段，建立卫生信息共享平台，做好医药信息的监测和预警。为保障突发公共卫生事件时应急医疗物资能及时供应，在常态下，全国卫生部门、各省级卫生部门、各地方卫生部门应该建立联合的信息平台，通过大数据、信息技术平台等手段建立医疗信息共享平台，掌握各地卫生部门的医药储备情况、医院规模、医务人员情况，同时可通过大数据反映的医药用品情况对应急医药用品供应进行监测和预警。在紧急情况发生时，国家卫生部门或某个省级卫生部门可通过信息共享平台，紧急调用全国各地的医药物资和医务人员，并发挥实物储备、技术储备、生产能力储备等各种机制的作用，保证及时、准确地响应药品需求，迅速、高效地响应紧急突发公共卫生事件。在新冠疫情期间，有些城市出现居民抢购口罩、消毒液等物资的情况，此时，相关部门应该鉴于对市场的监测，及时做出预警，对于此方面的物资储备和供应迅速开展物流应急准备工作。

在应急物资运输环节，卫生部和交通部联合发布的《突发公共卫生事件交通应急规定》中明确说明，突发公共卫生事件时应急物资运输原则是优先处理应对突发事件的人员群体、防疫人员、医护人员、消毒用品、医疗救护设备和器械，保证此类物品的运输畅通、及时。

充分利用现代科技手段和先进的物流技术，提高应急医疗物资运输的效率。在运输紧急医疗物资时，要充分利用 GPS 定位技术、5G 移动通信技术、射频识别技术等定位技术和物流技术，对于运输物资的车辆、药品等情况进行实时监督，及时掌握物资情况，提高物资运输效率。

在运输方面采用多种运输方式相结合的手段，缩短应急医疗物资的运输时间。紧急医疗物资的运输方式可以是公路、铁路、航空、水运等，无论采取何种方式，都是以最短时间将医疗物资和人员送达目的地为根本目的。为提高救灾运输的效率，尽量采用直达运输的方式；直达条件不允许的情况下，可以采取多种方式联合的运输方式。比如 2020 年 1 月，湖北省武汉市的新冠疫情出现快速蔓延的势头，国家医疗队紧急驰援武汉，铁路、航空部门为运输援鄂医疗队的医务人员和物资安排了大量的运力，保证医务人员和物资以最快速度安全抵达武汉。1月25日正值我国农历正月初一，浙江省、江苏省首批援鄂医疗队近300人需乘高铁到达武汉，国铁集团迅速安排医疗队从杭州、南京分乘高铁到合肥会合，再换乘前往武汉。在合肥南站中转时，52名铁路干部职工组成接应小组，及时转运医疗队随车携带的12吨医疗物资，仅40分钟就完成转运工作。2020年1月到3月下旬，全国铁路累计运送援鄂医护及救援人员约1.2万人，向湖北地区累计装运防控保障物资超过30万吨；空运方面，累计共有4400余架次飞机在武汉紧急降落起飞，3.6万名援鄂医护人员在这里降落。这样优先、高效的航空、铁路运力安排，为保障疫情的防控和感染者的生命救治都提供了最大的便利，也体现了我国在突发紧急事件时，"一方有难，八方支援"的凝聚力和全国人民众志成城抗击新冠疫情的决心。

开通交通绿色通道，保障医疗物资运输的畅通无阻。政府部门应协同相关各部门，为紧急运输医疗物资提供专用通道，应急运输车辆等持"绿色通行证"在通过海关、检查站、跨省关卡、卫生检疫站等地点时，简化检查程序，缩短检查时间，快速通过。交通部门还可以协调当地有关人员，紧急征用车辆、人员、设备等配合完成紧急医疗物资和人员的运输。

在重大传染性疾病发生的情况下，医疗物资的运输不仅要高效，还要安全。因此，承担运输紧急物资的飞机、轮船、车辆、班列要做到进入疫区前清洗消毒；运输工作人员应在上岗前进行紧急的卫生安全知识培训，并配备相应的防护工具；物资到达疫区，按照卫生部门要求进行静置和消杀；离开疫区时，运输工具要再次做好彻底的清洁、消毒工作，必要时要对运输人员和交通工具采取隔离措施。

## 7.6　突发公共卫生事件应急物资的配送和发放

突发公共卫生事件常涉及重大传染病，在此情况下，疫区外到疫区内的医疗物资配送适合采用无接触式配送。大件物资可以用无人机、无人车等运输设备进行城市内配送，疫区内的物品还可以用机器人代替人来配送。在无法实现无接触式配送的情况下，如大型车辆运输的医药物资需要送到某个医院或疫区，此时可以采取设立缓冲区的办法，在疫区与非疫区中间设立缓冲区，运输物资达到后，由专人采取防护措施进行卸载，在缓冲区静置后再运入疫区使用。

对于防控区居民防护物资的配送，可以采取直接售卖的方式，商家跟小区物业协调，在小区内设立自动售货机，售卖口罩、手套等防护物资。对于疫情防控区居民生活物资的配送，可以采用无接触式配送，快递员将各家各户通过网络平台采购的物品存放在共享快递柜，居民根据取货码自行安排时间取货，避免了居民在同一时间内一起接触快递员取货的聚集风险。从中长期来看，随着技术的发展，非接触式服务需求会大大增加，智能快递柜、机器人配送等新业态会迎来新的发展机会（陈镜羽、张立，2020）。

由于公共卫生事件的紧迫性，政府往往要协调运输企业与企业联动，让专业的物流企业参与到医疗物资的末端配送环节，这样可以大大提高配送的效率。

对于疫区内免费防护物资和医药用品的发放，政府也可以调动公众广泛参与，在做好必要防护的前提下，社区工作人员、社区网格员、志愿者都可以参与到医疗物资发放的工作中。在人力充足的情况下，防护物资的发放可以由网格员按楼、按单元发放，每个居民楼的楼长在此时就要发挥作用，为楼内居民协调防护物资的发放。

# 7.7　典型案例——新冠疫情防控生活物资应急保障供应实践

本章前几节所涉及的物资储备、运输、配送均为医药物资，但在重大公共卫生事件发生时，涉疫地区除了急需医药物资的保障，还需要正常的生活，因此，本节研究如何在重大公共卫生事件下保障居民的生活物资供应。

2020 年初，新冠疫情在我国暴发，疫情先从湖北省武汉市蔓延，后涉及全国多个省份。为控制疫情更大面积的蔓延，各地都采取了不同的疫情防控措施，其中包括对确诊病例的隔离、有确诊病例的小区隔离，某小区甚至某个城市的封控，这就给生活物资的保障供应提出了考验。本节探讨了疫情防控政策下，我国国家层面的生活物资保障供应政策和我国南方某城市的生活物资保障供应实践案例。

2020 年 2 月 3 日，中共中央政治局常务委员会的会议精神要求，"在加强疫情防控的同时，努力保持生产生活平稳有序"。会议强调要确保蔬菜、肉蛋奶、粮食的供应，要加强物资调配和市场供应，要保障煤、电、油、气、暖的供应。

2021 年 5 月，商务部市场运行和消费促进司制定了《商务部生活必需品市场供应保障工作手册（2021 版）》，手册为生活必需品的保障范围、消费量测算、信息化系统建设、储备管理、保供手段等提供了重要的参考。

2021 年 12 月，商务部和国家发展和改革委员会联合发布了《新冠肺炎疫情防控生活物资保障工作指南》（发改办运行 2021 年 1053 号）。指南强调要统筹做好粮油、肉类、蔬菜、方便食品、能源等生活物资的应急监测、生产调度、物资运输、储备投放等环节的工作，在疫情防控政策下也要满足广大人民的生活需求。指南对保障生活物资供应的措施、畅通物资运输的措施和做好终端配送的措施提出了指导性建议。

遵照上面两个重要的文件，我国南方某城市积极做出响应，为我国其他城市生活物资的应急保障供应工作提供了宝贵的经验。该市的主要做法有以下几个方面。

（1）迅速启动应急响应。

在 2020 年 1 月 25 日的中共中央政治局常委会议上，习近平总书记强调"生命重于泰山"。该市领导班子认真领会总书记讲话的精神，针对疫情发生以来出现的抢购口罩、抢购蔬菜和抢购防疫物资的现象，迅速召开生活物资保供的部署会议，会议根据国务院、商务部和省市关于疫情防控的文件，制定了具有针对性的应对措施，并建立组织机构，确保人员到位，明确了各部门的任务。

（2）高效组建应急体系。

该市组建了应急物资保供专班工作组，市长担任专班工作组组长，公共组包括5个小组，即综合组、保供组、协调组、督查组和各县区组。各组任务和职责明确，相互协同工作。

（3）完善应急监测机制。

该市对全市各区县的生活物资供应情况、全市菜市场的供应情况、全市多家重点生活物资保障单位都进行了每日数据的监测，全面掌握全市的生活物资运行情况。根据每日数据的监测，专班工作组对全市的物资需求进行了综合研判，及时调整储备、供应政策。

（4）积极推进应急保供。

为确保全市的农产品生产、销售、供应畅通，该市从多个方面采取措施。首先，每天召开专班工作组例会，各小组汇报具体情况。其次，与重点保供企业签订协议，保证生活物资的供应到位。最后，与公安交警支队协同作业，印发绿色通行证，保证运输生活物资保障车队的畅通无阻。

（5）保证应急储备供应。

为确保民生，该市制订了详细的储备计划，应急储备的内容主要为蔬菜和肉类产品。储备形式为政府储备和市场储备，政府储备的蔬菜和肉类总量各达到7天以上的供应量，政府储备的形式是安排重点企业进行储备；市场储备的蔬菜和肉类达3000吨以上。

为避免抢购现象发生，市政府在多家大型超市安排政府储备肉投放点，猪肉以低于市场价格10%的价格向市民供应，保证市民肉类产品需求得到满足。

政府还要向重点保供企业下达任务，要求企业按照保供专班工作组的要求供应商品的种类、数量以及供应的时间、地点等。企业还要每天向专班工作组汇报保供情况，以便及时调整储备和供应的方案。

该市在突发公共卫生事件即新冠疫情期间，采取多方位措施，做到了生活物资保障充足，确保了疫情期间人们生产生活的正常运行，也为全国各地其他省市在物资保供方面提供了良好的经验。

Theory

# Chapter 1    The Overview of
# Emergency Logistics

Emergency logistics is a special logistics activity, as opposed to conventional logistics. The term "logistics" originated from military and was originally used to meet the needs of military logistics support. With the development of social economy, and the increasing circulation of goods, logistics is gradually used to refer to the circulation of goods in human society. Its purpose is to meet human economic needs. In the face of natural and man-made disasters, apart from self-rescue, mutual assistance within neighbors or relying on the management and decision-making of the local government, the proverb "When one side is in trouble, all sides support" reflects the enhancement of the social and economic development, the progress of civilization and humanitarian awareness. Whether it is self-rescue or external rescue, it will inevitably involve the convening, flow, management, maintenance and other aspects of personnel and materials. This attention to logistics in the face of public emergencies is increasingly growing. In recent years, emergency logistics has gone through a process from scratch to development, from point to point, and then to the urgent need for systematization.

Before the concept of emergency logistics was put forward, scholars at home and abroad have studied many related concepts, such as military logistics, enterprise logistics, humanitarian logistics, disaster logistics, and so on, which provides research ideas and soil for the concept of emergency logistics. As many countries attach importance to emergency events such as natural disasters and accidents, they have gradually established emergency management organizations, which has promoted the planning and management of logistics activities in face of emergencies. The first country to establish an emergency management agency is the United States, which first established the Federal Emergency Management Agency ( FEMA) in the 1970s. Subsequently, Canada, Russia, Japan and other countries have successively established their own emergency management models ( Zou Yijiang, 2008). The establishment of emergency management or relevant organizations of governments in various countries has effectively promoted the development of logistics theory and practice in face of emergencies, and also provided theoretical support and policy basis for the final proposal of emergency logistics. By comparison, it was late for China to establish emergency management organization. It was in March 2018 that the Ministry of Emergency Management of the People's Republic of China was established according to the State Council's institutional reform plan.

However, the explicit expression of "emergency logistics" first appeared in China. The SARS epidemic in 2003 caused serious losses to the economy of China, Southeast Asia and even the whole world. Therefore, people are deeply aware that in the face of emergencies, not only the quality of material security will affect the success or failure of fighting against emergencies, but also the non-standard and imperfect logistics activities will directly cause economic losses. In China alone, the cost loss caused by logistics activities during the SARS epidemic reached at least US $3 billion ( He Mingke, 2003 ). In view of the strong impact of the SARS epidemic on the whole society, including the logistics industry, the second annual academic meeting of the China Logistics Association was held on October 17, 2003, which designed a research topic of "emergency logistics". Ten research papers written by the experts and scholars attending the meeting were published in the column of "special series of reports on emergency logistics" of the journal *China Logistics and Procurement* in December 2003, which is the earliest expression of this concept. In March 2004, Ou Zhongwen and others published a research paper just titled *Emergency Logistics*. In the abstract of this paper, it mentioned that it proposed the concept of "emergency logistics" for the first time at home and abroad. This view is still open to debate, but indeed the English terminology "emergency logistics" appeared for the first time. In contrast, according to China National Knowledge Infrastructure (CNKI), although similar concepts such as humanitarian logistics or disaster logistics were expressed in foreign studies as early as the 1970s and 1980s, such as logistics of emergency departments and emergency medical logistics even appeared in the late 1990s. However, the terminology "emergency logistics" made by foreigners appeared in July 2004, which was later than the research findings of Chinese scholars. It can be concluded that whether in Chinese or English, the concept of "emergency logistics" is indeed derived from the research findings of Chinese scholars, and thus becomes a terminology.

## 1.1　Definition of emergency logistics

In the first special reports on emergency logistics published in 2003, Chinese scholars elaborated on the understanding of the concept "emergency logistics", but they only limited their understanding to the interpretation of this concept, instead of forming a clear definition. He Mingke pointed out that "in this paper, emergency logistics refers to logistics activities caused by sudden factors, including emergency logistics demand caused by sudden factors and emergency logistics supply activities to meet these logistics demands" (He Mingke, 2003). Xu Dong argued that "As the name implies, emergency logistics is mainly a logistics activity implemented in response to major epidemic, serious natural disasters, military conflicts and other emergencies". Gao Liying held at the beginning of her paper that "emergency logistics can be literally understood as a series of emergency logistics support measures taken to deal with emergencies (including war, disaster and epidemic)" (Gao Liying, 2003). Gao Dongye and Liu Xinhua believed that "emergency logistics refers to a special logistics activity that provides emergency support for the needs of materials, personnel and funds in various emergencies" (Gao Dongye and Liu Xinhua, 2003). Zhao Xinguang et al. believed that "emergency logistics refers to a special logistics activity that provides emergency support for the needs of materials, personnel, funds, etc. in the event of a crisis" (Zhao Xinguang, Gong Weifeng and Zhang Yan, 2003). Although these explanations on the term "emergency logistics" are relatively simple, they all emphasize the core elements of "sudden and urgent" and "logistics guarantee". What is rarer is that some scholars have recognized that emergency logistics not only includes the support for materials, but also includes the support for personnel and funds since this term was first put forward.

In 2004, Ou Zhongwen and other scholars explored the implications of emergency logistics, that is, "emergency logistics refers to special logistics activities aimed at providing emergency supplies for emergencies such as sudden natural disasters and sudden public health events, with the goal of maximizing time efficiency and minimizing disaster losses" (Ou Zhongwen, Wang Huiyun et al. 2004). Although this definition is limited to material support, it has its own merits, for it points out that emergency logistics is different from other logistics in terms of "loss minimization".

With the concept of emergency logistics being widely accepted, this term has also been recognized by government agencies. In 2006, the *Logistics Terminology* (GB/T 18354—2006) published by the National Standardization Administration of China incoporated "emergency logistics" as a term and defined it as "logistics activities that have prepared plans for possible emergencies and can be implemented quickly when the event occurs". This definition emphasizes the need to prepare a plan for emergencies. Although it is difficult to achieve enough effective and accurate plans for some emergencies, it also expands people's understanding of emergency logistics. Emergency logistics is not a passive response after an emergency, but can be actively deployed and prepared in advance. The 2021 version of *Logistics Terminology* ( GB/T 18354—2021 ) revised the definition to "e-mergency logistics refers to the logistics activities which provide emergency production materials and living materials support for responding to emergencies". Compared with the previous version, the new definition clarified that the material support of emergency logistics activities includes both living materials and production materials. At the time of the COVID-19, facing the possible shutdown of production enterprises at any time, this new definition fully takes into account the emergency production and continuous and stable supply of living materials under the long-term impact of major public events.

In 2006, on the basis of previous studies, Meng Shen and Wang Changqiong imitated the definition of modern logistics and made the following definition as normative as possible. The definition is that "Emergency logistics refers to special logistics activities formed by integrating transportation, packaging, loading and unloading, handling, warehousing, circulation and processing, distribution and related information processing of emergency materials with the purpose of providing emergency materials required for sudden events such as natural disasters, public health events, major accidents, and other emergencies, and aimed at maximizing time efficiency and minimizing disaster losses with the help of modern information technology"(Meng Shen, Wang Changqiong, 2006). Although this definition is more standardized and comprehensive apparently, it mechanically applied all steps of material circulation in modern logistics, and unilaterally strengthened the whole process of material circulation, but ignored the financing and management of personnel and funds.

In 2007, Wang Feng and others defined emergency logistics as "a kind of special logistics activities that provide emergency protection for the needs of materials, personnel and funds in response to serious natural disasters, sudden public health events, public security events, military conflicts and other public emergencies" (Wang Feng, JiangYuhong, Wang Jin, 2007). This definition summarized the types of public emergencies comprehensively for the first time, and drew on the more comprehensive description of "materials, personnel, funds" made by the previous researchers.

The definitions on emergency logistics made by various researchers are either similar or have different emphases. It can be said that there are too many different opinions. However, due to the short history of emergency logistics development, the theoretical research still needs to be further deepened, and no unified and standardized definition has yet been formed. Based on the existing researches and practices, this book tries to define emergency logistics by learning from others' strong points and improving the omissions. The definition is as follows.

Emergency logistics refers to a kind of special purpose logistics by using modern information technology and participated by one or more parties such as the governments, the military, professional organizations, enterprises and the public with reference to corresponding or similar plans to provide emergency support for personnel, funds, materials and other needs, in order to minimize casualties, property losses, anddestruction of the ecological environment when in face of sudden crises such as natural disasters, accident disasters, public health events and social security events.

In this definition, "natural disasters, accident disasters, public health events, social security events" are the motivating factors of emergency logistics. This expression refers to the description of the types of emergencies in Item 3 of *the Emergency Response Law of the People's Republic of China*, which was implemented on November 1, 2007. "The government, the military, professional organizations, enterprises, and the public" are the main objects of participation, which are summarized according to practical experience. "With reference to corresponding or similar plans" not only takes into account the inevitability of emergencies, so it is necessary to have a plan, but also takes into account some predictable and unpredictable characteristics of emergencies, so it can refer to similar plans for some unpredictable emergencies. "Emergency support for personnel, funds, materials and other needs" draws on previous research results, and also conforms to the emergent needs in face of emergencies in reality. The goal of "minimizing casualties, property loss and and destruction of the ecological environment" is not only to reflect the importance of life and property, but also to creatively integrate the idea of ecological protection. Comparing the response and results of the forest fire in Australia in 2019 and the forest fire in Chongqing in 2022, we will realize the importance of emergency logistics to the ecological environment. "Special purpose logistics" is used to replace the "special logistics activities" in many scholars' definitions. First of all, emergency logistics is a branch of logistics and should be included in normal management. It's special for its special purpose. Just as there is English and English for special purposes such as logistics English, scientific English, and so on as branches in linguistics, the expression "special purpose" is adopted in the definition. Secondly, emergency logistics should not only be logistics activities involving transportation, packaging, loading and unloading, handling, warehousing, circulation processing, distribution and related information processing. Its scope is far greater than the functions of logistics activities, and integrates different fields such as organization, management, information and logistics. Therefore, emergency logistics cannot be simply defined as logistics activities.

## 1. 2    Attributes of emergency logistics

Based on the definition of emergency logistics, it is necessary to further explore the attributes of emergency logistics so as to have a deeper understanding of it. As mentioned earlier, emergency logistics cannot be simply understood as logistics activities. Compared with conventional logistics, emergency logistics also involves the physical flow of goods from the place of supply to the place of receipt, but its nature of responding to emergencies makes it different from ordinary logistics.

First of all, emergency logistics bears a social attribute. According to the different purposes of logistics, the purpose of military logistics is to meet the military's conventional logistics support or material support for emergency marching. So military logistics is essentially a military activity. The purpose of commercial logistics is to realize the economic value of goods. Even if there are emergency logistics activities such as emergency supply or product recall, it is still an economic activity in essence. Unlike the former two, the purpose of emergency logistics is to reduce casualties, property losses and destruction to the ecological environment. It is a reflection of the value of achieving social stability and humanistic spirit of society through emergency response to emergencies. It is essentially a social activity.

Secondly, emergency logistics is diversified. Although emergency logistics is still a branch of logistics, it is not limited to logistics. From the perspective of stimulating factors, the stimulating factors of military logistics are military activities such as marching and fighting, which are commanded by the military command center. The stimulating factors of commercial logistics are economic activities, which are managed by business chain participants such as factories, enterprises and consumers. The triggering factors of emergency logistics are diverse. Only natural disasters such as rainstorm, typhoon, locust disaster, forest fire and earthquake may need to be connected with different departments such as meteorological department, agriculture and forestry department, seismological bureau, let alone accident disasters, public health events and social security events. From the perspective of participants, the participants of military logistics are military logistics departments, and the participants of commercial logistics are logistics companies or logistics departments, while the participants of emergency logistics are not just a single department, but involve the collective participation and cooperation of various institutions or groups such as government, military, professional organizations, enterprises, and the public. From the perspective of demand guarantee, military logistics and commercial logistics are mainly the demand guarantee for materials, while the demand guarantee for personnel and funds in the military and commercial fields is within the responsibility of the personnel department and the financial department respectively. Only the demand for emergency logistics includes both the demand for materials and the demand for personnel and funds. The logistics department alone cannot meet all the needs, only the linkage of multiple departments can realize the guarantee of multiple needs. In short, the launch and connection departments of emergency logistics are diverse; the participants are diverse; the demands are diverse; and the security departments are diverse. The diversity of emergency logistics has become an attribute that is different from other logistics.

Thirdly, emergency logistics has the nature of instant public welfare. Commercial logistics takes the principle of economic benefits and cost analysis as its core consideration. In contrast, emergency logistics aiming at the safety of people's lives, property and ecological environment no longer takes economic benefits as the first choice, but adheres to the concept of "people first, life first", and even carries out rescue at no cost in order to ensure life safety after an emergency. Unlike military logistics, the economic cost of which is allocated by the government, although the economic cost of emergency logistics cannot be separated from the special relief funds of the government, there are often generous assistance or donations from enterprises, various institutions and the public. Even they work as volunteers, together with the government and army officers and soldiers, to provide the human, material and financial needs of the people in distress. Therefore, emergency logistics has immediate public welfare in a certain period of time in the emergency rescue.

# 1.3　Guiding principles for the construction of China's emergency logistics system

Nowadays, sudden crises such as natural disasters, accident disasters, public health and social security events that bring about serious harm will inevitably happen. How to deal with these crises is one of the powerful challenges that any country or region may face. In recent years, with China's economic development, scientific and technological innovation, considerable progress in transportation and logistics industry, the gradual increase of national strength, the ability to deal with emergencies has been continuously improved. However, many problems have been exposed at the same time. In terms of emergency logistics, take the Wenchuan earthquake in 2008 as an example. Although various rescue materials and equipment poured into the disaster area from all over the country and even the whole world after the earthquake, due to the serious damage of roads and other basic facilities, traffic and communication interruption, it had brought great difficulties for earthquake relief, and materials and equipment could not be transported to the disaster area in time. Different channels and different types of logistics lacked an unified command, so disorder existed. The needs of shelters in different earthquake-striken areas were also different, and the information was complicated and difficult to sort out, and it was difficult to match the supply and demand. Therefore, it is necessary to build a set of emergency logistics system with strong command, smooth information, good management, timely distribution, and perfect security. This is not only an urgent need to ensure the safety of people's lives and property in response to emergencies, but also a practical need for China's economic construction and social stability and development. It is also in line with the important development strategies of the country, which has very important practical significance. However, the emergency logistics system is a huge and complex system, involving many fields, many levels and many elements. In order to ensure the realization of its construction, we must abide by the scientific guiding ideology.

## 1.3.1   Human-oriented guiding principle

Being human-oriented is the core idea of the scientific outlook on development. In the process of establishing and improving China's emergency logistics system, we should abide by the human-oriented guiding principle, that is, we should be mainly aimed at maximizing the safety of people's lives and property , taking the interests of the people as the starting point and foothold of all work, safeguarding the dignity of the people, and implementing emergency humanitarian relief when the people are in danger.

Firstly , we should be human-oriented to help people. The emergency logistics system responds to the needs of the people and quickly provides the basic living materials such as food, water, clothing, bedding, tents, medicine and so on, which are urgently needed to ensure the life safety and health needs of the victims. At the same time, it should also take into account the differentiated material needs of special groups, such as baby milk powder, diapers, sanitary napkins for women, to truly respect the normal needs of people in life.

Secondly, we should be human-oriented to mobilize people. Based on the human-oriented idea, the emergency logistics system should effectively mobilize the government, the army, social organizations, enterprises, the public and other participants, give full play to their respective strong points, stimulate people's enthusiasm, initiative and creativity to carry out emergency logistics activities, and achieve multi-agent coordination.

Thirdly, we should behuman-oriented to cultivate people. The emergency logistics system should strengthen the training of professionals in all aspects of emergency logistics, improve the professional quality and working ability of professionals, and enhance their overall situation awareness, responsibility awareness and dedication awareness by consciously carrying out systematic theoretical training and practical experience in emergency logistics activities.

## 1. 3. 2 Guiding principle of sustainable development

In the process of establishing and improving China's emergency logistics system, we should adhere to the guiding ideology of sustainable development, that is, establish a long-term mechanism of emergency logistics, and realize the construction of emergency logistics capacity for sustainable development.

Firstly, sustainable emergency logistics decision-making and management system. Improving emergency logistics decision-making and management capacity is an important part of building sustainable development capacity. To train high-quality emergency logistics decision makers and managers, it is necessary to comprehensively use means of planning, law, administration, education and others to establish and improve the organizational structure of sustainable development, and form a mechanism for comprehensive decision-making and coordination management of emergency logistics.

Secondly, sustainable emergency logistics technology system. Only by applying high-level science and technology to the emergency logistics system can we achieve the goal of sustainable development. Science and technology can effectively provide basis and means for emergency logistics decision-making of sustainable development, promote the improvement of emergency logistics management level of sustainable development, improve the efficiency of emergency logistics supply chain, and provide power and assistance for emergency logistics support system.

Thirdly, sustainable emergency logistics supply chain system. The concept of green environmental protection should be applied to all links of the emergency logistics supply chain to improve the sustainable development capacity of emergency logistics, such as using recyclable packaging materials, reducing excessive packaging and secondary packaging, and accelerating the promotion and application of standardized emergency logistics turnover boxes.

Finally, the participation of multiple subjects in sustainable development. Multi-agent participation is the necessary guarantee to achieve the sustainable development of emergency logistics, because the goal and action of sustainable development is not enough to rely solely on the political and military forces of the government and the army, but also requires the extensive participation of enterprises, social organizations and the public. The way and degree of participation of enterprises, social organizations and the public will determine the process of achieving the sustainable development goal of emergency logistics.

### 1. 3. 3   Guiding principle of synergetic development

The theory of synergetic development has been identified by many countries and regions in the world as the basis for achieving sustainable social development. Synergetic development is not only the development means of the emergency logistics system, but also the development goal of the emergency logistics system. The emergency logistics system is a complex system. Its operation depends on the synergy of the government, the military, social organizations, enterprises, and the public, as well as the coordinated operation of various subsystems of the emergency logistics system. Following the guiding principle of synergetic development can ensure that all elements in the emergency logistics system give full play to their functional advantages, and promote the systematic, integrated and collaborative development of the emergency logistics system through mutual coordination and support.

# 1. 4   Main contents of constructing China's emergency logistics system

As a subsystem of the emergency management system in the event of an emergency, the emergency logistics system plays the role of logistics support in the entire emergency management system. Although the construction of the emergency logistics system has been given full attention, for example, at the press conference held by the joint prevention and control mechanism of the State Council on March 6, 2020, Gao Gao, the Deputy Secretary-General of the National Development and Reform Commission, mentioned that we are urgently studying and formulating policies to strengthen the construction of the emergency logistics system in China. He particularly stressed that for natural disasters, major public health emergencies, major safety accidents and other emergencies, it is necessary to establish a hierarchical response and security system for emergency logistics, make overall use of national storage resources and networks, give full play to the organization and coordination capabilities and professional advantages of industry associations and key enterprises, and improve the rapid response and security capabilities of emergency logistics, including rapid operation and cold chain logistics.

According to *The Outline of the 14th Five-Year Plan For Economic and Social Development and Long-Range Obectives Through The Year* 2035 ( referred to as *The 14th Five-Year Plan*) , the emergency logistics system refers to the logistics system that ensures the supply of emergency materials and the operation of production and living under the conditions of emergencies. During the *14th Five-Year Plan* period, we will accelerate the establishment of an emergency logistics system with sufficient storage, rapid response and strong impact resistance. We will make full use of various existing logistics resources, give priority to the improvement of mechanisms which are supplemented by hardware construction, and adhere to the government's overall planning, enterprise operation, peacetime and wartime integration, and the common participation of the whole society. We will also establish an emergency logistics team with enterprises as the main body, enhance the emergency support capability of logistics facilities, and improve the level of emergency logistics technology and equipment to improve the emergency logistics operation guarantee mechanism and strengthen the emergency logistics policy guarantee.

The construction of the emergency logistics system is of great significance. It is related to the national economy and people's livelihood. On the macro level, it is closely related to the country and governments at all levels, the stability and harmony of the country and society, and the consolidation of national defense security. On the micro level, it is related to the well-being of the people, and the safety of people's daily life and the safety of their property. In order to effectively respond to emergencies and avoid major damage and negative impact on social stability and the safety of people's lives and their property, there is no doubt that the construction of emergency logistics system is extremely important, and it is urgent to form a scientific, standardized, systematic, professional, intelligent and synergetic construction system.

Different experts and scholars have different perspectives and views on the construction of emergency logistics system. Wang Xuping, Fu Kejun and Hu Xiangpei (2005) believed that the emergency logistics system included four levels: control level, decision-making level, data level and environment level. Li Rui and She Lian (2007) studied the emergency logistics system in hub cities under emergencies, and designed the emergency logistics system as an integrated system of an organization and command system, a resource guarantee system, a traffic guarantee system and an information sharing system. Chen Fangjian (2008) believed that an effective and complete emergency logistics system must be composed of emergency logistics support system, emergency logistics command system, emergency logistics information system and emergency logistics distribution system. Yu Duogou and He Shiwei (2009) pointed out that the emergency logistics system should be built on three levels, namely, command and decision-making, operation framework and security mechanism. Li Yanqin, Zhang Liyi and Guo Chunsheng (2010) believed that the establishment and improvement of the emergency logistics system included the construction and improvement of infrastructure, the research on the financing and procurement mode of emergency supplies, the discussion on the storage and dispatching mode of emergency supplies, the formulation and implementation of policies and regulations, the training of professional and technical personnel, and many other aspects. Gao Xiaoying (2011) stated that an effective emergency logistics system should include four subsystems: emergency logistics command system, emergency logistics information system, emergency logistics support system and emergency logistics distribution system. Liu Tongjuan and Ma Xiangguo(2013) held the view that the construction of emergency logistics system should include at least five aspects: emergency material supply system, emergency logistics operation system, emergency logistics organization system, emergency logistics basic support system, emergency logistics laws, regulations and policy system. Chen Hui (2014) argued that emergency logistics generally consisted of organizational system, command and decision-making system, material storage system, logistics distribution system, information management system, professional system, theoretical system, policy and regulation system and other relevant elements. Either simplified or detailed, all views have their merits. Some only focus on the level of material logistics, while others extend their scope to command and decision-making, information management and policy and regulatory protection.

Based on the views of above scholars and conforming to the definition of emergency logistics in this book, the emergency logistics system can be divided into the following four subsystems: emergency logistics command system, emergency logistics information system, emergency logistics management system, and emergency logistics support system. The emergency logistics system is a complex and huge system, involving the participation of different institutions or individuals such as the government, the military, professional organizations, enterprises, and the public, covering the fields of collection, collation, sharing and use of information, distribution, scheduling, management, of people, property, and materials, as well as the support of laws and regulations. The elements of each different part come from different subsystems. At the same time, each subsystem complements each other and integrates organically to form a complete set of emergency logistics system from emergency startup to the realization of the purpose of rescue and guarantee under emergencies.

(1) Emergency logistics command system. Be responsible for initiating emergency logistics actions at corresponding levels according to the severity of the emergency, making rapid decisions and arranging, issuing and guiding instructions, so as to ensure the efficient and orderly operation of the entire logistics system.

(2) Emergency logistics information system. Computer network can be used to build a special emergency logistics information platform to provide technical support for the whole process of information transmission, collection, collation and sharing. The information system can provide information access and transmission for the command and decision-making system, the unified scheduling of personnel, funds and materials for management system, and information collection and sharing for security system.

(3) Emergency logistics management system. This system is a unified management of personnel, funds and materials related to emergency logistics. It is responsible for the recruitment and mobilization, training, assignment and transfer, assessment and pre-evaluation of emergency logistics personnel, the collection, use and supervision of emergency logistics funds, and the comprehensive management of the planning, procurement and production, storage, dispatching and requisition, transportation and distribution, recovery and processing of emergency materials.

(4) Emergency logistics support system. It not only provides the guarantee of laws, regulations and policies for the entire emergency logistics activities, but also provides logistics support and traffic facilities and other security coordination services for personnel involved in emergency logistics tasks.

# Chapter 2　Construction of the Command System of China's Emergency Logistics

When an emergency occurs, a large number of emergency supplies and emergency personnel are needed in a short time. How to coordinate the relevant departments to provide special equipment for disaster relief, communication equipment, medical equipment, daily necessities and other supplies, and how to allocate various levels of management personnel, rescue personnel and logistics personnel? It requires a top-down command system with division of labor and mutual cooperation. For example, when dealing with major earthquake disasters, the earthquake area needs the transportation, communication and power departments to carry out emergency repair of the infrastructure damaged by the earthquake, and the engineering equipment and supplies such as food, medicine, tents, cotton-padded clothes for emergency rescue, which requires the close cooperation of different departments such as the earthquake bureau, the government, the military, transportation, communication, electricity, medical treatment and enterprises. If these departments do not have a mature coordination mechanism among themselves, it is easy to cause unclear responsibilities, multiple command and fight independently, which is not conducive to the timely and effective realization of the purpose of emergency logistics.

The social nature of emergency logistics also inevitably requires the participation of the whole society, including the government, the military, professional organizations, enterprises, and the public. In order to achieve a reasonable division of labor for personnel at different levels and in different fields, give full play to their expertise and effective cooperation, it is essential for a unified command system to do the overall deployment and task planning. On the basis of integrating and screening various information, a unified command system can take the overall picture and effectively coordinate and allocate various resources.

The emergency logistics command system refers to the command and decision-making, liaison and coordination, supervision and evaluation on emergency logistics level, liaison organization, emergency logistics process, etc. according to the corresponding plan to respond to natural disasters, accident disasters, public health and social security events and other sudden public crises, in order to ensure the rapid response and smooth operation of emergency logistics.

The main tasks of the emergency logistics command system are as the following. First, it is to formulate corresponding emergency plans for predictable emergencies, and formulate targeted measures and plans according to the classification of the plans, such as natural disasters, accident disasters, public health events and social security events. Second, it is to launch emergency logistics actions timely to deal with emergencies, and make action deployment according to the corresponding plan and the actual situation. Third, it is to conduct overall monitoring, coordination and evaluation of the emergency logistics action process, and timely conduct necessary guidance and appropriate adjustment of the action plan.

# 2.1　Construction principles of China's emergency logistics command system

The command system of emergency logistics is the initiator of emergency logistics action and the guidance center of emergency logistics system. It plays a vital role in the efficient and orderly operation of the entire emergency logistics system.

To establish an effective emergency logistics command system, the following principles should be followed.

### 2. 1. 1    Unified command and scientific decision-making

Emergency logistics is the lifeline to deal with major public crises, and also the artery to ensure people's livelihood in a special period. It is the basic ability to maintain the healthy operation of the national economy. Its importance determines that it must be under the unified command of the government. The government's unified command of emergency logistics can give full play to the government's functional advantages, for it can effectively organize the party, government, army, enterprises and the public to form a joint force and combine professional and social forces to form an efficient emergency response mechanism. At the same time, under the leadership of the Communist Party of China and the government, it can give full play to the role of the expert pool as a think tank to form scientific decisions based on the professional opinions of experts, and ensure the scientific nature of emergency decision-making.

### 2. 1. 2    Flexible response and quick decision

In the process of responding to emergencies, the type and quantity of needed materials will also change as the emergencies may continue to escalate or change. The commanders need to respond flexibly and make quick decisions according to the changes in the situation, so as to ensure the support of emergency logistics within the golden time of rescue.

### 2. 1. 3    Overall planning and coordinated operation

Under the unified leadership of the government, early warning and overall planning of emergency logistics should be carried out throughout the country according to the types of disasters that are prone to occur. It is necessary to do a good job of sufficient material storage, but also to avoid repeated construction and excessive waste. When a disaster comes, it is necessary to supplement and allocate emergency supplies on time, widely mobilize various resources of the government, the army, enterprises and the society, give full play to the advantages of all forces, and form the overall efficiency and synergy to realize the effective operation of materials flow, information flow and capital flow.

## 2.2    Construction of organizing China's emergency logistics command system

The emergency logistics command system is the "brain" of the emergency logistics system and the leading organization of the emergency logistics action when an emergency occurs. In the implementation process of emergency logistics, several departments are often required to take unified action, but these departments have not formed a mature coordination mechanism among themselves. The communication channel is not smooth, the responsibility is unclear, and multi-level command leads to the failure of emergency logistics to reflect its fast and efficient characteristics and requirements, which often result in serious consequences. In China's current emergency management system, the National Emergency Management Ministry has set up a department of disaster relief and material support, whose main responsibilities are: to undertake disaster relief work such as disaster verification, loss assessment, disaster relief donations, etc., to formulate emergency material storage plans and demand plans, to organize the establishment of emergency material sharing and coordination mechanisms, to organize and coordinate the storage, allocation and emergency distribution of important emergency materials, and to undertake the management, allocation and supervision of disaster relief funds and materials from the central government, organize and coordinate the emergency relocation and resettlement of the disaster-affected people, the rehabilitation and reconstruction subsidies for the disaster-damaged houses and the living assistance for the disaster-affected people in cooperation with relevant parties. Although the department has assumed the core functions and roles of the national emergency logistics command organization, it also has part of the functions of disaster relief. In terms of emergency logistics, it focuses on making plans and coordinating materials and supplies, and has not yet played the due role of supervision and guidance for the entire emergency logistics system. In addition, a clear top-down command system has not yet been formed nationwide, which can not only achieve top-down guidance and supervision on the organization, but also provide more targeted leadership and command by the corresponding level of command organization according to the level of public crisis events.

## 2. 2. 1 Vertical construction

In the construction of the emergency logistics command system, attention should be paid to the hierarchical composition of the top-down emergency logistics command center to form an emergency logistics command system with smooth organizational mechanism. In the government-led emergency management system, the emergency logistics management department should be clearly established to meet the needs of the government more effectively in response to emergency public events. Corresponding to China's administrative regional system, the emergency logistics management department can be set at four levels: central, provincial, municipal and district (county). This system is flexible and can realize hierarchical command according to the degree of the disaster. When the scope of the disaster is small, the emergency logistics command center of the disaster area can formulate a plan to command the disaster relief. When there is a nationwide public hazard, the nationwide command center will unify the command departments at all levels and form a nationwide rapid response network. In response to the nationwide public health events of the COVID-19, China has formed an epidemic prevention and control network covering every corner of the country, from the central government to all provinces and cities, to districts and counties, and to towns or streets. Under strict prevention and control, China has effectively curbed several rounds of attacks of mutant strains from the original strain to Alpha, Beta, Gamma, Delta, Omicron, etc. to the greatest extent. It has delayed and minimized the serious harm caused by the virus to the people's health and life, and also accumulated valuable experience for the construction of the emergency logistics system under the large-scale public crisis in the country.

On the national level, relying on the National Emergency Management Ministry, China established a national emergency logistics department responsible for the unified leadership, unified command and emergency decision-making of particularly significant emergency logistics actions in the national or cross-provincial public security events. If necessary, China can alo form a special emergency logistics national command working group according to the type and impact of the disaster.

On the provincial level, under the guidance of the national emergency logistics command department, relying on the provincial emergency management department, the provincial emergency logistics command center should be established to be responsible for the unified leadership, unified command and major emergency decision-making of emergency logistics actions in great public security events in the province or in the cross-city regions within this province. If necessary, a special provincial emergency logistics command working group can be temporarily formed according to the type and impact of the disaster.

On the municipal level, under the guidance of the provincial emergency logistics command center, relying on the municipal emergency management department, a municipal emergency logistics command center should be established to be responsible for the unified leadership, unified command and major emergency decision-making of the emergency logistics actions in the major public security events in the city-wide or cross-district (county) areas of the city. If necessary, a special emergency logistics municipal command working group can be temporarily formed according to the type and impact of the disaster.

On the district (county) level, under the guidance of the municipal emergency logistics command center, relying on the district (county) level emergency management department, an emergency logistics command center at the district (county) level should be established to be responsible for the unified leadership, unified command and emergency decision-making of emergency logistics actions in the general public security affairs of the whole district (county) or the villages, towns or streets under the jurisdiction of the district (county). If necessary, a special emergency logistics area (county) command working group can be temporarily formed according to the type and impact of the disaster.

When the capacity and resources of emergency logistics on one level of government are insufficient, the government of the upper level can be requested to provide support, but the use of emergency resources of the central government needs to be reported to the Premier of the State Council.

## 2. 2. 2   Horizontal construction

Emergency logistics is the core organization undertaking emergency logistics services in the emergency management system. Based on the national conditions of China and the types and characteristics of public security accidents that may occur, we should give full play to the institutional advantages and set up 4 sectors including an emergency logistics headquarter, an emergency logistics office, an emergency logistics expert advisory committee, and an emergency logistics monitoring and feedback office within the emergency logistics command departments at all levels established under the unified leadership of governments at all levels.

### 2.2.2.1    Emergency logistics headquarter

Whether central or local, there should be a standing emergency logistics headquarter within emergency logistics command departments at all levels. After a disaster, a temporary special command group was formed by quickly organizing related departments that responded effectively to the incident. On the basis of collecting adequate information, the command group in the emergency logistics headquarter should discuss how to respond rapidly, and then the corresponding measures will be taken quickly and practically and the relevant actions will be specified. Let's take Sichuan Province as an example. Sichuan Province is a province with frequent earthquake disasters. The standing emergency logistics headquarters set up by the emergency logistics headquarters can be composed of special personnel sent by the government emergency logistics management department, the transportation department, the military logistics department, the seismological bureau and other agencies, or the temporary emergency logistics headquarters can be formed by relevant agencies according to other types of public disasters. If necessary, the commander can be sent to the scene of the disaster area to make decisions in person. Multi-department joint defense and joint control command center can form a unified command opinion and be responsible for the formulation of plans, disaster emergency response and other decisions, so as to avoid various problems caused by multiple command, command confusion, and poor information communication.

### 2.2.2.2    Emergency logistics office

Emergency logistics offices at all levels are responsible for the timely collection of the demand information of the disaster area, the emergency coordination among disaster-related departments under the direction of the leading group, and do a good job of multi-sectoral and multi-agent emergency logistics information communication and coordination, to ensure the emergency release of orders and decisions and the uploading and delivery of information.

### 2.2.2.3 Emergency logistics expert advisory committee

According to the needs of emergency logistics within the administrative region, the expert group on emergency logistics shall be composed of relevant experts and scholars to provide decision-making advice and action suggestions for the emergency logistics leading group. If necessary, an emergency logistics leader will participate in on-site emergency logistics command.

### 2.2.2.4 Emergency logistics supervision and feedback division

This division is to supervise and evaluate the whole process of emergency logistics actions, and timely report the new situation and new changes to the leading group, so as to make flexible adjustment of command and decision to achieve dynamic feedback mechanism of emergency logistics supervision and evaluation.

## 2.3 Working mechanism of China's emergency logistics command system

Based on the tasks of the emergency logistics command system and the basic principles of its construction, China's emergency logistics command system should form the following work mechanisms to achieve scientific command, rapid response, synergetic and efficient command.

### 2.3.1 Monitoring, early-warning and emergency-plan drill mechanism of emergency logistics

Monitoring and early warning is the premise to prevent all public emergencies from causing serious consequences. Similarly, in the emergency logistics system, it is also necessary to monitor the possibility of all public security emergencies, and be ready to start emergency logistics operations at any time, even before the governments start the disaster rescue operations. It is also necessary to start emergency logistics operations in advance, which is also known as the old saying "food and fodder should go ahead of troops and horses". Through an effective information sharing platform, emergency logistics offices of governments at all levels should pay attention to the disaster early warning information uploaded and shared by geological, meteorological, fire, health, epidemic prevention and other departments at any time, and report it to the emergency logistics leading group in a timely manner. The leading group, together with relevant experts of the expert advisory committee, will conduct risk prediction and assessment, provide early warning opinions, and take countermeasures as soon as possible. The monitoring and early warning mechanism of emergency logistics will predict and plan emergency logistics actions in advance, which can greatly improve the efficiency and response speed of emergency logistics command work, achieve the goal of "being prepared, being ready to fight", and form the flexibility of emergency logistics command system.

The monitoring and early warning mechanism can ensure the timeliness of emergency logistics actions, while the perfect emergency logistics plan practicing mechanism is the premise and key to achieve the effectiveness of emergency logistics command tasks. As the basis of an emergency logistics action, the emergency logistics plan is highly applicable and operable, and can provide an action plan quickly and effectively in the event of an emergency public event. Since the State Council issued the National Overall Emergency Plan for Public Emergencies in 2006, people's governments at all levels, relevant departments, key enterprises and institutions, schools, hospitals, and densely populated places have formulated relatively complete emergency plans, but the plan for emergency logistics has not been fully valued and has not formed a relatively complete plan system. In order to change this situation as soon as possible, the emergency logistics departments at the district (county) level and above shall, in accordance with the characteristics and laws of large-scale public security incidents in the region, work with the relevant departments to formulate emergency logistics plans in the administrative region. After the plan is formulated, relevant organizations and personnel should also be regularly organized to carry out emergency logistics plan practices, promote the cooperation and communications between departments, entities and subsystems, and timely improve, adjust, enrich and improve the plan according to the exposed problems. Due to the unpredictability and the impact of the emergency, the emergency logistics command organizations at all levels should also have the awareness of flexible response and command experience, and should not mechanically apply the plan completely, but adopt dynamic response strategies to adjust the plan according to the type and characteristics of the public emergency, the environment where it occurs, the scope of impact, and other conditions.

## 2.3.2 Hierarchical response and liaison mechanism of emergency logistics

Whether the response is rapid and timely is the key to the success of emergency logistics, and is also a basic requirement for the construction of emergency logistics system. First of all, an emergency logistics command system with rapid and timely response is indispensable. The vertically graded emergency logistics command system can not only meet the emergency needs of the local emergency logistics to start quickly, but also timely apply to the superior department for support and assistance from neighboring regions according to the extent and scope of the emergency public events. For regional and small-scale public emergencies, the local government generally leads the emergency logistics command department to respond in a timely manner, and at the same time reports to the higher level government to pay close attention to the development of the situation and provide coordination and assistance when necessary. For cross-provincial or nationwide public emergencies, the National Emergency Logistics Ministry will directly start the command task of emergency logistics. The hierarchical response mechanism, with clear responsibilities and scientific division of labor, reflects the speed and efficiency of hierarchical response of the emergency logistics command system. In addition to the hierarchical response of the organization mechanism, the emergency logistics command organization should also clarify the level of response according to the scale and situation of public emergencies. According to the Overall Emergency Plan for National Public Emergencies issued by the State Council, public emergencies can be divided into four levels according to the degree of harm, urgency and development trend that may be caused: Level I (especially serious), Level II (serious), Level III (larger) and Level IV (general). When formulating corresponding emergency logistics plans, governments at all levels should formulate corresponding four levels of emergency logistics according to the characteristics of the four levels of public emergencies, and define the implementation standards of emergency logistics at each level. When a public emergency occurs, the emergency logistics command organization should pay close attention to the level of the crisis, make a timely response based on the information of all parties, and launch the corresponding level of emergency logistics action. Of course, according to the development of the situation and the degree of material shortage, the level of emergency logistics action can be adjusted timely to command the emergency logistics action more scientifically.

The hierarchical response mechanism can improve the speed and efficiency of the emergency logistics command system, while the liaison mechanism is the key to improve the speed and efficiency of the entire emergency logistics system. Emergency logistics involves a wide range of participants, including the government, the military, enterprises, social organizations, the public, and even governments of other places, overseas organizations and institutions. The various links of emergency logistics are also very complex, including the convening, training and allocation of emergency logistics personnel, as well as the collection, use and supervision of emergency logistics funds, as well as the planning, procurement, storage, allocation and transportation of emergency materials, and even the protection of laws and regulations, infrastructure and transportation facilities, which almost involves all walks of life and all aspects of society. Only a strong emergency logistics command system under the leadership of the government can connect the power of all sectors of society, coordinate the resources of all sectors of society, and pave the way for the smooth implementation of emergency logistics. In order to effectively activate the liaison mechanism of the command system, special posts can be set up in the emergency logistics offices at all levels to strengthen the liaison and information sharing with other departments, such as the emergency management department, the military, the civil affairs department, the transportation department, the fire department, the flood or drought control and relief department, the seismological bureau, the industrial and commercial bureau, etc.

## 2.3.3 Supervision and evaluation mechanism of emergency logistics

The emergency logistics command system needs to have the ability to control the overall situation of the emergency logistics, not only at the macro level but also at the micro level. This requires the emergency logistics command department to play the role of evaluation and supervision in emergency logistics operations. Macro control means that the emergency logistics command system should have the ability to conduct a global assessment of the overall logistics situation of the occurrence, development and end of major emergencies, timely adjust the emergency logistics actions, and effectively coordinate and adjust the supply, so as to avoid the occurrence of inconsistent supply and demand, and the idleness or waste of a large number of emergency supplies. The overall control at the micro level means that the emergency logistics command system can effectively supervise the function of various elements in each subsystem, such as whether the number and training quality of emergency logistics professionals can meet the daily needs, and whether the structure and type of emergency supplies can meet the needs of the people in the disaster-stricken area. According to the assessment results and problems found in the supervision process, the emergency logistics headquarters can adjust the decisions and plans in time.

However, at present, China's emergency logistics system lacks a dynamic monitoring and evaluation mechanism. In addition to the planned emergency logistics behavior of the government and the military, the donations, human and material support of enterprises, social groups and individuals were not incorporated into the effective management system in a timely manner, resulting in management confusion and material waste. If the command department does not know the scale and capacity of the spontaneous volunteers on the scene and the actual situation of emergency supplies donated by the enterprise, it is impossible to effectively command and coordinate. To tap the potential of the supervision and evaluation mechanism of the emergency logistics command system, it is necessary to use modern information technology to intelligently process the complex information of all parties and timely incorporate it into the decision support information network. For example, for the demand of certain emergency supplies, the command department should formulate a guiding supply plan based on the number of people affected by the disaster and the estimated duration of disaster relief. At the same time, the command department will compare the emergency storage of the local government with the actual need, and timely release the interpretations to the society, so as to better manage the donations from the society.

# Chapter 3　Construction of the Information System of China's Emergency Logistics

The goal of the emergency logistics information system is to transmit all kinds of information needed by emergency logistics timely and accurately with the help of modern information technology so as to coordinate the whole process of emergency logistics actions. As a subsystem of China's emergency logistics system, the emergency logistics information system plays an important role in providing information services for the information collection and release, analysis and processing, communication and coordination, sharing and feedback of the entire system.

## 3.1　Construction principles of China's emergency logistics information system

The emergency logistics information system is the "neural network" of China's emergency logistics system, providing all kinds of necessary data or information for the entire system. To build an effective emergency logistics information system, the following principles should be followed.

## 3.1.1　Principle of integration

The smooth operation of each subsystem of the emergency logistics system is inseparable from the effective transmission of information. The information required by each subsystem is different, but it supports each other, forming a complex information ocean. The information system with single function cannot meet the information support within and between the subsystems. Therefore, it is necessary to design the information system as a whole, carry out integrated construction, integrate all kinds of effective information supporting different systems, eliminate the information transmission barrier, and ensure the smooth flow of information in the emergency logistics system.

## 3.1.2　Principle of standardization

Standardization not only means that the construction of information systems should follow scientific and normative standards, but also refers to the standardization of information collection and processing. There are many original information and many processing information in the emergency logistics system. To realize the sharing of information in multiple departments and fields, it is necessary to formulate unified standards and formats to ensure the smooth flow of information in the emergency logistics system.

## 3.1.3　Principle of dynamics

Information plays a vital role in emergency logistics operations. It is the foundation of various links including command, management, transportation, distribution and so on. Whether the information is accurate and reliable or not can even lead to the success or failure of the whole emergency logistics operation.

The unpredictability of emergency logistics makes some demands change at any time. To ensure the accuracy of information, it is necessary to update and adjust all kinds of information in time. Therefore, the principle of dynamic for construction is a powerful guarantee to ensure the reliability of the emergency logistics information system.

## 3.1.4　Principle of visualization

In order to effectively meet thes ervice guarantee for public emergencies, emergency logistics needs not only the broad participation of the society, but also the attention of the media and the public. Based on the principle of visualization, the openness and transparency of emergency logistics information system are not only conducive to the effective sharing of information within the system and between systems to improve the overall efficiency of the operation of the emergency logistics system, but also conducive to the realization of public supervision of the government's emergency response, in order to improve the ability of governments at all levels to respond to emergencies and the credibility of the government.

## 3.1.5　Principle of intelligence

The emergency logistics information system not only needs to collect the original data, but also needs to use a variety of technical means to intelligently process the original data to provide targeted information support for all aspects of emergency logistics, so as to improve the efficiency of the entire emergency logistics system. For example, the optimization method and simulation technology are used in the distribution of emergency supplies to reduce the inefficiency of manual processing of information and realize the decision support of information to the command system.

## 3.2    Hierarchy construction of China's emergency logistics information system

Emergency logistics information system is an indispensable neural network in China's emergency logistics system. It should not only form its own system, but also extend to all subsystems to provide information security for all parts of emergency logistics. China's emergency logistics information system can adopt the method of hierarchical construction, and build an intelligent emergency logistics information platform that integrates information from all parties based on a complete set of communication infrastructure, so as to realize the application of information in various fields of emergency logistics. According to this idea, China's emergency logistics information system can be built on three levels, that is foundation level, platform level and application level.

### 3.2.1    Foundation level

The foundation level refers to the infrastructure, equipment and systems supporting the dissemination of emergency logistics information. On the foundation level, a complete emergency logistics information system includes both hardware and software. Hardware refers to not only large infrastructure such as signal towers and lines, but also hardware resources and physical equipment of the system, such as computers, servers, communication equipment, etc. Hardware is the foundation of information system construction, and constitutes the hardware platform of information system operation. Software refers to the system composed of software systems and modules that maintain various functions of the information system. Software includes both data and programs shared by the whole system and special data and programs designed to support the function of a certain system. Software mainly includes system software and application software. Among them, the system software is mainly used for system management, maintenance, control and program loading and compilation. The application software is a program or file that commands the computer to process information, including a fully functional database system, a real-time information collection and processing system, a real-time information retrieval system, a planning, resource allocation, real-time monitoring, and situation prediction system ( Yuan Yuan, Yang Xilong, 2009 ).

The complete foundation level of an information system is the carrier of information flow and it plays a decisive role in the effective transmission of information. A good information system can transmit early warning signals and disaster relief logistics information in time, which can greatly improve the rapid response ability and efficiency of disaster relief, and shorten the time of disaster relief. The government can consider establishing a special channel for information transmission in disaster situations, setting up an emergency communication network independent of commercialand public communication networks, to ensure that this special channel can be started to command disaster relief and emergency logistics activities when the civil communication network is paralyzed. Since the information system plays an indispensable role in the emergency logistics process, the foundation level, as the basis of the emergency logistics information system, its role should be strengthened in particular. Therefore, "communication network operators should increase capital investment, speed up the construction of communication network infrastructure, optimize and strengthen network signals, expand the coverage area of signals, and enhance the carrying capacity of network data transmission. Especially in case of communication blind spots after disasters, they should repair facilities and equipment as soon as possible, eliminate the blind spots as soon as possible, and ensure smooth communication" ( Wei Qi, 2010 ).

## 3.2.2　Platform level

The platform level refers to the comprehensive collection platform of all kinds of information required by each link of emergency logistics. Although China classifies emergencies into four types: natural disasters, accident disasters, public health security events and social security events, each category covers several various emergencies, and the information required for emergency logistics activities related to each emergency is more complicated but indispensable. Information from any channel has certain value and plays a role for the implementation of emergency logistics activities. Unfortunately, China has not yet established a unified emergency logistics information platform, which has led to the dispersion of various information sources. Emergency logistics commanders and administrators sometimes suffer from the lack of key information, and sometimes face a large number of highly overlapping information. They have to spend a lot of time and energy on information collection and screening, which seriously reduces the work efficiency. Therefore, only by establishing a unified emergency logistics information platform, centralizing all kinds of information resources, and making it convenient for all links and fields to access and search at any time, can information resources play a maximum role in emergency logistics activities.

The main task of the platform level is to collect all kinds of information about emergencies, including the type of disaster, location, casualties, degree of disaster, climate conditions, damage to traffic facilities, material demand, etc. On the premise of not processing the original information as much as possible, the original information should be collected and entered according to the unified and standardized data collection format, and stored in the emergency logistics information platform. For the information of the platform, relevant departments are required to upload and update it at any time to ensure that the information is timely, reliable and rapid, so that relevant emergency logistics personnel can remake the work deployment according to the dynamic changes of the information. In the process of collecting the original information, due to the insufficient investment of emergency logistics funds, the lack of professional talents and the lack of awareness of secondary use of information, the utilization rate of information is low and the processing cost is high. Therefore, in the construction of the emergency logistics information system, we should also pay attention to information storage at the platform level in the form of original data, so as to facilitate secondary analysis and processing, improve the efficiency of data utilization, and improve the visual management of information resources.

According to the types of emergencies, the emergency logistics information system can be divided into emergency logistics information platforms of different disaster types, such as natural disaster emergency logistics information platform, accident disaster emergency logistics information platform, public health emergency logistics information platform and social security emergency logistics information platform. Each type of information platform can also be subdivided. For example, the natural disaster emergency logistics information platform can be subdivided into earthquake disaster emergency logistics information platform, snow disaster emergency logistics information platform, typhoon emergency logistics information platform, flood emergency logistics information platform, etc. The more goal-oriented the setting of the information platform, the more accurate the information collection will be, and the more effective the intelligence and integration of information services will be. Take the statistics of emergency supplies as an example. If the data of emergency supplies from different sources are collected according to the disaster types of natural disasters, accident disasters, public health events and social security events, the barriers to the sharing of materials resources between multiple levels and departments will be broken, and the original scattered, different formats and different types of emergency supplies resource data will be uniformly connected to the emergency logistics information platform. Strengthening the universal integration of various materials and resources data can lead to the whole process of tracking and management of emergency materials from collection to use, and ensure the effective use of national emergency materials and resources.

### 3.2.3    Application level

The application level refers to the application of information processed in the platform level in various fields of emergency logistics operations. At present, China's emergency logistics informatization is generally low, which greatly restricts the efficiency of all aspects of emergency logistics. In order to improve the informatization level of emergency logistics, it is necessary to strengthen the application of information technology in the emergency logistics system. *The Outline of the 14th Five-Year Plan* also stressed that "we should accelerate the construction of digital technology-assisted government decision-making mechanism and improve the level of accurate and dynamic monitoring, prediction and early warning based on high-frequency big data". Only by deeply integrating the information provided by the information platform with the professional fields, integrating the information of all links in the emergency logistics system by means of system integration, and realizing the intelligent application of emergency logistics information in a timely manner, can we provide strong information support for the specific work of emergency logistics command, management, coordination and so on.

The main task of the application level is to build a unified and efficient emergency logistics information application center that connects from top to bottom and from left to right according to the information needs of different links in the emergency logistics system on the basis of various disaster emergency logistics information platforms. According to the information requirements of each part of the emergency logistics system, the emergency logistics information system can be built into a system of information for serving each subsystem of the emergency logistics, such as the command information system of emergency logistics, the management information system of emergency logistics, the support information system of emergency logistics, and the comprehensive information system of emergency logistics for the information exchange between subsystems. For example, in the management of the transportation and distribution of emergency materials, the emergency logistics information platform can carry out real-time, accurate, and large-scale dynamic positioning of transportation vehicles carrying emergency materials around the clock through integrating modern information technologies such as Global Positioning System (GPS), Global System for Mobile Communications (GSM), Geographic Information System (GIS) to improve the operation efficiency and safety of vehicles and effectively improve the transportation capacity of emergency materials.

## 3.3 Function construction of China's emergency logistics information system

As the nerve center of the emergency logistics system, the information network of the information system is spread across all subsystems, so multiple functions need to be constructed to provide information guarantee for all links of the emergency logistics system. From the start of emergency logistics action to the command and decision-making of emergency logistics, to the communication and coordination of emergency materials management departments and the operation of emergency logistics support system, the efficient and reliable operation of all links of the emergency logistics system cannot be separated from the support of the information system. According to the function and role of information system in emergency logistics system, China's emergency logistics information system can be divided into command information system of emergency logistics, management information system of emergency logistics, support information system of emergency logistics and integrated information system of emergency logistics.

## 3.3.1    Command information system of emergency logistics

Command information system of emergency logistics is the application system of information technology in emergency logistics command work. Compared with many developed countries, although in some industries and fields China's informatization level and scale are relatively mature, it is still very low in the field of emergency logistics. In the aspect of emergency logistics command and decision-making, it is not only faced with problems such as untimely information transmission, low accuracy and limited data analysis ability, but also lacks a unified command information sharing platform. When facing an emergency, even with the timely collection of all kinds of information, there is no perfect and effective information platform support of emergency logistics. Therefore, the massive information resources cannot be effectively utilized, and the first-hand information is also difficult to be converted into the basis for decision-making. To establish a command information platform of emergency logistics and use advanced technical means to process various data and information can contribute to the realization of information integration and intelligent processing, which ultimately will greatly improve the efficiency of emergency logistics command. For example, after the occurrence of an accident or disaster, the application of remote sensing technology, database and network communication technology can accurately locate the disaster area and quickly obtain the disaster information, so as to quickly make emergency logistics decisions based on the relevant information and provide information security for the emergency logistics command.

It is necessary to build a four-level command information sharing system according to the vertical composition of the emergency logistics command organization at the central, provincial, municipal and district (county) levels. After the outbreak of an emergency, the regional emergency logistics command organization of the disaster area will quickly start the emergency logistics procedures according to the needs of the disaster area, and report to the superior emergency logistics command organization at the same time, and make decisions with the information support of the information system. If necessary, the regional emergency logistics command organizationa can apply for the guidance of its superior organization, or apply for the support and cooperation of the emergency logistics command center in other adjacent areas. In this process, all relevant departments need to exchange information in a timely manner and communicate effectively through video, We-Chat or telephone with the help of necessary equipment and software. At the same time, the command information system of emergency logistics should follow certain information sharing standards and improve the information sharing ability based on the network of information technology.

### 3.3.2 Management information system of emergency logistics

Management information system of emergency logistics is the application system of information technology in emergency logistics management. Emergency logistics management is not only the management of material circulation in a narrow sense, but also involves the comprehensive management of emergency logistics personnel, funds and materials. Without the support of information technology, such a complex management system will inevitably fall into a situation of management confusion, unclear entries and difficult coordination. Although the emergency logistics system integrates human, funds and materials into the unified management, the huge differences between the management objects make the management contents and methods very different. *The Fourteenth Five-Year Plan for the National Emergency Response System* pointed out that "to build a green and energy-efficient high-density data center, promote the construction of emergency management cloud computing platform, and improve the unified scheduling of multiple data centers and emergency support functions for important businesses". Only by using "big data", "cloud computing" and other modern information technologies to analyze the data of various management objects can we effectively grasp the information of all parties, carry out unified planning, scheduling, distribution and other management of human, funds and materials, and realize the needs and requirements of emergency logistics actions for personnel, funds and materials.

The management information system of emergency logistics can be divided into three parts: management information system of emergency logistics for personnel, management information system of emergency logistics for funds, and management information system of emergency logistics for materials. The management information system of emergency logistics for personnel integrates all management information about emergency logistics personnel, including the recruitment and mobilization, education and training, appointment and secondment, assessment and evaluation of emergency logistics personnel. By breaking the institutional barriers, the management information system for personnel can integrate emergency logistics professionals and volunteers from the government, the military, enterprises, social groups, the public, and so on into one system, to achieve the sharing of emergency logistics personnel information. In this way, it not only facilitates the unified command and scheduling of emergency logistics personnel, but also provides an open, fair and convenient information environment for emergency logistics practitioners. The management information system of emergency logistics for funds integrates special funds for emergency logistics from the government, funds of corporate sponsorship, and donations from social groups and individuals into a unified management information system. It is subject to supervision from the government and the public and provides information sharing, which is more conducive to achieving transparency in the use of emergency logistics funds and maximizing the efficiency of fund use. The management information system of emergency logistics for materials integrates all relevant information of emergency materials, including the planning, procurement and production, storage, dispatching and requisition, transportation and distribution, and even the recovery of emergency materials. Through the establishment of information sharing standards and specifications, the management information system of emergency logistics can realize the scientization of emergency materials at the preparation stage, the visualization of emergency materials in the process of transportation and distribution, and the environmental protection of emergency materials at the stage of recovery and processing.

### 3.3.3 Support information system of emergency logistics

Support information system of emergency logistics is the application of information technology in support system of emergency logistics. Emergency logistics requires not only the support of relevant laws, regulations, rules and other policy documents, but also the support of "transportation infrastructure, communication infrastructure, material storage infrastructure, logistics information network infrastructure, etc. " (Wang Ying and FanJiulin, 2022). Of course, emergency logistics also needs support from other aspects of society. The establishment of a unified support information system of emergency logistics can take advantage of the public sharing function of it to avoid the one-sided and repetitive support requirements effectively, and be fully prepared for the smooth operation of the emergency logistics system.

In terms of the guarantee of laws and regulations and other policies, integrating the national and local policies, regulations, plans and other relevant documents related to emergency logistics into the unified information system, will not only provide reference to emergency logistics related personnel, but also facilitate the mutual learning and reference of emergency logistics related institutions at all levels and places, and ultimately improve the corresponding laws, regulations, various plans and other policy documents.

From the aspect of infrastructure support, integrating infrastructures of transportation, communication, material storage, logistics information network and others into the support information system can help build a good physical environment for the implementation of emergency logistics activities. With the functions of the resource sharing and information transmission of the information system, it is not only helpful for the daily maintenance and improvement of the emergency logistics related infrastructure, but also can timely give feedbacks of relevant damage information of the infrastructure in the event of damage, so as to ensure the timely repair and reconstruction of the infrastructure after the disaster.

### 3.3.4    Integrated information system of emergency logistics

The integrated information system of emergency logistics is an application system that provides information support for the entire emergency logistics activities. It is to comprehensively solve the problem of information transmission from the information collection of various channels of disaster information, to the information coordination and communication of all links of emergency logistics activities, and to the evaluation and feedback information after the completion of emergency logistics activities. The integrated information system of emergency logistics should not only perform the function of supporting the operation of the information system itself, but also perform the function of maintaining the communication and cooperation between the information subsystems, and should also be a place for information exchange and communication among the relevant disaster prevention agencies.

First of all, the integrated information system of emergency logistics should perform the function of supporting the operation of the information system itself. As an information application system, the integrated information system of emergency logistics needs to have the functions of data collection, sorting, storage, processing, statistics and retrieval. This requires the integration of various advanced information technologies to maintain the normal operation of the information system.

Secondly, the integrated information system of emergency logistics should perform the function of maintaining communication and cooperation between information subsystems. *The Fourteenth Five-Year Plan for the National Emergency Response System* states that "we should systematically promote the construction of 'smart emergency', establish an emergency data management system in line with the development of big data, and improve the functions of supervision and management, monitoring and early warning, command and rescue, disaster management, statistical analysis, information release, post-disaster assessment and social mobilization". The emergency logistics information system is the emergency data management system that performs many functions. These functions are not independent, but complement to each other. A special integrated information system of emergency logistics is needed to communicate and cooperate among the subsystems, strengthen the "neural network nodes" among subsystems of the emergency logistics system, and form an emergency logistics information system with horizontally and vertically smooth flow of information.

Thirdly, the integrated information system of emergency logistics should also perform the function of providing information exchange and communication for various disaster prevention organizations. Based on the experience of Japan, the "disaster prevention mutual communication network built by the Japanese government can quickly allow the police station, the maritime security department, the land and transportation department, the fire department and other disaster prevention related agencies to exchange various on-site disaster relief information with each other at the scene, so as to carry out more effective and targeted disaster rescue and command work" (Zuo Xiaode, 2011). In order to strengthen the information exchange and cooperation of disaster prevention related institutions in China, the integrated information system of emergency logistics can link all disaster prevention related institutions together, build a "disaster prevention mutual communication network", create a platform for information communication and sharing for all disaster prevention institutions, and thus build a new platform for the information sources of emergency logistics command and decision-making departments.

# Chapter 4   Construction of the Management System of China's Emergency Logistics

As a subsystem of the emergency logistics system, the emergency logistics management system mainly involves the management of personnel, funds and materials related to emergency logistics. The central purpose is to meet the needs of personnel, funds and materials in emergency logistics operations at the best. Integrating all logistics-related needs into the emergency logistics management system is conducive to centralized planning, overall management, flexible matching and timely replenishment.

## 4.1   Construction principles of China's emergency logistics management system

From the perspective of emergency logistics, China's emergency logistics management system combines the characteristics of various elements and follows the scientific management methods of management science to integrates human, funds and materials of emergency logistics operations into unified management. In order to implement scientific and effective management of various elements, the following construction principles should be followed.

## 4.1.1 Combining unified leadership with hierarchical responsibility

Both the central and local governments should integrate the management of emergency logistics support personnel, funds and materials under the unified leadership of the Party and the government, so as to give full play to the advantages of centralized planning and overall management, and avoid confusion and poor communication caused by multi-party management. Specific management can be carried out by governments at all levels to facilitate the linkage between the upper and lower levels.

## 4.1.2 Strengthening standardized management by law

The management of human, funds and materials in emergency logistics should be standardized according to law, and the supply of human, funds and materials should be stable and reliable under the premise of complying with national laws and regulations, which can fully meet the emergency material guarantee of various public security events at all levels, thus laying a solid foundation for the implementation of effective management.

## 4.1.3 Saving resources and possessing both special and regular functions

The management of emergency logistics personnel, funds and materials should be both special and regular, and should be carried out according to the management characteristics in regular time as well as in urgent times. We should not only be prepared for danger while in peace times and do a good job in emergency management, but also optimize daily management and avoid wasting human, financial and material resources in regular days.

### 4.1.4    Relying on technology and being clear and transparent

The management of personnel, finance and materials in the emergency logistics management system is multi-level, multifaceted and multi-channel dynamic management. If not relying on the power of science and technology, the scientific and efficient management cannot be achieved. Only with the help of scientific management methods and strong technical support, can the management information and status of personnel, funds and materials be clearly displayed, and such a complex management system become clear and transparent.

### 4.1.5    Being quick and coordinated in response

In order to meet the needs of emergency logistics for personnel, funds and materials in a timely manner, it is necessary to respond quickly and deploy and allocate these resources in time. Due to the unpredictability of public emergencies, it is inevitable to involve the secondment and allocation of these resources within regions, between regions, and even between superior and subordinate departments. Rapid coordinated response is an important part of ensuring the demand of emergency logistics for personnel, funds and materials.

## 4.2    Personnel management of emergency logistics in China

Emergency logistics personnel are the human guarantee to maintain the smooth operation of all subsystems of the emergency logistics system and all links of emergency logistics activities. Emergency logistics personnel generally refer to all personnel who make efforts for emergency logistics actions. In terms of the functions of emergency logistics, it includes emergency logistics command and decision-making personnel, emergency logistics information technology personnel, emergency logistics management personnel, emergency logistics transportation and distribution personnel, emergency logistics support personnel, etc. From the perspective of personnel ownership and the nature of emergency logistics services, there are public service personnel belonging to the government and the military, business service personnel belonging to the market, charitable service personnel belonging to social organizations, and voluntary service personnel of the public. In the management of emergency logistics personnel, it is necessary to give full play to the characteristics of different kinds of personnel, integrate emergency logistics personnel with different functions and services into a unified management system, and form a management mechanism for emergency logistics personnel with complementary advantages and collaborative services. In the emergency logistics system, the management of emergency logistics personnel mainly includes the recruitment and mobilization, education and training, appointment and secondment, assessment and evaluation of emergency logistics personnel.

## 4.2.1 Recruitment and mobilization of emergency logistics personnel

The number of emergency logistics actions in a particular area can be few in China. Therefore, as a "contingency" service support team, emergency logistics requires not only permanent personnel support, but also the temporary participation of a large number of emergency personnel. Emergency logistics personnel have a wide range of sources and complex composition, including not only highly professional technical personnel, but also some grass-roots workers, social volunteers, etc. This requires a unified emergency logistics personnel management system to recruit and mobilize emergency logistics personnel from multiple entities and sources.

First of all, the urgency of emergency logistics needs to respond in time and carry out emergency logistics actions quickly, so there needs to be a "standing army" of emergency logistics personnel. The permanent emergency logistics team is usually set up by the government to maintain the normal operation of key posts in the emergency logistics system.

Secondly, in the event of a public safety incident, a large number of temporary personnel are also required to participate in emergency logistics operations, such as government agencies, the military, enterprises, social groups and the public, which requires an emergency personnel recruitment mechanism to complete the recruitment and mobilization of temporary emergency logistics personnel to ensure the timely replenishment of emergency logistics human resources. In line with the principle of saving resources and possessing both professional and regular functions, the government can establish a "human resource pool of emergency logistics", which includes professionals and volunteers in various fields involved in emergency logistics under various public safety emergencies for unified management. The personnel of the resource pool are mobile personnel who can be appointed or dispatched at any time. They are included in the emergency logistics management system with the agreement of their themselves and their units, and their personal information of emergency logistics personnel are established. According to the types of public safety incidents that may occur in the region, local governments can be responsible for the recruitment and mobilization of emergency logistics personnel in their own regions according to the principle of unified leadership and hierarchical responsibility. In addition to the full-time personnel required for daily maintenance, other non-daily positions can be filled by people from the personnel reserve base according to the type of disaster. The personnel of the resource pool shall serve their work units and posts on a daily basis, and comply with the emergency dispatch of the government when necessary for emergency logistics operations, and actively complete the assigned tasks.

In addition, in the face of major public safety events, it is also necessary to promote the enthusiasm of the public and mobilize the wide participation of the people to achieve the purpose of emergency logistics. During the COVID-19 pandemic in China, there were many cases where people spontaneously participated in emergency logistics operations, and even spontaneously organized mutual aid and self-help, which greatly improved the efficiency of emergency logistics.

## 4.2.2  Education and training of emergency logistics personnel

Most emergency logistics personnel are professional forces from various fields and can be competent for the assigned emergency logistics work, however, based on the professionalism of emergency logistics and the particularity and urgency of actions, it is still necessary to pay attention to the education and training of emergency logistics personnel in order to better display the advantages and characteristics of different personnel and better carry out emergency logistics actions.

First, it's necessary to strengthen the construction of emergency logistics major and related curricula in colleges and universities. With the increasing attention paid to emergency logistics in China, some colleges and universities have offered courses related to emergency logistics to meet the needs of the society for emergency logistics professionals, such as emergency logistics courses in the School of Logistics, and emergency logistics and supply chain management courses in the School of Emergency Management. However, the emergency logistics system is a huge system, and its operation involves the cross-discipline application of all walks of life and emergency logistics. At present, the training of emergency logistics talents is only limited to the few opening of individual relevant courses in individual schools, lacking comprehensive and systematic professional training, which will undoubtedly greatly restrict the effective supplement of emergency logistics professionals. To fundamentally and effectively cultivate emergency logistics personnel, it is necessary to start with higher education, accelerate the construction of emergency logistics major and related curricula, and comprehensively train emergency logistics personnel.

Secondly, it's necessary to establish a normal training system for emergency logistics personnel. At present, China has not built a unified emergency logistics personnel management system, so the management of existing emergency logistics personnel is in lack of targeted training system. To achieve effective management of emergency logistics personnel, it is necessary to classify and manage emergency logistics personnel in different links according to the plan, regularly carry out professional skills and process training of emergency logistics actions, and even conduct rehearsals of emergency logistics actions, so as to better promote the normal operation of the emergency logistics system. For example, "according to the capacity requirements of the emergency logistics post, focus on training command and management talents with strong overall planning ability, high management quality and full professional skills; focus on training key front-line positions such asrapid warehouse layout, port loading and unloading, container packaging operation, bulk cargo driver, etc. ; focus on supporting expert talents who have studied the security plan, practice guidance and assisted decision-making" ( Huang Jianwei, He Dian, Yang Chaojiang, 2021 ). At the same time, establish the training information database for emergency logistics personnel, carry out digital management for the education and training of emergency logistics personnel, and form a dynamic training mechanism for emergency logistics personnel.

## 4.2.3    Appointment and secondment of emergency logistics personnel

Emergency logistics personnel include not only specially prepared standing emergency management personnel, but also personnel from emergency logistics reserve pool, scientific research staff, professional technicians, military-civilian integrated logistics personnel, enterprise emergency logistics personnel and social volunteers. For each emergency public security event, various emergency logistics personnel need to be assigned and seconded urgently to form an emergency logistics team, and personnel allocation should be planned as a whole, and assigned and seconded according to personal expertise.

First of all, we should have a better understanding of the personnel and tap their potential. Personal files and educating and training records of emergency logistics personnel shall be open and transparent. All localities need to be familiar with the expertise and characteristics of the personnel in the human resources database in combination with the nature of the public security incidents that are prone to occur in all localities, so as to urgently convene the emergency logistics team, carry out task assignment and respond to emergency logistics actions.

Secondly, we should improve the recruitment system. In addition to the regular full-time emergency logistics personnel, most of the emergency logistics personnel are serving their original posts in daily life. Therefore, after the occurrence of an emergency, temporary secondment should be carried out according to the recruitment system to quickly meet the needs of emergency logistics personnel. In addition, emergency logistics operations often face cross-regional support, so in addition to intra-regional recruitment, we should improve the cross-regional recruitment system, handle affairs according to law, and standardize emergency logistics operations.

Finally, it is necessary to establish a compensation mechanism for employment. For emergency logistics personnel recruited in an emergency, compensatory measures should be formulated according to the local salary level. Reasonable salary subsidies and allowances shall be given to the emergency logistics personnel to ensure the legitimate rights and interests of the emergency logistics personnel and improve the work enthusiasm of the emergency logistics personnel.

### 4.2.4    Assessment and evaluation of emergency logistics personnel

To strengthen the management of emergency logistics personnel, we should also establish an assessment mechanism to assess emergency logistics personnel to ensure their quality, ability, attitude at work and their enthusiasm.

First of all, the personnel who have signed up for the emergency logistics human resource database shall be assessed for qualifications, and the qualified personnel shall be issued with the qualification certificate of emergency logistics personnel and included in the emergency logistics human resource database.

Secondly, local governments can formulate their own policies according to the actual situation, and conduct process assessment and evaluation on the personnel involved in emergency logistics operations. In the assessment, the participants of emergency logistics actions can be assessed for specific emergency logistics actions, and the annual assessment can also be carried out in combination with relevant training and other conditions. The purpose of the assessment is not only to encourage the advanced, but also to find out the problems, and reflect on the rectification in time, so as to enhance the overall situation awareness, responsibility awareness and dedication awareness of the emergency logistics personnel while ensuring their professional quality and work ability.

# 4.3    The fund management of China's emergency logistics

Emergency logistics funds are the financial guarantee to support the smooth operation of all subsystems of the emergency logistics system and all links of emergency logistics activities. The management of emergency logistics funds in China mainly includes three aspects: the raising of funds for emergency logistics, the use of funds for emergency logistics, and the supervision and evaluation of the fund use for emergency logistics.

## 4.3.1 The raising of funds for emergency logistics

Like emergency logistics actions, the raising of emergency logistics funds needs the joint participation and efforts of all parties. For the raising of emergency logistics funds, it should be carried out through the combination of government special allocations and social public donations, and establish a diversified funding mechanism.

Firstly, we should improve the emergency logistics fund reserve system. There is great importance of strengthening the system construction, establishing and improving the emergency logistics fund reserve and management regulations, and standardizing and guaranteeing the raising of emergency logistics funds into the legal system.

Secondly, we should strengthen special government allocations. It is important to give full play to the government's functions, integrate emergency logistics funds into the scope of special government allocations, strive to eliminate regional and urban-rural gap, establish emergency logistics funds pools to strengthen the reserve of emergency logistics funds.

In the end, we should guide diversified capital investment. It is important to play a policy-oriented role to encourage natural persons, juridical persons or other organizations ( including international organizations) to donate and assist in accordance with the provisions of the *Law of the People's Republic of China on Donations to Public Welfare* and other relevant laws and regulations, and guide enterprises, associations, individuals and other diversified capital investment.

## 4.3.2 The use of funds for emergency logistics

As a special fund, the use of emergency logistics funds must be closely related to emergency logistics actions. The flow of emergency logistics funds can cover the whole process before, during and after emergency logistics operations. In the use of emergency logistics funds, various resources should be integrated and optimized to form the synergy of a policy.

First of all, it's about the use of funds for preparations of emergency logistics operations. In order to prepare for emergency logistics, human, financial and material resources need to be invested, and human and material resources can not be separated from financial support. From the practice of emergency logistics, the training of emergency logistics personnel, the improvement of emergency logistics facilities and equipment, to the procurement and storage of emergency materials, all links need financial support to complete successfully.

Secondly, it's about the use of funds in emergency logistics operations. After the emergency logistics action is launched, there is urgent need for a large number of professionals and the advisory services from the expert committee. Also, vehicles are needed for shipment and transportation from the emergency materials storage warehouse and storage base. Sometimes, scarce materials need to be temporarily purchased. All these need fund supports to meet the cost of purchasing emergency logistics services.

In addition, it's about the use of funds after the completion of emergency logistics operations. Even after the emergency logistics operation is completed, the disaster area has received sufficient material support, and still needs capital investment to carry out the closing work. For example, the recovery and disposal of some emergency materials, the compensation for emergency requisitioned materials, and the repair, maintenance and maintenance of various relevant facilities and equipment, etc.

### 4.3.3　The supervision and evaluation of the fund use for emergency logistics

*The National Overall Emergency Plan for Public Emergencies* states that "the use and effect of financial emergency guarantee funds for public emergencies should be supervised and evaluated". With the special reserve system for emergency logistics funds, it is necessary to effectively supervise and evaluate the raising and use of funds to standardize the use of funds and improve the efficiency of fund use.

Firstly, we should improve the laws and regulations on emergency logistics fund management. On the basis of complying with the laws and regulations on the management of emergency logistics funds, establish the responsibility system for the use of emergency logistics funds, and seriously investigate and deal with violations of the emergency logistics funds management system. In addition, strengthen the special use of emergency logistics funds to avoid misappropriation and embezzlement.

Secondly, we should improve the supervisory mechanism and realize the dynamic supervision of emergency logistics funds. Establish a special supervisory department to strengthen the dynamic supervision of the whole process of emergency logistics funds, give full play to the role of emergency logistics management organizations at all levels, and improve the authority of emergency logistics funds supervision.

Finally, we should improve the evaluative mechanism of emergency logistics funds and carry out the normalization review and evaluation of emergency logistics funds. According to the division of responsibilities, organize the superior leading departments to review and evaluate the annual emergency logistics funds, submit the review and evaluative report, and take the review and evaluative results as an important basis for improving the management of emergency logistics funds.

## 4.4    The material management of China's emergency logistics

Emergency materials refer to all relevant materials, such as tools, articles, and equipment, etc. , used to control the occurrence of an accident before the occurrence of an emergency public security event, or used for emergency rescue such as evacuation and rescue after the occurrence of an accident. Emergency supplies are an important part of emergency logistics services, and also the core purpose of material security in response to emergency public emergencies. For different types of emergency public emergencies, emergency materials can be divided into different catalogues and uses. Yet China has not formed a unified classification standard, which also makes the management of materials difficult. According to *the National Overall Emergency Plan for Public Emergencies*, it is necessary to ensure the timely supply of emergency supplies and daily necessities, and do a good job to ensure the basic living and medical and health care for the affected people. To ensure the "basic living" is to ensure that the people in the disaster-stricken area have food, water, clothing, shelter and their diseases can be treated without delay. To do a good job in medical and health care, it is necessary to provide timely medical equipment such as drugs and instruments for the affected areas. According to the overall needs of the people in the disaster area, emergency materials can be basically divided into life rescue materials, living materials and post-disaster reconstruction materials ( Meng Xiangjuan, Xu Yaokun, 2016 ). For the management of emergency materials, the nature and characteristics of all kinds of emergency materials should be taken into account, and sufficient preparation should be made, resources should be saved, and the scientific and effective management of emergency materials should be realized. When an emergency occurs, the emergency logistics action should be started immediately. The command organization should initially judge the demand for emergency materials and make emergency logistics decisions based on the type of emergency, the scope of influence, the climate of the disaster area and other factors, and in combination with the data in the emergency logistics command information system. The emergency logistics management organization, based on the information stored in the management information system, inquires about the preparation of emergency supplies, including the distribution, variety and reserve of supplies, raises and purchases emergency supplies in an emergency manner according to the information obtained, conducts the dispatch and requisition of emergency supplies when necessary, organizes the transportation and distribution of emergency supplies through the green channel, and delivers emergency supplies to the disaster area in a timely manner. According to the progress of disaster relief and the use of emergency supplies, necessary emergency supplies should also be recycled and disposed. In short, the management of emergency supplies should at least include the planning, procurement and production, storage, allocation and requisition, transportation and distribution, issue and recovery of emergency materials.

## 4.4.1　The planning of emergency materials

The planning of emergency materials refers to the planning of the category, quantity, source and storage location of emergency materials. The emergency logistics organizations at all levels shall plan the emergency materials according to the emergency logistics plan, prepare the emergency materials catalogue according to the regional characteristics and the predictable types of hazards in the region, and clarify the type, quantity, source and storage location of the emergency materials in the region.

First, the categories of emergency materials should be scientifically planned. According to the categories and characteristics of local public safety incidents that are prone to occur, the list of emergency supplies should be developed. In addition to the commonly needed food, drinking water and other necessary supplies for life, each region should have targeted enrichment of specific categories of emergency materials, such as tents, campers, mobile houses, cotton-padded clothes, quilts and other living supplies in earthquake-prone areas, life jackets, life-boats (rafts), lifelines and other water rescue supplies in shipwreck-prone areas, cotton clothes, snow melting agents, anti-skid materials and other cold relief materials in snow-prone areas.

Secondly, the quantity of emergency materials should be scientifically planned. According to the nature and frequency of public safety emergencies in the region, as well as the service scope of each material storage center, an appropriate amount of reserves shall be made to ensure that the demand can be met after the occurrence of the event, and the loss or deterioration caused by excessive quantity shall be strictly controlled. For materials that are easy to store and have a long shelf life, such as tents, cotton-padded clothes, quilts, etc., there should be sufficient reserves. For materials with short shelf life that are not easy to store, such as food and medicine, the way of regular and quota replenishment can be adopted to maintain the cyclic replenishment and renewal of materials and avoid large-scale loss and waste.

Thirdly, the source of emergency materials should be scientifically planned. We should focus on reserves, supplemented by timely procurement, allocation and social donations. The local emergency logistics management departments shall, according to the local plan, reserve the conventional emergency materials conforming to the characteristics of the territory to a certain extent, to ensure that the medium level of public security emergencies are basically met. In the event of a major public security emergency, if the reserve is insufficient to meet the demand, the materials can be replenished in a timely manner by means of emergency procurement from cooperative suppliers and allocation from neighboring regions. At the same time, the donations from enterprises, associations and the public are also one of the important sources of emergency materials, which play an important role in disaster relief. However, the categories of social donations are complex, with different specifications and different quality, which will not only increase the additional burden of emergency logistics, but also cause the imbalance between supply and demand of materials. Therefore, the government should convey the focus of emergency material donation to the public according to the nature, level and material demand of the emergency.

Finally, the storage location of emergency materials should be scientifically planned. The location of emergency materials storage shall be set as close as possible to the accident-prone area, and the traffic convenience shall be considered. This can not only reduce the cost of emergency logistics activities, play a greater logistics effect, but also facilitate emergency transportation, timely transport emergency materials to the disaster area, and save valuable time to ensure the safety of life and property of the affected people.

## 4.4.2 The procurement and production of emergency materials

The procurement of emergency materials includes not only the conventional procurement of emergency material storage, but also the urgent procurement of scarce supplies in case of public safety emergencies. The routine procurement of emergency materials can be carried out according to the plan and the categories and quantity of emergency materials planning, so as to ensure the proper variety, reliable quality, sufficient quantity and constant readiness, and ensure the need of emergency materials. The urgent procurement of emergency materials needs to be targeted according to the nature and harm of the emergency, the specific needs of post-disaster rescue, the material storage and other factors. Because China has not yet established a complete emergency material storage system, in view of the unpredictability of emergencies, it will inevitably lead to the shortage of some emergency materials. Moreover, many basic living materials and medical and health materials are not suitable for a large number of storage, so conventional procurement cannot fully meet the needs of disaster relief. Especially in areas with relatively under-developed economy, there are various problems such as fewer emergency material storage, uneven distribution, imperfect hardware facilities, single type of storage materials, and insufficient quantity ( Chen Hui, 2016 ), and the material demand is even more difficult to guarantee. The emergency materials donated by the society are not only slow in response, but also prone to over-concentration, which leads to the shortage of some kinds of supplies at the early stage of the disaster and the over-saturation at the later stage, resulting in serious waste, while some emergency supplies in short supply are not effectively supplemented. Therefore, in addition to the regular procurement of emergency materials, emergency procurement is also required, which is also an important way of providing emergency materials in short supply.

The procurement of emergency materials shall be under the unified leadership of the government, and the emergency logistics management center of each region shall be responsible for the establishment of emergency material procurement plan and emergency material procurement system. Whether it is routine procurement or emergency procurement, the procurement of emergency materials is a government act, so it should be carried out according to the government procurement law. The conventional procurement method of emergency logistics is public bidding, but other procurement methods are also allowed, such as invitation to bid, competitive negotiation, single source procurement, inquiry procurement and other procurement methods, to realize the physical storage of emergency materials. For emergency procurement of emergency materials, more flexible procurement methods can be adopted. In addition to single-source procurement and inquiry procurement, the government can also cooperate with the market and establish a contract reserve system on the premise of improving emergency materials procurement laws and regulations. The contract reserve system refers to that the emergency logistics management center signs a pre-purchase contract with the enterprise that produces emergency materials in advance. Once an emergency occurs, the pre-purchase contract will be started immediately, and the contracted enterprise will rapidly provide high-quality and reliable materials at the contract price. This can not only reduce the cost of storing materials, but also meet the needs of emergency materials in time, and can also avoid the price rise of scarce supplies and reduce the benefit of emergency funds.

Whether the procurement of emergency materials can be successfully completed is closely related to the production capacity of emergency materials. During the three years of the COVID-19 in China, many people have experienced the shortage of medical masks, alcohol, drugs and other protective articles, which are inseparable from the production capacity of manufacturers. Therefore, while improving the emergency material procurement law, the government should also strengthen the establishment and improvement of the emergency material production law and other supporting laws and regulations, standardize the production behavior of emergency materials, and ensure the priority production of emergency materials. At the same time, implement the emergency product production capacity reserve project and build a regional emergency material production support base, guide enterprises to increase investment in emergency material production capacity construction, support enterprises with strength in the field of emergency materials to become stronger and better, cultivate a number of large emergency material enterprise groups with strong competitiveness in the international and domestic markets, and encourage small-and medium-sized enterprises to produce emergency materials with obvious characteristics to accelerate development by using existing capital channels. In addition, social resources should be directed to advanced, applicable and reliable production and service of emergency materials in the form of recommendation list and encouragement list.

### 4.4.3    The reserve of emergency materials

The reserve of emergency materials is crucial to the smooth operation of emergency logistics operations. At present, China's emergency material storage is faced with such problems as unreasonable proportion of stored materials, unscientific layout of reserve warehouse, inflexible types and quantities of reserve materials, unclear management of material storage, and unadvanced technology of material storage. The *14th Five-Year Plan for the National Emergency Response System* emphasizes that the central and local governments, the government and the society, the physical and the production capacity of the emergency material storage mode should be established. To establish a scientific and reasonable emergency material storage mode, it is necessary to strengthen the improvement and optimization of the proportion of stored materials, the layout of warehouses, the types and reserves of material storage, the management of material storage, and the technology used in material storage.

From the perspective of the proportion of stored emergency materials, we should establish a "five-level and five-section integration" emergency material storage system. Although China has formed a certain emergency material storage network at present, from the central to the local, from the government to the private, but the awareness of making reservation on different administrative levels and from different sections varies, especially in some regions and the public. To improve the main structure of emergency material storage, it is necessary to improve the five-level vertical emergency material storage system at the central, provincial, municipal, county and township levels as well as the five-section horizontal emergency material storage system with the government, the military, enterprises, social organizations and the public, and realize the "five-level and five-section integrated" emergency material storage network with the combination of the central and local governments and the cooperation among the government, the military, the enterprises, social organizations and the public.

From the perspective of the distribution of emergency material storage, we should build a new layout of emergency material warehouses scattered across the country. First of all, improve the layout of the central emergency supplies reserve. In 2003, China has established 10 central-level emergency supplies reserves and 31 provincial-level reserves. However, the central-level reserves are mostly distributed in the central and eastern regions, while it is only in Xi'an that one central-level reserve was set up in the western regions. The layout is very uneven and unreasonable. To expand the western radiation scope of the emergency material storage, three emergency material storage depots in Kunming, Chongqing and Lhasa can be added in the southwest region, and two emergency supplies reserve depots in Lanzhou and Urumqi can be added in the northwest region to cover the entire western region. At the same time, we need to improve the layout of reserves in other regions. Shijiazhuang needs to be the newly added one in North China, and is responsible for most of Shanxi, Beijing and Inner Mongolia together with Tianjin. While maintaining the status of Hefei reserve center, Fuzhou emergency material storage warehouse will be newly established in East China. With the addition of Guangzhou in South China, the Guangzhou Reserve can not only meet the needs of emergency supplies in the two regions, but also serve Hong Kong and Macao, and can better receive international support materials ( Sun Yongchun, 2013 ). Secondly, we should give full play to the professional reserve power of government and military enterprises, and strengthen the construction of local emergency material storage bases. On the government side, relying on the existing central and local material storage, a number of comprehensive emergency material storage will be built in transportation hub cities, densely populated areas, and areas prone to serious and special natural disasters. In terms of the military, we should build and improve the emergency material storage and combat support stations of the military rescue team. In terms of enterprises, we should rely on large express logistics enterprises to build a batch of emergency materials distribution platforms and regional distribution centers.

From the perspective of the categories and amounts of emergency materials, a reserve system of emergency materials combining physical and production capacity should be established. In addition to optimizing the layout of emergency materials storage and making good physical emergency material storage, we should also implement the production capacity storage project of emergency products, build a regional production support base of emergency materials ( the *14th Five-Year Plan of National Emergency System*), incorporate the production of materials with strong seasonality, short shelf life and short turnover cycle into the capacity reserve, and dynamically adjust the categories and quantity of physical and capacity reserves. First of all, we should improve the policy of encouraging, guiding the expansion of key emergency material capacity reserve enterprises, and continue to improve the industry chain of emergency materials. Secondly, the qualified enterprises will be included in the scope of capacity reserve enterprises, and the inventory of emergency material capacity reserve will be developed to strengthen the dynamic monitoring of emergency material production capacity. In addition, it is necessary to strengthen the pre-judgment, research and judgment of material demand for major disasters and accidents, and improve the emergency material storage and centralized production scheduling mechanism.

From the perspective of emergency material storage management, we should follow institutionalized management theories and use scientific management models. Because China has not yet developed a clear emergency material storage mechanism and management method, the emergency material storage is mostly carried out by the local government based on the actual situation of the region" (Chen Hui, 2014). In the absence of normative institutional guidance, China's emergency material storage management cannot be standardized and reasonable, but with greater level of subjectivity and randomness. In addition, in some areas, many problems occur such as unreasonable reserve categories of emergency materials, insufficience in quantity, poor storage environment, and low mechanization of storage operation. To strengthen the management of emergency material storage, first of all, we should establish a strict emergency material storage system. Only under the guidance of relevant laws, regulations and emergency plans can the material storage work be done well. Local emergency material organizations should scientifically adjust the category, scale and structure of emergency material storage and standardize the management of emergency material storage by abiding by the basic principles of emergency material storage, establishing emergency material storage directory, improving the use of report system and other measures. Secondly, the method of classified management of emergency material storage is adopted. In the process of managing the emergency material storage, we can learn from the ABC classification method of inventory management in logistics management of enterprises to scientifically determine the reserve scale of emergency materials and realize its inventory control. When classifying, attention should be paid to the different requirements of different emergencies for emergency materials, such as a large number of relief tents, medical equipment and other materials in earthquake-prone areas, and the key reserves of life-saving equipment, fire-fighting equipment and so on in mine disaster prone areas. According to different categories of emergency materials, different inventory strategies can be used to reduce costs, improve utilization and comprehensive benefits.

From the perspective of techniques of emergency material storage, we should strengthen the scientific and technological application of emergency material storage. First, professional storage equipment should be configured in hardware. At present, the mechanization of emergency logistics storage in China is relatively low. Many storage centers still rely on manual work, and specialized storage tools such as forklifts are rarely used, so the operation cannot be completed in a short time, resulting in delays in emergency logistics operations. Secondly, advanced sorting technology is adopted in software for centralized storage management. The sorting group technology is used to manage emergency materials and form a comprehensive unit module for accurate allocation and rapid distribution.

## 4.4.4　The allocation and requisition of emergency materials

The allocation and requisition of emergency materials is the concrete embodiment of the overall management of emergency supplies, which is conducive to improving the utilization rate and maximum benefits of emergency materials. When a public security incident occurs, if public emergency supplies at a local level or from the government or the military cannot meet the demand, the emergency materials can be allocated or requisitioned by making full use of the "five-level and five-section" emergency material storage network, in order to achieve the guarantee of emergency supplies in the shortest time. First of all, promote the construction of the command and allocation platform for emergency materials at the central, provincial, municipal, county and township levels, and realize the interconnection of emergency supplies allocation by governments at all levels. Secondly, establish the coordination and linkage of emergency materials among the government, the military, enterprises, society organizations and the public.

In addition to the public supplies of the government and the military, the social emergency supplies from enterprises, social organizations and the public are managed as a whole, and are allocated or requisitioned according to relevant policies, which is also the best interpretation of the spirit of "when disaster struck, aid comes from everywhere". Of course, we should also establish a compensation mechanism for social material requisition. Apart from the social materials of donation nature, the government should make appropriate compensation for social emergency materials uniformly allocated or requisitioned according to relevant policies, so as to realize the sustainable development of the "five-level and five-section" emergency material storage system.

## 4.4.5 The transportation and distribution of emergency materials

The transportation of emergency materials refers to the process of using various transportation modes to transport emergency materials from the emergency material storages at all levels, emergency production enterprises, social groups and even the public to the disaster area. This is an important link for the real realization of emergency logistics. For a long time, the main modes of emergency materials transportation in China are railway and highway, which are highly dependent on road facilities, traffic conditions and other factors. When natural disasters such as earthquake and debris flow cause road damage, the transportation of emergency materials is likely to be interrupted due to the impassability of the road. Waiting for the road to be repaired or finding an alternative transportation mode will greatly reduce the time efficiency of emergency logistics and increase disaster losses. In addition, due to the public welfare nature of emergency logistics, China currently mainly relies on the military as the main force of emergency materials transportation, which is obviously difficult to transport emergency supplies from different sources to the disaster area in time to achieve the overall utilization of emergency materials. To improve the current transportation situation of emergency materials, first of all, we should deepen the emergency transportation linkage mechanism and implement the emergency transportation guarantee measures for railways, highways and aviation. To deepen the linkage mechanism of emergency transportation is to give full play to the advantages of different modes of transportation in terms of scale, speed and coverage, and build a comprehensive emergency transportation network that is fast, accessible, powerful, functional, safe and reliable. Secondly, relying on the large logistics enterprises as the backbone, we should build emergency transport storage forces covering various modes of transportation, such as railway, highway, water transport, civil aviation, etc. , and give full play to the advantages of high-speed railway to build a rapid power transmission system to ensure the rapid and efficient delivery of emergency resources for major disasters and accidents. Relying on large logistics enterprises is to give full play to the professional advantages of logistics enterprises and promote the establishment of emergency logistics and transportation teams with enterprises as the main body. Thirdly, we should also strengthen the construction of the green channels for emergency transportation, and improve the preferential access mechanism for transportation vehicles carrying emergency materials and personnel ( *the Fourteenth Five-Year National Emergency System Plan*). To strengthen the construction of green channels for emergency transportation, we can provide "green channel" for emergency logistics in accordance with the principle of "priority planning, priority arrangement, priority transportation, priority entry, priority stop, priority release, priority loading and unloading" ( Chen Hui, 2014), and ensure that the transportation routes of emergency logistics are free and smooth all the time.

The distribution of emergency materials refers to the process of repackaging, sorting and delivery of large batches of emergency supplies that are transported by large vehicles to the disaster area, and then delivering them to various disaster areas according to specific needs. The distribution of emergency materials is the last key link of emergency logistics activities, and also a link that causes large logistics losses due to low efficiency in China. According to statistics, among the huge casualties and property losses caused by sudden natural disasters, the losses caused by inefficient emergency logistics distribution account for about 15% to 20% of the total losses ( Feng Haijiang, Zhang Weigang, Peng Chunlu, 2010 ). In order to improve the distribution efficiency of emergency materials and reduce the logistics loss caused by the distribution process, we should pay attention to the following important details in the management of emergency supplies. First of all, the packaging, classification, marking and other management details of emergency materials should be rigorous, scientific and standardized. Considering the special environment that emergency supplies may face, it is possible to use helicopter, unmanned aerial vehicle and other distribution methods when the road is interrupted. Therefore, it is necessary to pay attention to the sealing and impact resistance of the packaging to reduce the extent of damage of emergency materials when they are forced to be dropped by air, and it is also necessary to do a good job of classification, marking and other details in advance, so that the victims can quickly identify and find urgently needed supplies. Secondly, the distribution specification of emergency supplies should be "small and portable" ( Li Yanqin, Zhang Liyi, Guo Chunsheng, 2010 ). When large quantities of emergency materials arrive in the disaster area and are waiting for distribution, in order to facilitate various small means of transport and even manual emergency handling, the large packages should be transfered into small and portable small size packages, which is convenient for flexible division and distribution according to actual needs, and for hand-carrying work of distribution personnel and even volunteers, so as to ensure that the "last mile" of emergency materials distribution is completed as soon as possible.

## 4.4.6 The distribution and recovery of emergency materials

The distribution of emergency materials refers to the process of handing out emergency supplies to the victims who have gathered in the disaster-stricken area. This is the ultimate goal of emergency logistics activities and the last step to achieve emergency logistics material support. Generally, the site of distribution emergency materials is located near the gathering place or relief sie of the victims, or in public places such as schools, stadiums and squares. And the site of distributing emergency materials shall be at an appropriate distance from the living area of the disaster victims, so as to specify the access way for emergency materials handout, and avoid management confusion during the process, which may result in personal safety accidents or material property losses. In addition, the distribution of emergency materials should be planned as a whole according to the principle of "urgent first and highlight the key points". For example, priority will be given to emergency materials such as food, drinking water and medicine that are in urgent need. Consumable materials with low urgency will be handed out later, and non-critical supplementary materials will be handed out finally. In the early stage of disaster relief, the distribution of emergency materials should be done by the government to ensure that emergency supplies reach the victims in time. If the period of distributing materials is too long, the work can be entrusted to professional social groups or logistics enterprises in accordance with relevant laws and regulations. In this way, it can not only meet the needs of disaster victims in time, improve the issue efficiency of emergency materials, but also effectively avoid corruption or artificial injustice in the process. In addition, it can also reduce the burden of the government, give full play to the professional advantages of society and enterprises, and mobilize the supervision power of the public.

The recovery of emergency materials refers to the process of taking back emergency supplies that are surplus or reusable after the end of disaster relief for secondary use. Although the emergency materials have been planned according to the actual needs, the unpredictability of the development of the disaster and the multi-channel nature of emergency supplies will still cause too much emergency supplies transported to the disaster area. If they are not recycled in time, it will cause a great waste of materials. After summing up the experience and lessons, we should first formulate relevant rules and regulations. When emergency materials arrive in the disaster area, if some emergency supplies with short shelf life cannot be released smoothly due to some factors, they can be handled flexibly according to the regulations, such as being received and disposed by relevant enterprises or donated to charitable organizations. For the reusable emergency materials such as tents and lights, the reverse emergency logistics should be improved, and the necessary cleaning, maintenance and recovery should be carried out by relevant enterprises or social institutions after the disaster relief, which can not only avoid environmental pollution or waste of materials, but also further improve the management of emergency materials and improve the recovery rate of emergency materials.

# Chapter 5   Construction of the Support System of China's Emergency Logistics

Since the catastrophic flood in 1998, the Wenchuan Earthquake in 2008, the Corona Virus Disease in 2019, and the Flood in south China, China has accumulated a lot of experience in responding to natural disasters and public health emergencies. The emergency logistics system has been constantly improving and optimizing, but it is not difficult to see that there are still many problems in the system. For China, which is prone to natural disasters, it is essential to establish a comprehensive emergency logistics system to cope with climate change and public emergencies. The construction of a comprehensive emergency logistics system requires not only the cooperation of all relevant administrative departments and the establishment of a certain coordination mechanism among them, but also the improvement of relevant laws and regulations to provide legal protection for the construction. At the same time, the system should be able to mobilize the whole society to participate in the emergency work of major social public events. In addition, the construction of the system should include improving the information equipment and transportation facilities that support emergency logistics. This chapter combs the advanced experience of foreign countries in the construction of the support system of emergency logistics, focusing on the emergency logistics management mechanism, laws, regulations and policies that support the emergency logistics system, mobilization mechanism, and infrastructure construction supporting emergency logistics in China.

# 5.1 Construction of the support system of emergency logistics in the United States

As one of the developed countries in the world, the United States has a relatively complete response mechanism to sudden disasters. The research in this section includes the emergency management institutions, emergency management system, and legal and regulatory protection of emergency logistics.

## 5.1.1 The management system of emergency logistics in the United States

The Federal Emergency Management Agency (FEMA) implements unified response and disposal of all emergency affairs at the federal and state levels. The Federal Emergency Management Agency of the United States was established in April 1979. Its main responsibilities are to do a comprehensive job of disaster prevention, mitigation, preparedness and relief at the federal government level, and also tomake post-disaster reconstruction. The main goal of its work is to minimize the damage of sudden disasters and the loss of citizens' lives and property. After the 9.11 Event in 2001, the agency, together with 22 other agencies, was incorporated into the Ministry of Homeland Security and became an important independent agency of it. The agency can report directly to the President and is specifically responsible for major disaster emergency services. One of its main emergency response measures is to "provide shelter, clothing and food for the victims" in order to ensure the supply of subsistence goods for the disaster victims.

The emergency management system of the United States includes three levels of management and response agencies at the federal, state and local (municipal) levels. Its characteristics are: unified management, territory-based operation, hierarchical response, and standard operation. The responsibility of the federal government is to organize and coordinate disaster relief work at the national level. The specific practices of each state are different because the United States is a federal country, but the general emergency management is similar: the state government establish the emergency service offices, and the local government is responsible for managing and coordinating the emergency response and disaster recovery within its jurisdiction. When there is an emergency, it is the local government who takes command of emergency action. When there is a trans-regional emergency, the superior government provides support only when the local government asks for help it. However, the superior government cannot completely take over the local government's right of emergency response, it can only help the local government coordinate emergency resources, and support the local government in carrying out post-disaster recovery. The superior government can audit and supervise the local government's use of relief materials and funds after the disaster.

The core forces of emergency rescue are the fire department, police department and medical department. The main departments involved in the rescue include the Federal Emergency Management Agency, the Red Cross, and the departments of transportation, communications, agriculture, and national defense.

The emergency logistics management system also follows the organizational principles of emergency management. The Federal Emergency Management Agency has a special unit to take charge of the management and storage of disaster relief materials, and to monitor and predict the demand for them. In the event of a national public emergency, the special unit will respond quickly to ensure the preparation and transportation of disaster relief materials. According to the laws of the United States, the right to deal with emergency belongs to the local government. When the local government's emergency resources are insufficient and it cannot manage disaster relief, it should submit a request for support to the state government. However, the state government cannot completely take over the right to deal with the local government's emergency supplies and other resources. When the state government encounters problems in disaster relief or emergency resources, it shall submit a request for support to the federal government.

## 5.1.2 Legal and regulatory guarantee of emergency logistics in the United States

As early as 1988, the United States enacted the *Robert T. Stafford Disaster Relief and Emergency Assistance Act*, abbreviated as the Stafford Act. This law outlines the outlines of relief in the event of natural disasters, and the coordination mechanism among the federal government, the state and local governments. The law clearly states the procedures for disaster prevention, disaster mitigation and emergency assistance, the establishment of major disaster and emergency assistance agencies, assistance plans of major disaster and emergency, and making of emergency plan. Article 307 of the act clearly stipulates that the federal government's relief funds should first ensure the supply of subsistence goods, reconstruction and other relief operations in the affected areas. Article 309 clearly stipulates that, with permission, the President can ask the American Red Cross and many other relief agencies to distribute emergency materials, food and medicine. The above articles of the act ensure the smooth transportation and distribution of emergency materials in the event of major hazardous events in the country. The United States also issued the National Earthquake Disaster Mitigation Act in 1977 and the Federal Response Plan (FRP) in 1992. These regulations describe the distribution of emergency supplies, ensuring the smooth operation of emergency logistics.

# 5.2   Construction of the support system of emergency logistics in Japan

Japan is an island country in the Pacific Ocean. Due to its special geographical location and conditions, the whole country is located in an earthquake-prone zone, so natural disasters such as earthquakes and typhoons occur frequently. In view of such geographical factors, Japan has rich experience in dealing with natural disasters, and its emergency support system has been established earlier and developed relatively well.

## 5.2.1   The management system of emergency logistics in Japan

The management system of Japan's emergency logistics has developed through three stages: preliminarily-established, fairly-established and well-developed stage (Jiang Xu *et al.*, 2021). At present, Japan's emergency management system is relatively perfect. Japan has set up Central Disaster Prevention Committee. The emergency management is conducted through a three-level mechanism of the central government, the prefectural government, and the municipal government. The management system of emergency logistics is implemented by a system of "government-dominated, supplemented by government-enterprise cooperation". The government plays the role of commander in chief. At the same time, it attaches importance to mobilizing the major logistics enterprises and various associations, including Japan's Truck Association, the International Aviation Federation, the Transport Union, and the Air Cargo Transport Association. In case of emergency events, such as natural disasters, the government cooperates with these enterprises and associations to allocate emergency supplies. The allocation order of emergency supplies is from "outside the disaster area—the first-level regional logistics center in the disaster area—the second-level municipal logistics center in the disaster area—the refuge" (Jiang Xu *et al.*, 2021). The central government cooperates with these logistics enterprises and associations to ensure that the emergency supplies are delivered in the shortest time.

## 5.2.2 Legal and regulatory guarantee of emergency logistics in Japan

In view of the special geographical factors in Japan, the laws related to the emergency logistics system in Japan are also relatively perfect. Laws related to emergency logistics can be divided into general legislation and special legislation according to their nature. According to their content, the laws can be divided into the basic law, the disaster prevention law, the disaster emergency law and the post-disaster reconstruction and recovery law. In general legislation, the main laws are the *Disaster Relief Law* promulgated in 1947 and the *Basic Law on Disaster Countermeasures* promulgated in 1961.

The provisions of the *Disaster Relief Law* on emergency logistics management include the allocation of emergency food, drinking water and medical supplies for disaster relief, as well as rational allocation of emergency supplies and temporary requisition of local civil resources by local governments.

*The Basic Law on Disaster Countermeasures* stipulates the responsibilities of the state, the prefectures, the municipalities and public authorities at all levels and all citizens in the prevention and emergency response of sudden disasters. The provisions concerning disaster prevention in Chapter IV stipulates that the reserve plan of disaster prevention materials must be included in the disaster prevention plan. The provisions also include the reserve, allocation and transportation of disaster prevention and emergency materials. The matters to ensure emergency transportation are also specified in the provisions of Chapter V on disaster countermeasures.

In addition to the provisions on disaster prevention and emergency measures, Japan also has relatively perfect laws on post-disaster reconstruction and compensation mechanisms. Chapter VI of the Basic Law on Disaster Countermeasures specifically includes detailed provisions for post-disaster reconstruction, including the implementing subject of post-disaster reconstruction, the use of reconstruction funds and financial measures. Article 82 and 84 of the Law respectively stipulate the compensation for the subjects engaged in emergency disaster relief and the injured, disabled or dead persons who have been engaged in emergency disaster relief.

# 5.3    Construction principles of China's emergency logistics support system

Emergency logistics is an activity in which the circulation of human, financial and material resources is involved in response to various unexpected public events. In order to improve the efficiency of emergency logistics operation and reduce the loss of people's lives and property caused by public emergencies, it is necessary to establish a complete emergency logistics support system, including emergency logistics management system, legal and regulatory support system, social mobilization mechanism on emergency logistics and infrastructure construction supporting emergency logistics. The construction of the supporting system must comply with the following four principles:

## 5.3.1    Government leading, enterprises participating

China's various emergency laws and regulations stipulate that in the event of a national major public event, the emergency response shall be led and organized by the central government. In the event of a local major public event, local governments shall organize and implement emergency response. Under the leadership of governments at all levels, major logistics enterprises participate in the operation of emergency logistics, give full play to their advantages in logistics operation, apply the professional knowledge of logistics to emergency logistics operation, and thus to improve the efficiency of emergency logistics.

## 5.3.2  Improving related regulations and policies

In order to ensure the efficient operation of emergency logistics, laws, regulations and policies related to it must be completed to provide legal guarantee for the operation of emergency logistics. In *National Emergency Response Plan for Public Emergencies, Management rules of Contingency Plan for Public Emergencies* and other documents, only a few words about emergency logistics can be found. Later, in *Medium and Long-term Plan for the Development of Logistics Industry (2014-2020), The 13th Five-Year Plan for the Construction of National Emergency Response System,* "*The 14th Five-Year Plan for Modern Logistics*" and other documents, emergency logistics planning is taken as an important national task. It can be seen that the construction of emergency logistics system is gradually improved due to the protection of laws, regulations and national policies.

## 5.3.3  Government mobilizing, the whole people participating

In addition to coordinating and organizing the logistics enterprises to complete the operation of emergency logistics, when major public events occur, the government must also attach great importance to mobilizing the public to participate in disaster relief under its unified leadership. Mobilization includes the cultivation of national crisis awareness and emergency logistics talents in the stage of disaster prevention. At the stage of disaster resistance and mitigation, the government should widely mobilize all sectors of society to participate in the disaster relief work. In the stage of post-disaster reconstruction, the government should mobilize all social forces to participate so as to restore the economic vitality of the disaster-stricken areas as soon as possible.

### 5.3.4    Standardizing the construction and improving the utilization of facilities

The construction of emergency logistics infrastructure includes the construction of transportation channels, logistics parks, storage equipment, handling equipment, logistics information technology, etc. On the premise of the reasonable layout of transportation channels, emergency logistics should make good use of highway, railway and air transportation. When constructed, the transportation channel of ordinary logistics should be rapidly converted into emergency transportation channels in case of emergencies to improve the utilization of infrastructure and then avoid of rescources. The construction of emergency logistics equipment and information technology should rely on high-tech means. At the same time, we should pay attention to the construction of special facilities for emergency logistics, such as the construction of apron and emergency shelter.

## 5.4    Construction of China's emergency logistics management system

The definition of the emergency logistics management system in this book is based on the definition in Jiang Xu *et al.* (2021): a system that can correctly evaluate, effectively predict, and effectively guarantee the circulation of materials and information during the occurrence of accident disasters, natural disasters, social security events and public health events. China's emergency logistics started late, and the development of emergency logistics management system can be divided into two stages. The period from 1949 to 2003 was the stage of classified management of public emergencies. There was no concept of emergency management in China at that time. When natural disasters and other emergencies occurred, the departments of Water Conservancy, or the departments of Earthquake, or other related departments were responsible for the response to natural disasters. After the end of the SARS epidemic in 2003, China began to build an emergency logistics management system. China is gradually forming an emergency management system with "contingency plan, emergency management system, mechanism and legal system" as the core (Jiang Xu *et al.*, 2021). China's emergency logistics management system is in the process of exploration and gradual improvement.

In case of major public emergencies in China, the management of emergency logistics follows the mode of unified leadership under the Party Central Committee and the State Council, and graded responsibility of local governments at all levels. At present, China implements the four-level joint-action mechanism of the central government, provincial, municipal and county government ( district ) ( Yang Shanfeng, 2020), and establishes management institutions of emergency logistics at all levels. Under normal conditions, the Emergency Management Office of the State Council takes the lead in coordinating the Ministry of Transport and the Ministry of Commerce to develop a complete emergency logistics plan. During a major public emergency, the Emergency Management Office of the State Council will coordinate the operation of emergency logistics with the Ministry of Transport, the Ministry of Public Security, the Ministry of Commerce and other departments. The operation of emergency logistics is under the leadership of the government. It also encourages the participation of various logistics enterprises to apply their experience to emergency logistics, and gives play to their advantages in logistics operation. At the same time, the government can mobilize the participation of military forces when necessary to improve the efficiency and shorten the time of the operation of emergency logistics with the help of military transport forces, facilities and channels, thus minimizing the loss of life and property of the people in the disaster-affected areas.

## 5.5    Construction of China's legal and regulatory guarantee of emergency logistics

The operation of emergency logistics should rely on the protection of perfect laws and policies in the related fields. The development of emergency logistics laws and regulations in China has gone through a long time and is also a process of gradual development and improvement. This section sorts out the important emergency logistics laws, regulations, policies and other documents in China, providing important reference for researchers in this field.

China issued and implemented the *Overall National Emergency Plan for Public Emergencies* on January 8, 2006. The plan divides public emergencies into natural disasters, accident disasters, public health events, and social security events. The plan emphasizes that all relevant departments should cooperate in response to public emergencies according to the division of responsibilities and certain contingency plans, manage to meet the needs of people's emergency materials and daily necessities, and do a good job in medical and health security, and transportation security.

On June 15, 2006, *The State Council's Opinions Concerning Strengthening Emergency Management Work in an All-Round Way* ([2006] No. 24) stressed the need to strengthen the capacity to respond to public emergencies. It includes promoting the construction of the national emergency system, improving the capacity of the grass-roots' emergency management, strengthening the construction of emergency rescue teams, strengthening the management of various emergency resources, and doing a good job in emergency response and aftermath.

At the 29th meeting of the Standing Committee of the Tenth National People's Congress on August 30, 2007, the *Law of the People's Republic of China on Emergency Response* was adopted. Article 17 stipulates that "the State Council shall formulate the overall national emergency response plan and organize the formulation of the special national emergency response plan. Each related department of the State Council shall formulate its own emergency response plan according to their respective responsibilities and the emergency response plan of the State Council". It is emphasized in Article 32 that the state should establish and improve the support system for emergency supplies reserve and improve the system of supervision, for production, reserve, allocation and distribution system of important emergency supplies. The second paragraph of Article 45 emphasizes "mobilizing materials, equipment and tools needed for emergency rescue, preparing emergency facilities and refuge places, and ensuring that they are in good condition and ready for emergency use". Paragraph 7 of Article 49 stipulates that the government shall guarantee the supply of basic necessities of disaster-affected victims, such as food, drinking water, fuel, etc.

In 2009, the State Council issued the *Logistics Industry Adjustment and Revitalization Plan*, which proposed the "emergency logistics project" for the first time, and then emergency logistics became a part of the national strategic planning.

*The 2009 Survey Report of the Research and Development Center of the State Council* pointed out that we should speed up the construction of emergency logistics system and enhance the ability to ensure emergency supplies.

In 2013, China promulgated *Management Rules of Contingency Plan for Emergencies* (GBH [2013] No. 101), which divided the emergency plans into two categories, including the emergency plans of the government and its departments, and the emergency plans of grass-roots organizations. The management rules divides the emergency plans of the government and its departments into four levels, namely, special and departmental emergency plans at the national level, special and departmental emergency plans at the provincial level, special and departmental emergency plans at the municipal and county levels, and special and departmental emergency plans at the town and sub-district levels. The emergency plans at each level has different priorities. The special and departmental emergency plans are divided into four categories, including plans for the protection of important infrastructure, lifeline projects and other important objects, for major activities, for unexpected events, and for joint emergency plans. Among them, in the emergency plan for unexpected events, it is mentioned that guarantee of emergency materials, equipment, capital and other resources should be included in it to ensure the deployment of resources when the emergency occurs.

In 2014, the State Council issued the *Medium and Long-term Plan for the Development of Logistics Industry 2014-2020* ( GF〔2014〕No. 42 ), which defined the concept of " emergency logistics engineering ". Among the 12 key projects planned, one is the emergency logistics project. The plan requires "to establish a unified, coordinated, responsive, orderly, efficient and reliable emergency logistics system, to build a logistics center that meets multiple emergency needs, to form a group of backbone logistics enterprises with strong emergency logistics operation capabilities, to strengthen the construction of emergency storage, transfer, and distribution facilities, to improve the standardization and modernization of emergency logistics facilities and equipment, to improve the efficiency of emergency logistics and emergency support capabilities, to establish and improve emergency logistics information system, to standardize the coordination procedures, to optimize the process of information, business and management, and to promote the informatization of emergency production, circulation, storage and transportation, and information exchange and data sharing. "

In 2014, the General Office of the State Council issued the *Opinions on Accelerating the Development of Emergency Industry* ( GBF〔2014〕No. 63 ), which took emergency logistics as an important part of emergency services. In the 10th Paragraph "Emergency Services" of Article 3 "Key Services", it is emphasized to improve the level of socialized services for emergency prevention and disposal, and, in terms of socialized rescue, to develop emergency services such as emergency medical rescue, traffic rescue, emergency logistics, etc. In the 15th Paragraph of Article 4 "Main Tasks", it is required "to improve the management system of physical reserve, social reserve and production capacity reserve of emergency product, build a comprehensive information platform for emergency product and production capacity reserve, drive the application of emergency products, strengthen the construction of emergency storage, transit and distribution facilities, and improve the logistics efficiency of emergency products". The opinion also details the tasks of improving the reserve and transit of emergency supplies, and logistics efficiency of emergency products to specific departments.

In August 2015, the National Development and Reform Commission issued the *Notice on Accelerating the Implementation of Major Modern Logistics Projects*, which requires that "emergency logistics projects" be one of the main tasks, with the focus on building emergency storage, transfer and distribution facilities, and improving the standardization and modernization of emergency logistics facilities and equipment.

In 2017, the General Office of the State Council issued the *13th Five-Year Plan* for the Construction of the National Emergency Response System, which set out the overall goal of the *13th Five-Year Plan*: by 2020, to build an emergency response system that is compatible with the effective response to the challenges of public security risks and the requirements of building a moderately prosperous society in an all-round way, covering the whole process of emergency management, and involving the whole society. In the classified objectives, it is clearly proposed that the rapid improvement of the comprehensive support capability of emergency materials should be a main goal, and that the improvement of the emergency material support system and transportation support capability should be the main tasks of the planning.

In 2021, China promulgated *Outline of the 14th Five-Year Plan(2021 – 2025) for National Economic and Social Development and Vision 2035 of the People's Republic of China*, the two important objectives in it are to "implement the reserve project of emergency supplies production capacity, build a regional production base of emergency material" and "to implement and accelerate the establishment of an emergency logistics system with sufficient reserves, rapid response and strong impact resistance".

On May 17, 2022, the *14th Five-Year Plan of Modern Logistics*, China's first five-year plan in the field of logistics, , was issued. The plan proposes to improve the safety emergency capability of modern logistics, improve the support capability of strategic materials and emergency logistics, give full play to the role of social logistics, and promote the establishment of emergency logistics teams with enterprises as the main body. The plan also emphasizes the need to improve the development of emergency logistics, the layout and the network of emergency logistics facilities, coordinate and strengthen the matching and organic connection of various emergency material storage facilities and emergency logistics facilities in terms of layout, function and operation, and improve the emergency dispatching capacity.

To sum up, it can be seen that *the Overall National Emergency Plan for Public Emergencies* only mentions the requirements of "doing a good job in material and transportation support", and does not provide specific guidance for emergency logistics. *The State Council's Opinions Concerning Strengthening Emergency Management Work in an All-Round Way* also only emphasizes strengthening the management of various emergency resources. Since the *emergency logistics engineering* was first proposed in the "*Logistics Industry Adjustment and Revitalization Plan*" issued by the State Council in 2009, various laws and policies on the development of the logistics industry began to attach importance to the development of emergency logistics. The concept of "emergency logistics engineering" was defined in the "*Medium and Long-term Plan for the Development of the Logistics Industry 2014-2020*". Then "emergency logistics engineering" was taken as one of the main tasks of China's economic development. Later, to improve the emergency support of material and transportation was clearly put forward as the main task of the *13th Five-Year Plan*.

Then *14th Five-Year Plan* of Modern Logistics in China's logistics field was issued to emphasize the need to improve the development, the layout and the network of emergency logistics facilities.

The construction of China's emergency logistics system is gradually improved due to the protection of laws and regulations. However, the laws, regulations, policies and documents related to emergency logistics are all reflected in the laws, regulations and policies of emergency events or general logistics. China has no special emergency logistics law. Today, with more and more experience in handling emergency events in China, the country should issue special emergency logistics laws, regulations and policies and other documents. For the organization of emergency logistics, the storage, management, transportation, distribution of emergency materials, the responsibilities and authorities of emergency workers and social participants should be clarified and legal guarantees should be provided.

In the process of improving emergency logistics laws and regulations, we should improve the emergency logistics compensation system. In China's various laws and regulations on emergency response, the compensation mechanism has not been systematically and clearly regulated. In the Overall National Emergency Plan for Public Emergencies it is only mentioned that "pensions, subsidies or compensation shall be given to the injured, dead and other staff members in the emergency response work according to the regulations". In the Law of the People's Republic of China on Emergency Response, it is stipulated that governments at all levels "formulate and implement relief, compensation, comfort, pension, resettlement and other post-disaster work plans" according to the disaster situation. Other relevant laws also rarely mention the issue of compensation system. Therefore, in the process of perfecting the emergency logistics laws and regulations in China, the compensation system, including the standard, scope and form of compensation, should be clearly defined. In the process of improving the compensation system, it is necessary to fully mobilize social and market resources to make up for the lack of national financial compensation capacity ( Liu Jingfang, 2014 ), and establish a diversified compensation mechanism based on government compensation (Shang Xiqiao, 2017). In addition to government compensation, insurance companies should also play a compensation role after emergencies, and fulfill their responsibility for settling claims for personal and other organizations' accident insurance and property insurance, and fulfill their social responsibilities by setting up special disaster compensation departments and disaster reserves to shorten the time for the payment of post-disaster compensation (Xu Huimin, 2014).

In addition to government compensation and insurance company compensation, the government can also play the role of social mobilization, call for social donations, and use social donation funds for compensation. Through the improvement of relevant laws, regulations and systems, the compensation system can be legally based, the interests of individuals and units involved in the rescue can be guaranteed, and the social forces can be positively mobilized.

## 5.6   Construction of social mobilization mechanism for emergency logistics in China

When dealing with natural disasters, public healthor security emergencies, it is difficult to respond quickly and accurately by the power of the government alone. Therefore, the government must carry out emergency mobilization, fully mobilize all forces, and give full play to the enthusiasm of all forces, so as to comprehensively improve the ability and effect of response to emergencies. A strong mobilization mechanism plays a vital role in dealing with various emergencies. The Law of the People's Republic of China on Emergency Response promulgated in 2007 also stipulates that the country should establish an effective social mobilization mechanism to enhance the public security and risk prevention awareness.

## 5.6.1  Emergency mobilization

The term "mobilization" was once used only as amilitary term, specifically referring to war mobilization. Baidu Encyclopedia defines "mobilization or war mobilization" as: the armed forces of a country or political group are transferred from peacetime to wartime, and the focus of all economic sectors (industry, agriculture, transportation, etc.) are transferred to the work required by the war, that is, the mobilization of human, material and financial resources to serve the war. In a broad sense, mobilization refers to the process in which the government mobilizes all aspects of society to actively respond to social or national emergencies, including human mobilization, technology mobilization, production capacity mobilization, logistics mobilization, and so on.

The three major tasks of war mobilization are to mobilize forces from all sides to carry out armed operations and combat, maintain the stability of social production, and minimize war disasters. In a broad sense, the task of emergency mobilization can also be divided into three aspects. The first is to minimize the impacts of disasters on people's lives and property. The second is to maintain the stability of social production while fighting disasters. The third is to minimize secondary disasters and derivative crises.

Mobilization is divided into mobilization in the warning stage, emergency preparation stage, emergency response stage and disaster recovery stage (Xue Yingying, 2018). In the emergency warning stage, the main task is to intervene in avoidable emergencies to prevent their further deterioration. For food safety incidents, the main task in this stage is to stop the large-scale occurrence of the incidents when very few problems are found. For the inevitable events, such as natural disasters and public health events, the mobilization in the warning stage is mainly reflected in the government's propaganda and education of disaster prevention and mitigation knowledge for the masses, the cultivation of public awareness of the crisis to make sure that they can actively cooperate with the government's mobilization efforts in the event of a crisis, so as to play the role of social forces in disaster prevention and mitigation.

The main tasks in the emergency preparation stage are to improve relevant emergency laws and regulations, emergency plans, emergency warning system, emergency education and training, and to mobilize social forces to clarify their tasks in emergency response.

The main purpose of the emergency response stage is to save lives and reduce the loss of people's lives and property. The main task of this stage is to mobilize social forces and resources to participate in the work of disaster prevention and reduction. The government departments can timely convey disaster information to the society through media, networks and other channels, and mobilize social forces and guide social forces in disaster prevention and relief. Effective mobilization can give full play to the advantages of social forces and resources and is also conducive to strengthening the unity of the whole society. Another task at this stage is to mobilize the forces of the armed forces. When natural disasters occur, the local garrison, the armed police and fire-fighting officers are the main forces to fight and reduce disasters. In the process of fighting disasters, the armed forces play their role of "coming as soon as they are called, fighting as soon as they come". Through the mobilization of social and military forces, the party, government, army and people can effectively play a concerted role in fighting disasters. The main task of the disaster recovery stage is post-disaster reconstruction. At this time, social forces are the main forces. The government should mobilize all social forces to participate in post-disaster recovery and enhance social cohesion. At this stage, the government also has an important responsibility to coordinate with relevant organizations to intervene in the psychological recovery of the disaster-affected people and help them to overcome the psychological crisis as soon as possible. The participation of social forces in disaster prevention and reduction is also protected by the relevant laws of China. *The Law of the People's Republic of China on Emergency Response* stipulates that when citizens participate in emergency rescue work or stability maintenance work during disasters, the wages and benefits of their work units remain unchanged.

## 5.6.2　Emergency logistics mobilization mechanism

Emergency logistics mobilization is one aspect of emergency mobilization. Emergency logistics mobilization refers to the behavior of the government in the process of emergency logistics to mobilize non-governmental resources to respond to the demand for materials, personnel and funds required by public emergencies (Wang Feng *et al.*, 2007).

Major natural disasters or public health events are unpredictable. Usually, when an emergency occurs, a large number of disaster relief materials are needed in a short period of time. From life support supplies to special disaster relief materials and medical materials, they need to be delivered to the disaster area at the first time. Usually, there will be road interruption, communication equipment damage and other situations in the disaster area, which will bring greater difficulties to the emergency logistics operation. In case of emergency, logistics mobilization can concentrate all forces of society and ensure the continuous supply of resources in the process of disaster relief and post-disaster reconstruction through continuous logistics mobilization. In the process of mobilizing the strength of the whole society, the government has gathered the strength of all aspects of the country and improved the emergency response efficiency in the special period.

Emergency logistics mobilization is divided into three aspects: mobilization preparation, real-time mobilization and post-disaster mobilization (Wang Feng *et al.*, 2007).

The main task of preparation stage is to develop and reserve emergency logistics resources, and implement emergency logistics mobilization preparation in the construction of logistics potential at ordinary times, so as to make better, faster and more efficient use of logistics resources in case of emergencies. In this stage, preparation should be done well for natural disasters or public health emergencies before they occur. The preparation includes the reserve of emergency materials and financial guarantee of emergency logistics. Because of the unpredictability of emergency events and the materials needed for emergency logistics, the reserve includes not only the physical reserve of conventional disaster relief materials, living materials and medical materials, but also the reserve of production capacity and production technology, and the contract reserve with suppliers. The logistics mobilization preparation combines the emergency resources with the normal logistics system construction. When an emergency occurs, the normal logistics resources can be quickly converted into emergency logistics resources through the normal social mobilization procedure. The government should also support the reserve of emergency logistics resources from the financial budget and increase the investment in emergency logistics resources. The financial support can be the reserve of physical goods, production capacity, production technology or contract reserve. In addition to the reserve of resources and funds, the government should also train professional and technical personnel in emergency logistics management and efficient emergency support team. The implementation of emergency logistics mobilization requires management personnel with special emergency logistics knowledge and emergency support teams that can respond quickly. Therefore, the government should pay attention to the training of emergency logistics personnel and the reserve of personnel with emergency logistics knowledge. Like ordinary emergency mobilization, emergency logistics mobilization also needs to carry out crisis awareness training, emergency handling ability training, and other popularization work for the public at ordinary times to improve citizens' crisis prevention awareness and crisis response ability.

The preparation of logistics mobilization also includes the formulation of emergency logistics plan. Only by formulating a reasonable and complete emergency logistics plan according to the National Overall Emergency Plan for Public

Emergencies can the emergency logistics resources and the security forces of all parties efficiently and orderly complete the logistics support tasks in the event of an emergency. Local governments and relevant departments at all levels should formulate corresponding emergency plans based on the actual situation of the location and the previous disasters. Especially in areas prone to earthquake and flood, the government should make multiple plans for one emergency when necessary on the premise of predicting possible emergencies. For example, the reserve plans for emergency material involve not only the physical reserve, but also the plans of contract suppliers, technology research and development units and production reserve units. For example, the transportation plan of emergency materials should also take into account all kinds of emergencies caused by natural disasters, including road interruption, damage to communication facilities, etc. into the emergency logistics plan.

The real-time mobilization of emergency logistics occurs after the occurrence of an emergency, and the government departments allocate and mobilize non-governmental resources. According to the *Law of the People's Republic of China on Emergency Response*, people's governments at all levels should immediately mobilize all relevant departments, mobilize emergency rescue teams and social forces, organize citizens to participate in emergency rescue work, and have the right to require special professional personnel to participate in emergency rescue work. After the occurrence of an emergency, governments at all levels should quickly establish an efficient logistics support team in combination with specific emergency rescue tasks, and formulate a reasonable emergency logistics operation plan according to the nature of disasters, such as earthquake, flood, ice and snow disasters, to transport emergency supplies to the disaster area at the first time. In case of emergency, according to the Regulations on the Mobilization of Civil Transport Capacity for National Defense, the government can take temporary traffic control, implement traffic mobilization, uniformly control the transport routes and means of transport, and requisition the means of transport of social forces when necessary.

Emergency real-time mobilization also includes publicity. Diplomatic publicity can be carried out to present the real situation of the disaster to the international community, which can not only prompt the international community to respond to similar disasters in advance, but also win broad international recognition, sympathy and international support. Internally, the real disaster information will be released to the general public, and so the citizens' right to know will be respected. At the same time, the national mobilization will be carried out to mobilize the general public to actively participate in the emergency logistics support work.

At the mobilization stage of post-disaster rehabilitation and reconstruction, the disaster-affected areas basically recover to the normal state, and the emergency treatment support team withdrew in an orderly manner. The disaster-affected areas begin to assess the disaster situation, casualties and property losses, and to compensate for the civilian materials urgently requisitioned, and begin to rebuild the areas, so as to restore the economic vitality of the affected areas. At this time, the government needs to mobilize the masses to participate in the reconstruction work, and reward the units and individuals actively participating in the emergency rescue. By rewarding meritorious personnel, the government can mobilize more people to participate in the post-disaster reconstruction task again

## 5.7    The construction of emergency logistics infrastructure and equipment in China

Laws, regulations and mobilization mechanism are the mechanism guarantee for the operation of the emergency logistics system, while the improvement of infrastructure is thematerial guarantee.

According to the classification method of Li Hong and Chen Yuchai (2021), logistics infrastructure includes logistics parks, logistics centers, highways, railways, waterways, aviation and other transportation channels, transportation hubs, stations, storage facilities, etc. Logistics equipment includes transportation equipment, storage equipment, loading and unloading equipment, circulation processing equipment, logistics information technology equipment, etc.

The contents of the book focus on emergency logistics under public health emergencies and natural disasters, so this section mainly studies the infrastructure construction of roads, railways and aviation. By 2022, the total mileage of highways in China has reached 5. 28 million kilometers, forming a highway network based on expressways as the skeleton, common trunk lines as the vein, and rural roads as the base. The mileage of expressways in china ranks first in the world. By December 2020, China's railway operating mileage has reached 146, 000 kilometers, including 38, 000 kilometers of high-speed railway, which ranks first in the world. By 2021, China has a total of 5581 scheduled flight routes, with 237 domestic navigable cities. From the perspective of the national layout of transportation channels, China's railways have formed a "five vertical and three horizontal" railway network, and highways have formed a "five vertical and seven horizontal" national trunk line and a highway network connecting the main line and the connecting line. China's air transport network has also formed a crisscross and relatively complete transport network. In the *14th Five-Year Plan* formulated by the Civil Aviation Administration in 2021, it is clearly stated that "the three systems of domestic air transport network, international air transport channel and aviation hub function" should be improved. China's railway hubs mainly include Beijing hub, Tianjin hub, Shenyang and Harbin hub, Zhengzhou hub, Wuhan hub, Guangzhou hub, Lanzhou hub, Chongqing hub, Kunming hub, Guiyang hub, etc. Highway transport hubs are mainly distributed in 45 large and medium-sized cities such as Beijing, Tianjin, Shijiazhuang, etc. All railway and highway hubs are distributed in large cities or water transport centers with developed transport network, concentrated traffic power and relatively developed economy. The rapid development of transportation channel infrastructure such as highways, railways and air routes in China has provided a strong material basis for the efficient transportation of emergency supplies and emergency personnel. These transportation channels provide convenience for ordinary logistics under normal conditions, and can be rapidly converted into emergency transportation channels under emergency conditions. When formulating emergency plans for various emergencies, the emergency management department should make a plan to quickly convert the ordinary transportation channel into emergency channel, plan the emergency route in advance in advance, and then improve the efficiency of emergency transportation.

On the basis of the construction of the existing transportation channels and hubs, the future construction of the transportation channels of China's emergency logistics should try to establish the war-readiness reserve mechanism of infrastructure (Chen Yuan, Li Jing, 2011), build the freight stations, transit stations and other infrastructure according to the regional characteristics and climatic conditions of various places, reasonably arrange the logistics nodes, and make reasonable use of the existing main transportation roads and main network lines, establish the connection between the auxiliary highway and the main road, so that the transportation network can cover a wide range. In case of an emergency, the transportation channel should be quickly converted into the emergency transportation channel, so that the relief materials can reach the disaster area in time.

The construction of emergency logistics centers or logistics parks should be aimed at providing fast and convenient services for emergency rescue. The location of the center or park should be in a place with convenient traffic near the areas with frequent natural disasters. Meanwhile, the emergency logistics center or park should have a certain scale to ensure that there is space for loading and unloading emergency materials, and that multiple transport vehicles can pass at the same time. The scale of the emergency logistics center and the park is determined by the population of the surrounding cities, for the population determines the number of emergency materials stored or transported. The degree of urban economic development is also one of the factors that should be considered in the construction of the emergency logistics park.

The construction of emergency logistics equipment and technology should apply modern scientific and technological means, so as to further improve the efficiency of emergency logistics and minimize the damage caused by emergencies. From the perspective of the development of logistics equipment, China has developed a large automated three-dimensional warehouse, which applies computer science to the operations of roadway stacking, automated warehousing and transportation, and warehouse management, etc. In March 2008, China issued the *Standard for Main Dimensions and Tolerances of General Flat Pallets for Intermodal Transport* ( GB/T 2934—2007), which specifies the material and size of general pallets and facilitates the combined transport of emergency supplies. The use of the automatic sorting system can identify the quality, quantity, location and owner information of the goods according to the labels on the goods when the goods are warehoused, and send the goods to the location set by the system through the automatic conveyor, or even leave the main conveyor to enter the passage of the cargo collection area. At the same time, the upgrading of shelves and conveying equipment, the application of automatic carriers guided by electromagnetism, laser or magnetic gyroscope, as well as the application of electronic labels, bar code printers, and data acquisition technology have greatly improved the efficiency of emergency materials storage and warehouse management. From the perspective of the development of logistics information technology, barcode technology and radio frequency identification technology are widely used in modern physical systems, providing convenience not only for ordinary logistics, but also for emergency logistics to quickly identify items and respond to sorting and transportation systems in operation. The achievements of common logistics technology and equipment should be used in the operation of emergency logistics, in an all-round way, which not only saves the resources for developing emergency logistics technology and equipment, but also improves the efficiency of emergency logistics operation.

The development of logistics transportation channels, logistics equipment and technology provides the material basis for the efficient operation of emergency logistics. In addition, the construction of special facilities and equipment for emergency logistics is also essential. The first is the construction of regional emergency rescue sites. The planning and construction of the rescue sites are designed according to the local needs. Under normal conditions, they can be used for other purposes, such as sports grounds, cultural plazas, etc. After an emergency, these sites can be converted into emergency rescue sites or refuge sites for storing emergency supplies or for distributing emergency supplies. Secondly, in order to establish a three-dimensional rescue network, some areas prone to natural disasters can plan to construct large aprons with complete fire-fighting and rescue equipment, meteorological equipment and other equipment according to the provisions of the National Civil Aviation Administration, so that helicopters can take off and land safely in case of emergency events, and win valuable time for emergency rescue.

To sum up, the logistics transportation channel and most of the logistics equipment and information technology are constructed on the basis of the general logistics. However, under the premise of good planning at the initial stage of construction, and with the coordination of the emergency logistics management departments, transportation channel, the facilities and equipment should be quickly converted into those of emergency logistics in an emergency state, and they can only play the role of emergency logistics with the cooperation with the special emergency logistics facilities.

# Chapter 6 China's Natural Disaster Emergency Logistics System

China has a vast territory and a complex geographical environment. It is a country with frequent and various natural disasters. The losses caused by disasters restrict China's social and economic development to a certain extent. Therefore, China has also formulated many relevant laws and regulations to tackle natural disasters, so that any measure to tackle natural disasters has a legal basis. At the same time, in response to natural disasters, the state and local governments at all levels have also formulated many natural disaster emergency plans, including plans for the storage, management and transportation of emergency supplies. In addition, the efficient transportation of emergency materials is an important part of the disaster relief work, which can win valuable time for the disaster relief work, thus greatly reducing casualties and property losses. This chapter studies the construction of natural disaster emergency logistics system from the classification, storage, management, transportation and distribution of emergency materials.

## 6.1 Overview of natural disasters

Ge Quansheng (2008) believes that all kinds of events that endanger human life, property and living conditions can be called disasters. Huang Chongfu (2009) defined natural disasters as events that occur in nature and can cause casualties and loss of human social property. This book believes that any natural phenomenon that causes losses to human life and property and the natural environment can be called natural disasters.

China's Classification and Code of Natural Disasters (GBT 28921—2012), which was implemented on February 1, 2013, classifies natural disasters into five categories, namely, meteorological and hydrological disasters, geological and seismic disasters, marine disasters, biological disasters, and ecological and environmental disasters. Meteorological and hydrological disasters include 13 kinds of natural disasters, such as drought, flood and typhoon. Geological and seismic disasters include 9 kinds, such as earthquake disasters and volcanic disasters. Marine disasters include 5 kinds, namely, storm surge, wave, sea ice, tsunami and red tide. Biological disasters include 7 kinds, such as plant diseases, insect pests and rats. Ecological and environmental disasters include five kinds, such as water and soil loss and salinization. According to the causes of disasters, Xi Menghao (2021) divided natural disasters into six categories, namely, meteorological and hydrological disasters, marine disasters, geological disasters, earthquake disasters, biological disasters, and land degradation disasters.

For the definition and classification of natural disasters, many scholars and experts have different descriptions, but the essence is basically the same. The content of this chapter is the construction of emergency logistics in response to natural disasters. Due to space constraints, the natural disasters involved in this chapter mainly include earthquake disasters and flood disasters. Earthquake disaster refers to the natural disaster that the strong ground vibration caused by earthquake causes cracks and deformation of the ground, collapse or damage of various buildings or facilities and equipment, and thus causes fire, explosion, site damage and other human life and property and livestock casualties. Flood disaster refers to the hydrological phenomenon that the water volume caused by rainstorm and sudden melting of icebergs exceeds the holding capacity of rivers, lakes, reservoirs, oceans and other waters, resulting in a sharp increase in water volume or water level. Flood disasters usually bring losses to normal production and even human life and property.

# 6.2 Overview of major earthquake and flood disasters in China in recent decades

This section outlines several major natural disasters with large impact and serious disaster losses in China in recent decades, and briefly combs the role of emergency logistics in respouding to these disasters.

## 6.2.1 1998 catastrophic floods

The 1998 catastrophic floods occurred in the Yangtze River, Nenjiang River, Songhua River and other river basins. It was a major flood in the whole basin. According to statistics, 29 provinces (regions and cities), including Jiangxi, Hunan, Hubei and Heilongjiang, suffered different degrees of flood disasters, with direct economic losses of 166 billion Yuan. The first flood peak of the flood occurred in Nenjiang on June 27, and in the upper reaches of the Yangtze River on July 2. On July 14, the National Flood Control Administration issued *the Notice on Further Improving the Flood Control Work*, requires that all flood control measures should be fully implemented, and all cadres, labor and materials should be in place. In August, there was a shortage of rain-proof and cold-proof clothing for officers and soldiers at the front line of flood fighting in Harbin, a shortage of life-saving equipment in Daqing, and a shortage of cold-proof clothing in Inner Mongolia. The then Premier Zhu Rongji instructed that the problem of material shortage should be solved immediately, and that planned production should be organized to ensure the supply of emergency relief materials. On September 25, the water level in the middle and lower reaches of the Yangtze River fell below the warning water level, and the national people's disaster relief work was successfully completed. In the process of disaster relief of this catastrophic flood disaster, there was a temporary shortage of materials, exposing problems in the storage and transportation of disaster relief materials. At that time, China did not have the experience of emergency logistics, so in the event of a natural disaster, it failed to respond in material storage and transportation.

## 6.2.2 2008 Wenchuan Earthquake

The Wenchuan earthquake, also known as the 5.12 Wenchuan earthquake, occurred in Yingxiu Town, Wenchuan County, Aba Tibetan Autonomous Prefecture, Sichuan Province, at 2:28 p.m. on May 12, 2008. The China Seismological Bureau has determined the magnitude of the Wenchuan earthquake as 8.0, which has affected most areas of China and many countries and regions in Asia. The area damaged by the earthquake covers an area of 500000 square kilometers, with more than 69000 people were killed by the earthquake, more than 17000 missing and 46.25 million affected by the earthquake. The Wenchuan earthquake was the worst earthquake since the founding of the People's Republic of China. The houses, school buildings, transportation, geomorphology, water conservancy, and minority culture in the disaster area were seriously damaged.

After the earthquake, the Central Committee of the Communist Party of China, the State Council, the General Headquarters for Earthquake Relief of the State Council and the Sichuan Provincial Government led the Sichuan people to take an active part in earthquake relief. Under the deployment of the General Headquarters, all relevant departments have urgently allocated a large number of relief materials to the disaster areas, and a large amount of relief funds were also allocated to rescue the Sichuan disaster areas. After the earthquake, the Sichuan

Provincial Government quickly launched the Level I Emergency Response, and the provincial party committee and provincial government immediately established the earthquake relief headquarters to quickly, actively, effectively and orderly organize the earthquake relief work. The Sichuan Provincial Headquarters implemented effective traffic control and guarantee after the earthquake to ensure the smooth traffic of relief materials and relief personnel, and concentrated efforts were made to ensure the smooth flow of the "lifeline". Sichuan Provincial Party Committee and Sichuan Provincial Government actively organized and coordinated all parties in the process of material collection and management and traffic support to ensure smooth communications for disaster relief, so that the quick and safe arrival of rescue materials and disaster relief teams can be guaranteed.

### 6.2.3    Southern flood in 2020

The "2020 Southern China Flood Disaster" was announced by the Ministry of Emergency Management as one of the ten natural disasters in 2020. The flood disaster in South China in 2020 refers to the serious flood disaster caused by multiple rounds of heavy rainfall in South China since the flood season in 2020. By June 2020, rivers in 16 provinces and regions across the country had exceeded the warning water level. Shanghai, Chongqing, Sichuan, Guangxi, Guizhou, Zhejiang and other provinces and cities had launched emergency response respectively. Zhejiang Province had once adjusted the emergency response to Level I. In facing the flood, the Emergency Management Department has organized meetings for many times to study and judge the disaster and relief work. It has allocated disaster relief tents, folding beds and other central relief materials to Guizhou, Guangxi, Guangdong, Sichuan, Chongqing, Guizhou and other places to support local flood relief work. As of July 9, this flood disaster has affected more than 30 million people in Anhui, Jiangxi, Hunan and other provinces, and more than 600000 people need emergency living assistance, with a direct economic loss of more than 60 billion Yuan. The flood disaster was not relieved until the end of July. During the period of the disaster relief, China has accumulated rich experience in emergency logistics. The central government has repeatedly deployed emergency supplies to the disaster areas. From the central government to the local government, the whole country has united to actively deal with the flood disaster and achieved the final victory.

## 6.3 China's natural disaster emergency logistics guarantee mechanism

The key to the successful operation of emergency logistics is to build the support mechanism of each subsystem of the emergency logistics system (Yu Duohe, He Shiwei, 2008). A perfect support mechanism of natural disaster emergency logistics should include following aspects, namely, government coordination mechanism, disaster monitoring and warning mechanism, emergency plan mechanism, disaster information release mechanism, reserve mechanism of emergency material, social mobilization mechanism and "green channel" mechanism.

The organizational mechanism of government coordination, enterprise participation and military-civilian unity is applied. *China's Emergency Response Law stipulates* that the people's government shall uniformly lead and organize the handling of emergencies. The government departments coordinate the government, military and logistics enterprises to provide emergency supplies. The government uniformly organizes and allocates emergency supplies and funds, organizes the mobilization of the society, and organizes forces to ensure the smooth transportation and distribution of emergency supplies. In an emergency, the government can not only use the emergency supplies and transportation capacity of the government, but also use those of military forces, logistics enterprises and other social forces.

Importance is attached to the monitoring and warning mechanism. The monitoring mechanism refers to the collection and verification of information on the nature, regularity and hazards of previous disasters, the long-term monitoring, capture and prediction of possible natural disasters and other emergencies, and also the timely reporting of monitoring information. Early warning mechanism refers to the warning of possible natural disasters based on scientific prediction methods and technologies and long-term monitoring data, and reporting to relevant departments, so that the government and the public can take appropriate measures in time. At the beginning of a natural disaster, the market monitoring and warning information department should predict the number of emergency supplies based on the detected data and the actual number of people affected by the disaster. For example, in some earthquake-prone areas, the local government should develop a warning mechanism that combines the monitoring of the local population and the management of emergency supplies. When an earthquake disaster occurs, the local emergency department should rapidly predict the number of life-saving and life-support supplies needed according to the number of the affected population, and then provide emergency supplies at the fastest speed.

Emergency plan mechanism is needed. For some areas where natural disasters are frequent or prone to occur, the local government should formulate corresponding emergency logistics support plans according to the characteristics of local disasters, including how to reserve, manage, transport and distribute emergency supplies. It should also regularly organize drills to deal with natural disasters and strengthen the training of logistics support personnel. Governments at all levels can thus effectively respond to natural disasters by integrating disaster reduction work in daily preparations and applying the emergency plan to the actual emergency.

A long-term disaster information release mechanism should be developed. The release of disaster information includes information about the disasters and loss of it, as well as information about the demand, use and management of relief material, so that the whole society can grasp the disaster information. It is conducive for the government to raise relief materials, and also facilitates the social donation of relief materials.

A multi-dimensional reserve mechanism of disaster relief emergency material is implemented. The state reserves and manages materials according to the possibility of natural disasters in various regions by establishing a central disaster-relief material reserve center and provincial centers. In addition to physical reserves, the government should also sign contracts with enterprises to reserve. In case of disasters, enterprises can quickly implement contracts and carry out the production of disaster relief materials. The reserve of emergency supplies for disaster relief should also include the reserve of funds. The government can reserve funds to deal with various natural disasters in the annual financial budget, especially in some areas inflicted by frequent natural disasters, so as to effectively respond to natural disasters.

A wide range of social mobilization mechanisms is implemented. When a natural disaster occurs, the government informs the disaster situation through various media and networks, and mobilizes the whole society to participate in the relief work and to raise relief materials, mobilizes all logistics enterprises to participate in the transportation and distribution of relief materials, and thus unites the whole society to carry out disaster relief. In addition to the mobilization of the whole society to participate in disaster relief and resistance work, the mobilization work also includes psychological counseling for the people in the disaster-affected areas, so that people there can smoothly go through the anxiety and tension period and minimize the possibility of post-traumatic stress disorder among them.

The green channel mechanism is strengthened. In the event of a natural disaster, in order to ensure the smooth arrival of disaster relief personnel and materials in the disaster area, China has implemented a "green channel mechanism" to provide fast access for vehicles transporting those personnel and materials and improve the efficiency of emergency logistics. At this time, the aviation, railway, highway, waterway and other transportation departments have the responsibility to organize and coordinate the relevant epidemic prevention and inspection departments to issue "green passes" to reduce the inspection procedures and shorten the inspection time to ensure the smooth transportation of disaster relief personnel and materials.

When natural disasters occur, effective social mobilization is conducive to efficient logistics command, reasonable resource allocation, effective resource flow, and smooth logistics operation. It plays a key role in saving lives, reducing losses caused by disasters, and maintaining social stability. In the future, social mobilization should grasp the focus in the dynamic changes of disasters, and then the huge material flow and strength will be orderly transformed with the change of the main task (Zhang Hongrui, Wu Hongqiang, 2009). The dynamic mobilization is also the development direction of China's natural disaster emergency mobilization.

# 6.4   Construction of natural disaster emergency logistics information system

The emergency logistics information system is a subsystem of the emergency logistics system. The natural disaster emergency logistics information system includes monitoring and warning system, information sharing platform and logistics tracking system. Through the establishment of a complete logistics information system, the role of the command system can be effectively played. Through the construction of the information system, all emergency logistics enterprises can realize real-time sharing of logistics information resources to facilitate the deployment and transportation of emergency materials. Through the construction of the information system, the public can also timely grasp the demand and use of emergency supplies. It plays a role in mobilizing emergency supplies, and also in monitoring the use of emergency supplies by the whole society. The construction of emergency logistics information system should also follow the principle of government-led and enterprise-participating. Under the organization and coordination of the government, all logistics enterprises should actively participate in the disaster relief work of natural disasters. The construction of information system should rely on modern scientific and technological means, which is more conducive to accurate disaster relief.

The emergency logistics information system can realize the warning and monitoring functions by collecting, processing and analyzing big data. Market monitoring and warning provide strong data support for effective response to natural disasters. When natural disasters occur, the demand for emergency living materials can be estimated according to the market monitoring data under normal conditions. Under normal conditions, the government departments should cooperate with the market supervision department to collect the demand data of citizens' life supplies through the data management system, market real-time monitoring and data processing analysis system. In case of natural disasters, the government can supply living materials according to the market data under normal conditions. For the demand of life rescue materials, the allocatim is usually determined under the guidance of the government according to the number permanent residents in the area and the number of actual victims.

The emergency logistics information system can perform the function of releasing and sharing information by using the information sharing platform. The government should establish an information sharing platform among government departments at all levels and between governments and enterprises. Through the sharing of core data, vertically between the central government and local governments, horizontally among different local governments and between governments and enterprises, the information can be shared. The demand and allocation of relief materials in the disaster-affected areas can also be grasped in real time, and the allocation of the materials can be optimized. When a natural disaster occurs, the affected area can make the request for relief materials through the government's official platform and request support from the local and central government. In addition to the request for emergency supplies, the release of emergency logistics information should also include the information of the use of emergency supplies, so that the public can supervise the use and quality of disaster relief supplies.

Using modern scientific and technological means such as GIS and GPS and modern communication technology, the emergency logistics information system can realize the tracking of disaster relief materials. By installing the composite navigation system of GPS and GIS on the emergency transportation vehicles, technical and equipment support for the route planning can be realized. At the same time, the vehicle-mounted GPS safety monitoring system or terminal positioning system, which is now very popular in the market, can not only plan the route, but also locate the vehicle in real time, so that the command center can understand the location of the vehicles and the materials transported, so as to further arrange the disaster relief work. The system can also track and monitor the vehicle speed and the driving conditions of drivers. The alarm will be triggered in case of speeding or fatigue driving, which greatly ensures the safety of the vehicles, materials and drivers. Certainlly in addition to positioning technologies such as GIS and GPS, modern communication technologies such as telephone and video calls can also be used to directly track logistics vehicles and personnel, so as to timely and directly grasp the situation of them.

## 6.5   Reserve of emergency supplies for natural disasters

As early as 1998, China issued relevant laws and regulations on the reserve of disaster relief materials, which regulated the reserve of disaster relief materials at the national level, including the types of the materials, the construction of reserve points, etc. , and the laws and regulations have be revised for several times. As of July 2023, China has established 126 central level reserves for disaster-relief materials in 31 provinces and cities. China's reserve system of disaster relief material is also being further improved. This section will elaborate on the types of disaster relief materials for natural disasters, the establishment of disaster relief reserves and the reserve system of disaster relief materials.

## 6.5.1 Concept and classification of emergency supplies

Emergency supplies refer to the material necessary in the whole process of responding to public emergencies, including serious natural disasters, accident disasters, public health events and social security events. In broad sense, all materials used for public emergencies can be called emergency materials, including materials for disaster prevention and preparedness before disasters, materials for disaster relief and rescue when emergencies occur, and materials used in the process of post-disaster reconstruction. In narrow sense, emergency supplies refer to the materials needed for disaster relief.

The classification of emergency supplies can be carried out from several angles. According to the nature of public emergencies, they can be divided into emergency supplies for natural disaster, accidents, public health events and social security events. According to the severity of emergencies, they can be divided into general emergency supplies, serious emergency supplies and emergent emergency supplies (Wang Feng etc., 2007). General emergency materials refer to those materials with low disaster relief difficulty and relatively small demand, which are conducive to reducing the loss of emergencies, such as environmental protection treatment and engineering equipment. Severity emergency materials refer to the materials that are very necessary and can play a very important role in reducing the losses caused by the emergency or reducing the scope of the event, such as protective materials. Emergent emergency materials refer to the necessary and extremely important materials that play a key role in the implementation of emergency rescue work, saving the life and property losses of the victims and stabilizing the situation, such as life rescue, life support, and temporary accommodation materials.

The *National Development and Reform Commission's Classified Catalogue of Key Emergency Support Materials* (〔2015〕No. 825) classifies emergency support materials into 13 categories according to their use, namely, protective articles, life rescue, life support, rescue and transportation, temporary accommodation, pollution cleaning, power fuel, engineering equipment, equipment and tools, lighting equipment, communication and broadcasting, transportation and engineering materials. The 13 categories of products covers 250 kinds of materials.

This chapter only covers materials for earthquake relief and flood prevention and relief. The earthquake relief materials can be divided into life-saving materials and living materials, such as life detection instruments, demolition tools, small lifting equipment, cold-proof blankets, quilts, unlined tents, cotton tents, sleeping bags, life-saving food, etc. Flood control and disaster relief materials include life-boats, life buoys, life jackets, fuel appliances, cold-proof blankets, quilts, unlined tents, cotton tents, sleeping bags, life-saving food, etc. To sum up, it is necessary to reserve both life-saving materials and living materials for both earthquake and flood prevention.

Different natural disasters require different emergency supplies. In order to deal with different types of sudden natural disasters, classification of emergency suppliesis is helpful in managing the inventory of emergency supplies, efficiently transport and allocate different types of supplies, and also facilitate the distribution of materials at the end.

## 6.5.2　Establishment of China's reserve center of disaster relief material

In response to major natural disasters, China issued the *Notice on the Establishment of a Central-level Disaster Relief Material Reserve System* in 1998, and after several revisions, and after several times' revisions, formulated the currently applicable

*Interim Measures for the Management of Central Emergency Rescue and Relief Material Reserves*, which regulate the procurement, storage, and allocation of central disaster relief materials.

In 1998, the Ministry of Civil Affairs and the Ministry of Finance jointly issued the *Notice on the Establishment of the Central-level Disaster Relief Material Reserve System*, which tentatively determined the quality of the central-level disaster relief materials Such asunlined tents and cotton tents, and set up eight storage sites throughout the country. The reserve materials of each storage site are as follows ( Table 1 ).

**Table 1    China's eight central-level disaster relief materials reserve sites ( 1998 )**

| Region | City | Disaster relief materials |
|---|---|---|
| Northeast China | Shenyang | Cotton tent, unlined tent |
| North China | Tianjin | unlined tent, unlined tent |
| Central China | Zhengzhou | unlined tent |
| Central China | Wuhan | unlined tent |
| Central China | Changsha | unlined tent |
| South China | Guangzhou | unlined tent |
| Southwest Region | Chengdu | unlined tent |
| Northwest Region | Xi'an | Cotton tent, unlined tent |

According to the "Guiding Opinions on Strengthening the Construction of Natural Disaster Relief Material Reserve System" jointly issued by nine central ministries and commissions including the Ministry of Civil Affairs, as of 2015, the Ministry of Civil Affairs has established 19 central disaster relief material reserve warehouses in the cities of Beijing, Tianjin, Shenyang, Harbin, Hefei, Fuzhou, Zhengzhou, Wuhan, Changsha, Nanning, Chongqing, Chengdu, Kunming, Lhasa, Weinan, Lanzhou, Golmud, Urumqi, and Kashgar. In terms of the layout, it meets the basic requirement of "within 12 hours after the occurrence of a natural disaster, the basic living conditions of the affected will receive preliminary assistance". According to the News Office of the State Council on July 25, 2023, as of July 2023, China has established 126 central level disaster relief material reserves in 31 provinces and cities.

In addition to central-level disaster relief reserve centers, there are 31 provinces, autonomous regions, municipalities directly under the Central Government, and Xinjiang Construction Corps have also established provincial-level and city-level disaster relief material reserve warehouses. For example, Yunnan Province has established the Yunnan Provincial Disaster Relief Material Reserve Center, which was officially put into use on May 11, 2010. The center has five large warehouses, which can meet the basic needs of 700000 disaster victims when they are filled with disaster relief materials at the same time. The center has a 4800 square meter apron, which can accommodate two large helicopters.

Whether from the perspective of economic or social benefits, the establishment of a sound disaster relief reserve center can quickly respond to the disaster and win valuable time and resources for saving people's lives and property losses. To sum up, the central-level disaster relief reserve centers established in China are mostly concentrated in the east and the south. Such a layout is very unfavorable for northwest provinces with weak emergency forces to cope with sudden natural disasters. This book suggests that new disaster relief material reserve centers should be added to strengthen the disaster relief capacity of western provinces or autonomous regions such as Gansu, Tibet, Qinghai and Xinjiang. At the same time, in addition to the central-level disaster relief material storage center, the number of emergency storage warehouses of governments below the provincial level should also be increased to form a complete layout of emergency logistics infrastructure (Wang Minxi, 2009).

## 6.5.3   Management and form of disaster relief materials reserve in China

The reserve management of disaster relief materials is very important. The geographical layout of the disaster relief materials reserve center, the storage layout, material type and reserve quantity in the warehouse of the reserve center, as well as the daily maintenance and effective management of emergency materials all play a very important role in the reserve management of disaster relief materials.

The reserve management method of emergency supplies can fully use for reference of the inventory control management method in enterprises' logistics management, and then scientifically customize the reserve scale. The scientific classification of emergency materials can refer to ABC classification method in enterprise logistics management ( Meng Can, Wang Changqiong, 2006 ). In reserve management, the inventory can be divided into three levels according to the type of emergency supplies or the type of certain natural disasters and the amount of funds occupied, namely, special important inventory ( Class A), general important inventory ( Class B) and unimportant inventory ( Class C). The inventory can be managed and controlled according to the level of importance, so as to effectively reduce the total amount of emergency supplies inventory and release a certain amount of funds, making emergency material inventory management more efficient.

In terms of the form of disaster relief material reserve, in addition to the physical reserve, the provincial and other local governments can also carry out the contract reserve by establishing the directory of disaster relief material manufacturers and signing agreements of the emergency procurement with the manufacturers. In the event of a natural disaster, the contract manufacturers can immediately put the disaster relief materials into production.

## 6.6　Transportation of natural disaster emergency materials

In case of earthquake or flood disaster, reasonable transportation planning is the premise to ensure smooth transportation of emergency materials. The planning principle of emergency material transportation is to give priority to ensuring the rapid arrival of disaster relief personnel and disaster prevention and relief materials. When evacuate the masses in an emergency is needed, it is necessary to ensure the smooth deployment of evacuation, evacuation vehicles and traffic roads. The planning of emergency materials transportation includes the planning of transportation channels, transportation modes and routes and transportation forces.

The construction of natural disaster emergency materials transportation system can be divided into normalization construction and construction of the system when disasters occur. Under normal conditions, perfect traffic and transportation channels should be established, and their ability to rapidly transform into emergency channels under emergency conditions should be improved. Without a perfect and effective transportation channel, it cannot meet the requirements of timelines for emergency logistics (Chen Hui, 2014). Therefore, at the beginning of the construction of the transportation channel, it is necessary to design the function of transforming it into an emergency channel. The big data analysis of historical natural disasters can be used in the planning of transportation channels, and multiple emergency transportation channels should be planned in areas where natural disasters are more likely to occur, so the impediment of the transportation resulting from the obstruction of single-line channels can be avoided. In addition, various ports, stations, warehouses and distribution centers should improve their normal traffic hub functions and emergency traffic hub functions. In addition to the construction of transportation channels and transportation hubs, unconventional standby channels such as aprons should also be built to meet the needs of emergency logistics and ensure the timely arrival of emergency supplies by air in case of road disruption (Chen Hui, 2014).

Reasonable transportation mode and route of emergency materials can greatly improve the transportation efficiency of disaster relief materials. The mode of transportation can be highway, railway, airlines, water way and other transportation modes. The planning of transportation mode and route should be based on the basic purpose of delivering disaster relief materials in the shortest time. At this time, the difference between emergency logistics and ordinary logistics is reflected. In emergency logistics transportation, the transportation cost cannot be considered, but improving efficiency is the only purpose. When an earthquake or flood disaster occurs, the transportation mode and route can be planned according to the actual road conditions. For example, the materials transported from other parts of the country to the periphery of the disaster area can follow the daily transportation mode and route because the roads, routes and waterways are smooth. When transporting materials from the periphery to the center of the disaster area, there will often be road interruption or even communication interruption due to flood or earthquake disasters. At this time, the transportation mode and route should be re-planned according to the road conditions. If the road is completely interrupted and vehicle transportation cannot be realized, air transportation is the preferred mode. If necessary, helicopter, unmanned aerial vehicle and other transportation modes can also be used. In order to improve the efficiency of disaster relief transportation, direct transportation should be adopted as far as possible. If conditions do not permit, multiple modes of transportation can be adopted.

Reasonable arrangements for transportation forces should be made. When a natural disaster occurs, all transportation forces should be arranged in the main principle of ensuring the smooth and safe arrival of relief supplies. Under the leadership of the government, the transportation capacity of water, land and air can be used. At this time, some conventional transportation capacity arrangements can also be changed. The transportation capacity of conventional routes, trains and long-distance buses can be temporarily requisitioned for disaster relief, or some non-emergency conventional transportation can be suspended to facilitate the transportation of disaster relief materials. The transportation department can also ensure the safe and efficient transportation of disaster relief materials by means of special handling, emergency handling and simplified procedures ( Wang Feng et al. , 2007 ). In the case of insufficient civil transport capacity, the government can also coordinate to use military transport equipment and routes and related facilities to complete the transportation of emergency supplies.

On the third day after the Wenchuan earthquake in 2008, the Ministry of Transport issued an emergency notice, requesting the provincial transportation authorities to fully cooperate in the transportation of Wenchuan earthquake relief materials and relief personnel. At that time, the transportation departments at all levels of aviation, railway and highway urgently mobilized planes, locomotives and vehicles, strengthened the combined transportation of railway and highway, and implemented the combined transportation mode of air and ground. Rescue materials from all parts of the country entered the disaster area through railway, air transportation and air delivery. In the disaster area, due to the damage of roads, some relief materials were transported into the disaster area by motorway. Disaster relief officers and soldiers also flew to the disaster area day and night. After arriving at the periphery of the disaster area by plane, they used vehicles, walking and other means to enter the center of the disaster area. Through the comprehensive use and reasonable arrangement of various transportation modes, the loss of life and property caused by the earthquake disaster has been greatly reduced.

On February 6, 2023, two 7. 8 magnitude earthquakes occurred in Türkiye and Syria. As of February 10, 288 Chinese rescue workers had flown to Türkiye for rescue. China's relief supplies arrived in Türkiye by air on February 8 and February 12 respectively. On February 8, the materials arrived with the relief workers were mainly food and warm goods, with a total weight of 20 tons. On February 12, more than 50 tons of relief materials, mainly relief tents in urgent need, arrived in Türkiye by air. The rapid arrival of rescue personnel and materials reflects China's traditional virtue and international humanitarian spirit, and also reflects the ability of China's efficient emergency logistics operation.

Emergency material transportation can also give play to the professional advantages of logistics enterprises, adopt the professional technology of industry experts, andthen improve the efficiency of emergency logistics transportation. When a natural disaster occurs, although the government is the leading force, it can organize and coordinate all forces to carry out disaster relief. The government departments can mobilize and unite logistics enterprises, adopt the suggestions of experts in logistics, let enterprises and experts participate in the formulation of emergency material transportation plan, participate in the transportation, give full play to the professional advantages, and improve the efficiency of emergency logistics transportation.

With the help of modern scientific and technological means such as big data and information network, smart emergency logistics can be built and the efficiency of it can be improved. For the transportation of emergency logistics, various high-tech means such as 5G and other modern communication technology, modern network technology, GPS/GIS positioning technology, database system and so on can also be used to realize real-time monitoring and dispatching of vehicles in the transportation fleet, to realize positioning and remote management of the quantity, type and location of emergency materials, to realize intelligent emergency logistics, and to improve the efficiency of emergency logistics.

Based on the principle of "seven priorities and one free" "green channel" and "green pass" for emergency logistics should be provided. "Seven priorities" refer to the principle of priority planning, priority arrangement, priority transportation, priority entry, priority parking, priority release and priority loading and unloading in order to ensure the smooth flow of emergency logistics transportation routes at all times. "One free" means the principle of free passage for emergency materials transportation (Chen Hui, 2014). In case of natural disasters, the government departments shall cooperate with relevant departments to provide special access for emergency transportation. When emergency transportation vehicles pass through customs, checkpoints, cross-provincial checkpoints and other places with "green passes", the inspection procedures should be simplified, the inspection time should be shortened and then the vehicles can pass quickly. Under the leadership of the government, we will crack down on local protectionism such as setting up checkpoints and toll stations privately to ensure the smooth the transportation of emergency supplies.

## 6.7   Distribution of natural disaster emergency materials

The purpose of distribution of disaster relief materials, on the one hand, is to put the living materials on the market to meet the needs of the people in the disaster area, and on the other hand, it means the distribution the free disaster relief materials to the victims.

For the market launch of living supplies, the government can grasp the market demand through market monitoring and warning, and put the materials most needed by the people into the market. In terms of distribution, the government can coordinate experienced logistics enterprises to temporarily complete the distribution task, or sign a distribution agreement with logistics enterprises under normal conditions. Once an emergency occurs, the enterprise can quickly undertake the task of distributing emergency materials. These enterprises often have rich experience, fixed transport capacity, mature supply chain network, etc., and can effectively complete the market launch of such goods in a short period of time.

The distribution principle of free disaster relief materials is "first urgent, then slow, and the key points highlighted". The distribution of materials should be arranged as a whole and the materials should be used reasonably ( Wang Minxi, 2009 ). The Ministry of Civil Affairs of the People's Republic of China issued the *Regulations on the Reception, Distribution, Use and Management of Disaster Relief Materials* in as early as 1991, which stipulates that food, vegetables, and daily necessities must be distributed to the victims who lack such goods. Drinks and nutrition should only be distributed to the elderly, children or patients. The drugs and medical devices must be handed over to the medical units in the disaster area for unified management. For building materials, priority should be given to the repair of houses in nursing homes, welfare homes and other institutions, followed by the repair of houses of the homeless victims. Vehicles and communication tools must be uniformly distributed and used by the civil affairs department, and shall not be distributed to individuals. The content of the regulation fully reflects the principle of "first urgent, then slow, and the key points highlighted". Althought this regulation has been abolished by the *the Notice of the Ministry of Civil Affairs on the Abolition of Some Civil Affairs Regulations and Normative Decuments* ( 2000 ), the principle of "first urgent, then slow, and the key points highlighted" has always been applicable to various types of emergency disaster relief work.

For the free materials distributed to individuals, the previous practice is that the government staff and rescuing traps directly distribute them to the masses, but this practice is not efficient when disasters actually occur. This book suggests that the method of distribution can be implemented at different levels, such as from the municipal government to the county level, from the county level to the village level government, and then each village government subdivides the whole village into units according to certain rules. Each unit designates a person in charge to distribute free materials, so that the primary unit can count the number of victims and distribute materials according to the number to avoid material waste.

The places where free materials are distributed should generally be set up in open areas such as stadiums, schools, village squares, etc. , and the queuing routes should be well planned. The entrance and exit should adopt two routes to avoid crowding and stampede when receiving materials.

# Chapter 7　China's Emergency Logistics System for Public Health Emergencies

In the past decade, China has been affected by sudden major public health events such as SARS virus and COVID-19 pandemic. Sudden public health events are usually unpredictable and often cause very serious harm to people's lives and social stability. Therefore, China has formulated the National Emergency Plan for Public Health Emergencies as early as 2006. The former Ministry of Health also required local governments at all levels to formulate local emergency plans for public health events according to the actual situation of each region, and to respond quickly and actively to emergencies. In response to major public health emergencies, the efficient allocation of medical resources and medical personnel can win valuable time. This chapter discusses the management and organization of emergency logistics in China under public health emergencies, the storage of emergency medical materials, the transportation of medical personnel, and the transportation, distribution of medical materials from the perspective of the construction of emergency logistics system in response to public health emergencies. This chapter introduces the measures taken by a city in southern China to ensure the supply of living materials during the prevention and control of COVID-19 pandemic, which provides valuable experience for other cities in the country. The construction of emergency logistics information system in case of public health emergencies is similar to the construction of emergency logistics information system in case of natural disasters, which will not be discussed in this chapter.

# 7.1  Definition, classification and characteristics of public health emergencies

Wang Feng et al. (2007) defined public health emergencies as infectious disease outbreaks that have occurred or may occur and have caused or may cause major losses to public health, group infectious diseases of unknown causes, major food poisoning and occupational poisoning, and other public health emergencies. Zhou Xuankai (2006) defined sudden public health events as major infectious diseases, group diseases of unknown causes, major food and occupational poisoning, and events affecting serious public health that occur suddenly and cause or may cause serious damage to the public health.

The classification of sudden public health events can be divided into following six categories. ①major infectious disease, ②group disease of unknown cause, ③major food poisoning and occupational poisoning, ④new infectious disease, ⑤group vaccination and drug reaction, ⑥casualties and disease caused by major environmental pollution accident, nuclear and radiation accident, biological, chemical and nuclear radiation caused by terrorists, as well as other events affecting public health.

Characteristics of public health emergencies are as following: ①Public health emergencies are usually unpredictable, and some events may occur without any signs. ②The cause is complex. Public health emergencies may be caused by natural disasters, traffic accidents, environmental pollution, and sometimes animal transmitted diseases. ③The transmission speed is fast. A sudden infectious disease may spread rapidly in a short period of time due to the large population mobility in modern society. ④There are various types of public health emergencies. Sudden public health events can be sudden infectious diseases, major poisoning events, food safety events, drug safety events, health and safety events caused by major environmental pollution, which may involve in all fields of society. ⑤They may do serious harm to society. Once a public health and safety event occurs, it is likely to cause severe cases or death, and the scope of the event is large, which may cause severe group cases or death, and therefore will cause social instability events.

## 7.2    Overview of emergency logistics measures in response to major public health emergencies in China

During the spread of the SARS virus, the Chinese government has also taken a number of measures to ensure the smooth flow of logistics and transportation. For example, on May 6,2003, the Ministry of Public Security issued the "five prohibitions". It is not allowed to block road traffic on the grounds of preventing SARS. Traffic control is not allowed at the provincial boundary of the highway. It is not allowed to set up blocks on the road to hinder the normal passage of vehicles. It is not allowed to persuade the normal driving vehicles to return. The implementation of this policy has played a key role in ensuring the smooth iransportation of emergency supplies during the period of the spread SARS. The transportation of emergency materials also played a great role in fighting against SARS. For example,on May 6,2003, the State Council allocated materials to fight against SARS to assist Hong Kong. More than 80000 pieces of protective clothing were allocated, and the weight of materials exceeded 145000 tons. The materials were transported by air. The plane took off from Hangzhou, Zhcjiang to Shenzhen, and from Huanggang Port to Hong Kong. Both air transport and shipping were smooth. Efficient transportation has made great contributions to the anti-epidemic work in Hong Kong.

During the COVID-19 pandematic, many provinces in China issued various policies to ensure the production,supply and transportation of emergency supplies.

In the early days of the outbreak of COVID-19, it was the Chinese New Year. Many employees of manufacturers of epidemic prevention materials sacrificed their time reuniting with their families and worked overtime to produce medical masks and protective clothing, which ensured the supply of epidemic prevention materials. Some provinces and cities have issued various policies to ensure the smooth transportation of emergency supplies, which mainly include three categories: important agricultural products, important life support products, and important epidemic prevention and medical supplies. Several provincial governments have ordered the Transportation Commission and the Public Security Bureau to jointly issue a "pass" to provide quick inspection and "green passage" policy for emergency supplies and vehicles. Some provinces and cities have also announced the material security telephone number to the whole society, and citizens can track information about the material supply through the telophone. The central and local governments have issued a number of policies to give priority to the transportation of emergency supplies from all aspects.

# 7.3　Modes of public health emergency management in China

According to the *National Overall Emergency Plan for Public Emergencies and the National Emergency Plan for Public Health Emergencies*, the management and organization for major health emergencies in the country is under the unified leadership of the State Council, and the National Health Commission (formerly the Ministry of Health) is responsible for organizing, coordinating, managing and responding to public health emergencies in the country. The important responsibilities of the National Health Commission are to formulate and organize the implementation of the disease prevention and control plan, the national immunization plan and the intervention measures for the public health problems that seriously endanger the people's health, and formulate and monitor the list of quarantinable infectious diseases. It is also responsible for organizing and guiding the prevention and control of public health emergencies, and medical rescue of various public emergencies. When a major public health event occurs nationwide, the National Health Commission is responsible for the prevention, control, diagnosis and treatment of the disease. If necessary, the State Council will establish the national public health emergency headquarters.

In case of local public emergencies at all levels, the local government shall lead the health administrative departments and epidemic prevention agencies at all levels, and be responsible for organizing, coordinating and responding to the public health emergencies in its own administrative region. If necessary, the local government should establish provincial or municipal emergency command departments for public health emergencies.

The national and local public health emergency headquarters at all levels are responsible for the unified command and leadership of emergencies and making major decisions to deal with emergencies.

Under normal conditions, the Medical Emergency Department (formerly the Health Emergency Office) and the health departments of local governments at all levels are responsible for the management of prevention, monitoring and warning of public health emergencies. Under normal conditions, the National Health Commission and local governments at all levels can establish expert advisory committees to help make decisions and advice on the response and prevention of public health events. In the event of an emergency, the emergency headquarters can set up an expert group to provide decision-making consultation and cooperate with governments at all levels to deal with public health emergencies.

In the event of public health emergencies, in addition to the epidemic prevention and control measures of the Health Commission, the state and local governments should also ensure the supply and transportation of emergency supplies, including living supplies and medical supplies, under the premise of prevention and control of public health emergencies. At this time, it is necessary for the state and local governments to work together with multiple departments across the country. The Ministry of Commerce, the Development and Reform Commission, the Ministry of Transport, the Ministry of Emergency Management and other departments under the State Council need to coordinate and organize various departments of emergency material supply and transportation to achieve the efficiency of logistics and minimize the losses caused by public health emergencies.

# 7.4 Reserve of emergency supplies for public health emergencies

Emergency supplies refer to the material guarantee necessary in the whole process of responding to public emergencies, including serious natural disasters, accident disasters, public health events and social security events. The concept and classification of emergency supplies have been detailed in Chapter 6, and will not be stated here.

There are many kinds of emergency supplies involved in public health emergencies. This chapter focuses on the storage, transportation and distribution of medical supplies and the transportation of medical personnel. Different public health emergencies require different emergency medical supplies. In order to deal with different types of public health emergencies, emergency medical supplies are managed and stored by classification, which can effectively manage the inventory and efficiently transport and allocate different types of medical supplies.

## 7.4.1   China's reserve system of medical supplies for public health emergencies

The reserve of emergency supplies studied in this section mainly involves the reserve of medical supplies and life support supplies. Strengthening the management of medical reserves can not only ensure the adequacy of public medication under normal conditions, but also actively respond to public health emergencies, which plays a very important role in maintaining social stability.

According to *China's Measures for the Administration of National Pharmaceutical Reserves* (*revised in 2021*), China's pharmaceutical reserves include government reserves and enterprise reserves. The government's medical reserves are divided into central and local, medical reserves (province, autonomous region and municipality directly under the menagement of the Central Government). A security system capable of responding to various public emergencies, and accordingly effective market supply should be established. Enterprise reserve is the enterprise inventory established according to the production and operation status of pharmaceutical products. The management of government medical reserves is jointly managed by the Ministry of Industry and Information Technology, the National Development and Reform Commission, the Ministry of Finance, the National Health and Health Commission and the State Drug Administration. In case of public health emergencies, in principle, the local medical reserve is responsible for the supply of local medical products. When the local medical reserve is insufficient, it can request support from the central medical reserve. The central medical reserve has the right to use other local medical reserves with compensation.

## 7.4.2 The form of medical reserve for public health emergencies in China

Public health emergencies, whether they are major infectious diseases, mass diseases of unknown causes, major food and occupational poisoning, mass vaccination reactions or drug reactions, or casualties and epidemics caused by major environmental pollution accidents, nuclear accidents and radiation accidents, terrorist events of biological, chemical, nuclear radiation, and natural disasters, the most important task is timely save the lives of the victims, timely prevent the spread of the events and reduce the scope of impact of the event as soon as possible. Therefore, the types of medical reserves can be divided into following four aspects. Drugs and equipment for the inspection, detection and investigation of epidemiology, isolation and protective articles for patients with infectious diseases, drugs, diagnostic reagents and instruments needed for the treatment and disposal of infected patients (Wang Feng, 2007).

According to the provisions of *China's Measures for the Administration of National Pharmaceutical Reserves* (*Revised in 2021*), the form of government reserve of pharmaceutical products is a combination of physical reserves, production capacity reserves and technical reserves. The reserve task is undertaken by qualified pharmaceutical enterprises or health institutions. In addition, there must be a certain amount of information and capital reserves.

Some medical supplies with predictable demand shall be stored in physical goods. Physical storage refers to the storage of medical supplies in the warehouse of each medical enterprise as required in the form of physical goods. When an emergency occurs, the enterprise provides medical supplies to the disaster areas at the first time according to the relevant agreement. The advantage of entity reserce is easy to call, and can be put into use immediately when an emergency occurs, but its disadvantages are also obvious. On the one hand, some drugs that are not commonly used may be wasted due to expiration. Or some drugs are stored as reserve drugs, causing some drugs on the market not to be effectively circulated. On the other hand, the storage conditions of drugs are strict, and the cost of inventory management is high. Therefore, in addition to physical reserves, there are other forms of reserves to supplement.

The shortage of physical reserves can be supplemented with production capacity reserves, which is suitable for the special medical products responding to the major disaster or epidemic situation with uncertain demand. Production capacity reserve refers to a form of reserve in which the production capacity can be guaranteed by ensuring the stability of its production line, production technology and supply chain. The production and emergency supply can be organized according to the needs of the disaster or epidemic situation when necessary. The production capacity reserve has certain requirements for the production capacity and production equipment of the drug manufacturing enterprises. The enterprises need to ensure the normal production capacity, and can also undertake the emergency drug production in case of public health emergencies.

The government can cooperate with research institutions to jointly implement technology reserves. Technical reserve refers to the development and storage of production and research technology of some potential epidemic drugs without normal demand by the government through supporting the construction of its research platform. When necessary, this technology can be rapidly converted into medical products when it is needed by the epidemic. The technology reserve is applicable to the production of certain special drugs by rapidly transforming production technology into productivity when a public health emergency occurs and a certain area is in short supply of drugs. The advantage of technology reserve is that it will not cause the waste of physical objects or production lines, but its disadvantage is that the production technology may fall behind due to the development of epidemic situation and other events, resulting in technology waste, and also waste of the human, financial and material resources invested in technology research and development.

With the help of big data, internet technology and other means, information reserve can be established. Information reserve is to establish an information system of medical reserves so as to collect and master the structural layout, production capacity, inventory scale, and other information of the national pharmaceutical enterprises, realize the sharing of information resources, and provide medication guarantee for emergency response (Yuan Han Shibi *et al.*, 2018). The advantage of information storage is that it can strengthen the information communication among government departments at all levels, among pharmaceutical enterprises, and among governments and enterprises, so that the government can grasp the information of relevant medical supplies across the country, and help to quickly grasp the inventory of drugs in case of public health emergencies, and immediately make use of them. Its disadvantage lies in the need for special personnel to carry out information statistics and update information in real time. If the information is not updated in time, the delayed information will bring inconvenience to the response to emergencies and even mislead the formulation of response strategies.

The government reserves funds for emergency medical supplies as the last guarantee. Capital reserve means that the government reserves the funds used to purchase drugs for public health emergencies when making the annual budget. The capital reserve is applicable when the physical reserve, production capacity reserve and technical reserve cannot meet the current public health emergencies, the government can start the fund to purchase or produce the required drugs. The biggest disadvantage is that if there is no physical reserve, technical reserve or production capacity reserve, capital reserves cannot fulfill its role to buy the drugs needed to deal with emergencies.

Each of the above forms of medical material reserves has its own advantages or disadvantages. In case of public health emergencies, various forms of medical material reserves may be launched at the same time maximize the advantages of various forms of reserves and provide sufficient medical supplies for responding to public health emergencies.

### 7. 4. 3    Suggestions on improving China's medical reserve mechanism in response to public health emergencies

Firstly, in terms of reserve management and guarantee mechanism, we should emphasize the cooperation mechanism of multi-sectoral cooperation, which is under the responsibility of the National Health Commission. The Ministry of Science and Technology, the National Development and Reform Commission, the Ministry of Commerce, the Food and Drug Administration, the Medical Insurance Bureau and other departments should implement the linkage mechanism, and work together in terms of physical reserves and technical reserves. The National Health Commission proposed the central medicine reserve directory according to the needs of public health emergency and other aspects. The Ministry of Industry and Information Technology and other departments will provide guidance on the policies and scale of local medical reserves. The local and central departments will complement each other to form a centralized and unified national medical reserve system.

Secondly, in terms of physical reserves, the central and local governments coordinate scientifically and dynamically to adjust the inventory of drug reserves, and use the internationally-used exploration of emerging technology and other methods to develop an appropriate inventory of drug reserves in combination with the disease risk prediction model, expert evaluation, domestic and foreign intelligence information and the current capacity of responding to public health emergency ( Zhao Rui *et al.* , 2020 ). In terms of physical reserve management, it can be managed according to the type of risk, such as drug reserve in case of sudden influenza, avian influenza, SARS, novel coronavirus pneumonia and other major epidemic diseases, or drug reserve in case of sudden food poisoning events, sudden occupational poisoning events, and sudden mass vaccination response events. Different drug reserve directories can be developed according to different risk types, and various kinds of drugs and devices are stored in the relevant medical institutions. In case of public health emergencies, these drugs and devices can be quickly transferred according to the inventory without waiting for purchase. However, the biggest problem of physical storage is that the cost of storage and inventory management is high, and it may also cause waste due to the expiration of drugs.

Thirdly, in terms of technical reserves, the technical reserves of medical supplies can effectively solve the problem of waste of expired drugs. The government can sign contracts with scientific research institutions and pharmaceutical manufacturing enterprises to research special drugs in advance and store the technology in response to public health emergencies. Therefore, the government can encourage and support research institutions and pharmaceutical enterprises to carry out research, development and production of drugs in response to public health emergencies in terms of policies and funds. In addition to scientific research institutions and pharmaceutical enterprises, the government can also encourage universities with research foundation to carry out research of life safety and biosafety medicine (Zhao Rui *et al.*, 2020).

## 7.5   Supply and transportation of emergency supplies for public health emergencies

When a public health event occurs, the emergency logistics transportation usually involves the transportation of drugs, medical devices, protective articles, and medical personnel participating in the rescue.

In order to ensure the supply of emergency supplies after public health emergencies, under normal conditions, we should make full use of information technology means, establish a health information sharing platform, and monitoring and early warning of medical information. In order to ensure the timely supply of emergency medical supplies in the event of public health emergencies, under normal conditions, the national health departments, provincial health departments and local health departments should establish a joint information platform to share medical information through big data, information technology platform and other means, and to master the medical reserves, hospital size, and medical staff of local health departments. At the same time, the supply of emergency medical materials can be monitored through the information reflected by big data. In the event of an emergency, the national health department or a provincial health department can use the information sharing platform to urgently mobilize medical supplies and medical personnel from all parts of the country. Various mechanisms such as physical reserves, technical reserves and production capacity reserves can be fully used so as to ensure timely and accurate response to drug demand and to public health emergencies now. During the period of COVID-19 pandemic, residents in some cities rushed to buy masks, disinfectants and other materials. At this time, relevant departments should give early warning in time in view of market monitoring, and quickly carry out logistics emergency preparedness for material storage and supply of such material.

In the transportation of emergency materials, the Ministry of Health and the Ministry of Transport jointly issued the *Traffic Emergency Provisions* for Public Health Emergencies on November 25, 2003, which clearly states that the principle of emergency materials transportation in the event of public health emergencies is to give priority to the groups of people responding to emergencies, epidemic prevention personnel, medical personnel, disinfections supplies, medical aid equipment and instruments, and ensure the smooth and timely transportation of such goods.

Modern scientific and technological means and advanced logistics technology can be fully used to improve the transportation efficiency of emergency medical materials.

When transporting emergency medical materials, it is necessary to make full use of GPS positioning technology, 5G mobile communication technology, RFID ( Radio Frequency Identification) technology and other positioning technology and logistics technology to carry out real-time supervision on the vehicles and drugs transported, and improve the efficiency of material transportation.

In terms of transportation mode, a combination of multiple modes can be adopted to shorten the transportation time of emergency medical materials. The mode of transportation of emergency medical materials can be highway, railway, airline, water route and other modes. Whatever mode is adopted, the basic purpose is to deliver medical materials and personnel to the destination in the shortest time. In order to improve the efficiency of disaster relief transportation, the priority should be given to direct transportation. If it is impossible to use direct transportation, multiple modes can be adopted. For example, in January 2020, the COVID-19 pandemic in Wuhan City of Hubei Province, showed a trend of rapid spread. The national medical team rushed to Wuhan urgently. The railway and aviation departments arranged a large amount of transportation capacity for the medical personnel and materials to Hubei Province to ensure that the medical personnel and materials arrived in Wuhan safely and as quickly as possible. On January 25, on the first day of the first lunar month in China, nearly 300 medical teams from Zhejiang Province and Jiangsu Province needed to travel to Wuhan by high-speed trains. China Railway Group quickly arranged the medical teams to travel from Hangzhou and Nanjing respectively to Hefei Province, and then transfer to Wuhan. During the transfer at Hefei South Railway Station, 52 railway cadres and employees formed a team to transfer 12 tons of medical materials carried by the medical team in time, and the transfer was completed in only 40 minutes. From January to late March 2020, about 12000 medical and rescue workers have been transported by the national railway. More than 300000 tons of prevention and control support materials have been shipped to Hubei Province . In terms of air transport, a total of more than 4400 aircraft have taken off in Wuhan, and

36000 medical and nursing personnel have landed here. Such priority and efficient airline and rail way transport arrangements provide the greatest convenience for the prevention and control of the epidemic and treatment of infected people, which also reflects the cohesiveness of "support from all sides when one side is in trouble" and the determination of the people of the whole country to fight against the COVID-19 pandemic.

The "green traffic channel" should be opened to ensure the smooth transportation of medical materials. The government departments shall cooperate with relevant departments to provide special channels for emergency transportation of medical materials. When emergency transportation vehicles pass through customs, checkpoints, cross-provincial checkpoints, health quarantine stations and other places with "green passes", the inspection procedures should be simplified, the inspection time should be shortened and then the vehicles can pass quickly. The transportation department can also coordinate with local relevant departments to complete the transportation of emergency medical materials and personnel through the requisition of vehicles, personnel and equipment.

In the case of major infectious diseases, the transportation of medical materials should not only be efficient, but also be safe. Therefore, the aircraft, ships, vehicles and trains that are responsible for the transportation of emergency materials should be cleaned and disinfected before entering the epidemic area. The transportation staff should receive health and safety knowledge training and be equipped with corresponding protective tools before go to work. When the materials arrive at the epidemic area, they shall be kept still, disinfected according to the requirements of the health department. With the leaving from the pandemic area, the vehicles shall be thoroughly cleaned and disinfected again, and if necessary, the transport personnel and vehicles should be isolated.

# 7.6   Distribution of emergency supplies for public health emergencies

Public health emergencies often involve major infectious diseases. In this case, the distribution of medical supplies from non-affected area to affected area is suitable for non-contact distribution. Large goods can be distributed within a city using unmanned aerial vehicles, unmanned vehicles and other transportation equipment, and goods within epidemic areas can also be distributed by robots instead of people. In the case that contactless distribution cannot be realized, for example, the medical materials transported by large vehicles need to be sent to a hospital or the epidemic area, a buffer zone can be set up. A buffer zone can be set up between the epidemic area and the non-epidemic area. After the transportation materials arrive, special personnel taking protective measure will unload them, and then they will be transported to the epidemic area for use after they have been kept in the buffer zone for a certain period of time.

For the distribution of protective materials for residents in the prevention and control area, the direct selling method can be adopted. The sellers coordinate with Property Management Office in the community to set up vending machines in the community and sell protective materials such as masks and gloves. For the distribution of living materials for residents in epidemic prevention and control areas, contactless distribution can be adopted. The courier deposits the goods purchased by each household through the network platform in the shared cabinets, and the residents arrange their own time to pick up goods according to a special code, thus avoiding the risk of gathering of the residents to pick up goods together at the specified time by the courier. In the medium and long term, with the development of technology, the demand for non-contact services will greatly increase, and new business forms such as intelligent express cabinet and robot distribution will usher in new development opportunities (Chen Jingyu, Zhang Li, 2020).

Due to the urgency of public health events, the government often needs to coordinate transportation enterprises and cooperate with them to let them participate in the terminal distribution of medical supplies, which can greatly improve the efficiency of distribution.

For the distribution of free protective materials and medical supplies in the epidemic-stricken area, the government can also mobilize the public to participate widely. On the premise of protecting themselves well, community workers, community grid members and volunteers can participate in the distribution of medical supplies. In the case of sufficient manpower available, the distribution of protective materials can be distributed by grid personnel by building and by unit. The head of each residential building should play a role at this time to coordinate the distribution for the residents in the building.

# 7.7　Typical case-emergency supply practice during the period of prevention and control of COVID-19 pandemic

The material storage, transportation and distribution involved in the previous sections of this chapter are all medical materials. However, in the event of a major public health event, the epidemic area needs not only medical materials but also living material. Therefore, this section studies how to ensure the supply of living materials for residents in the event of a major public health event.

At the beginning of 2020, the novel coronavirus epidemic broke out in China, first be found in Wuhan, Hubei Province, and then in many provinces across the country. In order to control the spread of the epidemic, different epidemic prevention and control measures have been taken everywhere, including the isolation of confirmed cases, the isolation of communities with confirmed cases, and the closure of a community or even a city, which put the supply of living materials to the test. This section discusses the supply policy of domestic materials at the national level under the epidemic prevention and control policy, and the practical case of the supply of domestic materials in a city in the south of China.

The gist of the meeting of the Standing Committee of the Political Bureau of the CPC Central Committee on February 3, 2020 required that "while strengthening epidemic prevention and control, efforts should be made to keep production and life stable and orderly". The meeting stressed the need to ensure the supply of vegetables, meat, eggs, milk and grain, strengthen the allocation of materials and market supply, and ensure the supply of coal, electricity, oil, gas and heat.

In May 2021, the Department of Market Operation and Consumption Promotion of the Ministry of Commerce formulated the *Handbook of Market Supply Guarantee for Daily Necessities* (2021 Edition), which provides important reference for the guarantee scope, consumption measurement, information system construction, reserve management, supply guarantee means, of daily necessities.

In December 2021, the Ministry of Commerce and the National Development and Reform Commission jointly issued the Guidelines for the Support of Living Materials for the Prevention and Control of COVID-19 pandemic (No. 1053 in 2021). The guide emphasizes that the emergency monitoring, production scheduling, material transportation, storage and delivery of grain and oil, meat, vegetables, convenience food, energy and other living materials should be well coordinated, and the daily needs of the people should also be met when the cantrol and prevention of the pandemic was underway. The guide puts forward suggestions on measures to ensure the supply of living materials, smooth material transportation, and efficient terminal distribution.

In combination with the above two important documents, a city in the south of China responded positively, providing valuable experience for the emergency supply of living materials in other cities in China. The main practices of the city are as follows.

(1) Start emergency response quickly.

The leading group of the city grasped the spirit of the General Secretary's speech, and quickly held a meeting to arrange the supply of living materials in response to the phenomenon of rushing to buy masks, vegetables and epidemic prevention materials since the outbreak of the epidemic. According to the documents of the State Council, the Ministry of Commerce and provinces and cities on epidemic prevention and control, the meeting formulated targeted response measures, and established an organization to ensure that personnel are in place and the tasks of each department are clarified.

(2) Establish an efficient emergency system.

The city has set up a special work group to ensure the emergency supplies. The mayor serves as the head of the special working group. Five groups are concluded, namely, the comprehensive group, the supply guarantee group, the coordination group, the supervision group and the county and district groups. The tasks and responsibilities of each group are clear, and they cooperate to work together.

(3) Improve the emergency monitoring mechanism.

The city has carried out daily data monitoring on the supply of living materials in all districts and counties of the city, the supply of food markets and a number of key living material support units in the city, so as to comprehensively grasp the operation of living materials in the city. According to the detection of daily data, the special working group studies and judges the city's material demand, and adjusts the reserve and supply policies in time.

(4) Promote emergency supply guarantee actively.

In order to ensure the smooth production, sales and supply of agricultural products in the city, the city has taken measures from various aspects. Firstly, regular meetings of special work groups are held every day, and each group will report the specific situation. Secondly, the government signs agreements with key supply guarantee enterprises to ensure the supply of living materials in place. In addition, it cooperates with Traffic Police Detachment of Public Security Bureau to issue green passes to ensure the smooth transportation of living materials.

(5) Ensure emergency reserve supply.

In order to ensure people's livelihood, the city has formulated a detailed reserve plan. The emergency reserve mainly includes vegetables and meat products. The form of reserve is government reserve and market reserve. The total amount of vegetables and meat stored by the government can support the whole city more than 7 days each. The form of government reserve is to arrange key enterprises to reserve. The market reserves more than 3000 tons of vegetables and meat.

In order to avoid the phenomenon of panic buying, the municipal government has arranged delivery points of government reserve meat in many large supermarkets, and the pork price is 10% lower than the market price to supply the citizens, so as to ensure that the citizens' demand for meat products is met.

The government should also assign tasks to key supply guarantee enterprises, requiring them to supply certain types and quantities of tommodities at the given time analplane according to the requirements of the special work group for supply guarantee. The enterprise should also report the situation of supply guarantee to the work group every day, so that the work group can adjust the reserve and supply plan in time.

During the period of public health emergencies, namely the COVID-19, the city took various measures to ensure adequate supplies of living materials, ensure the normal production and life of people during the epidemic, and provide good experience for other provinces and cities across the country in terms of supplies.

# 参考文献

[1] 陈方建. 对健全我国应急物流体系的几点思考 [J]. 物流技术, 2008, 27 (10): 29 – 32.

[2] 陈慧. 我国应急物流体系存在的主要问题与优化建议 [J]. 中国流通经济, 2014 (8): 20 – 24.

[3] 陈镜羽, 张立. 疫情背景下应急生活保障物资末端物流配送模式研究 [J]. 物流科技, 2020 (10): 47 – 50.

[4] 陈媛, 李婧. 应急物流系统初探 [J]. 中小企业管理与科技, 2011 (11): 141.

[5] 冯海江, 张卫刚, 彭春露. 面向突发性自然灾害的应急物流配送系统研究 [J]. 中国物流与采购, 2010 (6): 76 – 77.

[6] 高东椰, 刘新华. 浅论应急物流 [J]. 中国物流与采购, 2003 (23): 22 – 23.

[7] 高丽英. 应急物流与军事物流: 准军事化物流系统的建设与构想 [J]. 中国物流与采购, 2003 (23): 21.

[8] 高晓英. 日本大地震对我国应急物流的启示 [J]. 江苏商论, 2011 (6): 77 – 78.

[9] 葛全胜. 中国自然灾害风险综合评估初步研究 [M]. 北京: 科学出版社, 2008.

[10] 何明珂. 应急物流的成本损失无处不在 [J]. 中国物流与采购, 2003 (23): 18 – 19.

[11] 黄崇福. 自然灾害基本定义的探讨 [J]. 自然灾害学报, 2009 (5): 41 – 50.

[12] 黄定政. 应急物流教程 [M]. 北京: 中国财富出版社, 2018.

[13] 黄剑炜, 贺电, 杨朝江. 持续推进我国应急物流体系建设落地见效 [J]. 快运物流, 2021 (4): 13 – 14.

[14] 姜旭, 胡雪芹, 王雅琪. 社会化应急物流管理体系构建: 日本经验与启示 [J]. 物流研究, 2021 (1): 14 – 20.

[15] 黎红，陈御钗. 物流设施设备基础与实训 [M]. 北京：机械工业出版社，2021.

[16] 李睿，佘廉. 枢纽城市紧急事态下应急物流系统研究 [J]. 中国管理科学，2007
    (15)：737 - 739.

[17] 李艳琴，张立毅，郭纯生. 谈科学发展观指导下的我国应急物流体系建设 [J].
    商业时代，2010 (3)：28 - 29.

[18] 刘晶芳. 我国应急物流系统法律保障机制研究 [J]. 研究与探讨，2014 (12)：
    25 - 27.

[19] 刘同娟，马相国. 应急物资物流方案的选择与优化 [J]. 商业时代，2013
    (30)：40 - 41.

[20] 孟参，王长琼. 应急物流系统运作流程分析及其管理 [J]. 物流技术，2006
    (9)：15 - 17.

[21] 孟祥娟，许耀坤. 浅谈应急物流的特点及物资分类 [J]. 市场周刊，2016 (9)：
    18 - 19.

[22] 欧忠文，王会云，等. 应急物流 [J]. 重庆大学学报，2004 (3)：164 - 167.

[23] 秦星红，魏光兴，周靖. 基于甲型 H1N1 流感疫情的应急物流体系流程研究
    [J]. 重庆交通大学学报（社科版），2010 (2)：23 - 27.

[24] 尚希桥. 我国应急物流法律保障体系的构建 [J]. 物流技术，2017，36 (6)：
    24 - 26.

[25] 孙永春. 我国应急物流体系的构建与优化研究 [D]. 兰州：兰州交通大学，2013.

[26] 王亮，党伟涛，朱琳琳等. 基于新冠肺炎疫情的应急物流特点与保障机制分析
    [J]. 青海交通科技，2020 (6)：15 - 19.

[27] 王敏晰. 基于供应链思想的应急物流体系的构建及管理，铁道运输与经济 [J].
    2009，31 (12)：61 - 65.

[28] 王丰，姜玉宏，王进. 应急物流 [M]. 北京：中国物资出版社，2007.

[29] 王旭坪，傅克俊，胡祥培. 应急物流系统及其快速反应机制研究 [J]. 中国软科
    学，2005 (6)：127 - 131.

[30] 汪莹，樊九林. 应急物流管理 [M]. 北京：应急管理出版社，2022.

[31] 韦琦. 面向自然灾害的应急物流信息系统构建 [J]. 中南财经政法大学学报，
    2010 (4)：60 - 64.

[32] 郗蒙浩. 应急物流管理 [M]. 北京：应急管理出版社，2021.

[33] 谢如鹤，宗岩. 论我国应急物流体系的建立 [J]. 广州大学学报（社会科学

版），2005（11）：55－58.

[34] 徐慧敏. 美日灾害事件应急物流体系法律保障机制分析及对我国的启示 [J].
物流技术，2014（5）：64－67.

[35] 薛莹莹. 突发事件中的应急社会动员机制研究 [J]. 现代商贸工业，2018
（30）：133－134.

[36] 杨山峰. 基于突发事件救援的我国应急物流保障机制构建 [J]. 商业经济研究，
2020（17）：89－92.

[37] 叶峻. 协同发展论与科学发展观 [J]. 鲁东大学学报（哲学社会科学版），2011
（5）：16－19.

[38] 余朵苟，何世伟. 应急物流体系构建研究 [J]. 物流科技，2008，31（11）：1－5.

[39] 袁韩时弼，黄业明，范玫杉，等. 我国医药储备形式的完善 [J]. 中国医药工业
杂志，2018（6）：869－874.

[40] 袁渊，杨西龙. 应急物流指挥信息系统的构建 [J]. 物流技术，2009，28（6）：
128－131.

[41] 张红. 我国应急物资储备制度的完善 [J]. 应急管理，2009（3）：44－47.

[42] 张洪瑞，吴宏强. 打赢现代应急动员"三大战役" [J]. 国防技术基础，2009
（1）：58－62.

[43] 张敏洁. 重特大突发事件下城市应急物流体系建设 [J]. 研究与探讨，2022
（5）：25－28.

[44] 赵锐，石秀园，王兴邦，等. 我国建立突发公共卫生时间医药研发储备机制的思
考 [J]. 卫生经济研究，2020，37（6）：6－9.

[45] 赵新光，龚卫锋，张燕. 应急物流的保障机制 [J]. 中国物流与采购，2003
（23）：24.

[46] 周宣开. 卫生检验检疫 [M]. 北京：人民卫生出版社，2006.

[47] 周尧. 自然灾害应急物流能力评价体系研究 [D]. 武汉：武汉理工大学，2009.

[48] 邹逸江. 国外经济管理体系的发展现状及经验启示 [J]. 灾害学，2008，23
（1）：96－101.

[49] 邹晓美，樊守林. 论《突发事件应对法》与应急物流研究 [J]. 中国流通经济，
2008，（8）：38－40.

[50] 朱东红，朱红. 关于福建省应急物流体系构建的若干思考 [J]. 物流工程与管
理，2014（11）：104－105.

[51] 左小德. 应急物流管理 [M]. 广州：暨南大学出版社，2011.